DEER & DEER HUNTING

A Hunter's Guide To Deer Behavior And Hunting Techniques

Al Hofacker, *Editor*

Valerie B. Smith, *Designer*

KRAUSE PUBLICATIONS
IOLA, WISCONSIN

Published by

700 E. State Street • Iola, WI 54990-0001

Photo Credits

Front Cover: *Charles J. Alsheimer*
Pages 2-3: *Denver Bryan*
Pages 14-15: *Ian McMurchy*
Pages 72-73: *Charles J. Alsheimer*
Pages 134-135: *Leonard Lee Rue III*
Pages 168-169: *Mike Biggs*

Library of Congress Number: 93-77552
ISBN: 0-87341-270-2
Printed in the United States of America

*This book is dedicated to all my former
co-workers at Deer & Deer Hunting magazine.
Their talented assistance and professionalism
made my duties as editor far easier
and more enjoyable than I deserved.*

Foreword

I was tempted to begin by assuring you that if you like *Deer & Deer Hunting* magazine, you will like this book. Then I realized that is not quite true. If you like the magazine, you will treasure this book even more because it contains some of the best work that appeared in the magazine during its 16-year history.

If you are unfamiliar with *Deer & Deer Hunting* magazine, you are in for an even bigger treat because this anthology includes some of the best material written over the past 10 years about white-tailed deer, how to hunt them and those who hunt them.

It's easy to make those claims because I've been a field editor for the publication during most of the years it has existed. During that time, I read the chapters included in this book as well as reader reactions to them. I have even written one of the chapters. Since my contribution only makes up a small part of this book's contents, that isn't enough to cloud my objectivity. In fact, my assessment would be the same even if my writing were excluded from the pages that follow.

Another reason for my confidence in the quality of this book's contents is that I trust the judgment of the man who made the chapter selections more than my own. Al Hofacker, a co-founder of the magazine, has been an important part of *Deer & Deer Hunting* magazine since it first appeared in 1977 and served as editor of the publication until Krause Publications acquired the magazine in 1992. He made the day-to-day decisions regarding the magazine's contents that increased the publication's popularity and credibility, allowing it to become one of the best magazines of its kind.

Because Al was the editor of the magazine during those 15 years, he is intimately familiar with everything that went into it and has the best qualifications for selecting those exceptional gems that made the magazine special and will make this book special, too.

Thanks to Al, and co-founder Jack Brauer, *Deer & Deer Hunting* magazine was the first national periodical devoted exclusively to whitetails and white-tailed deer hunting. That set a trend that others have tried to imitate, but throughout the years the magazine has maintained an identity of its own. An identity that lends itself to this book.

Hofacker and Brauer began the magazine with the objective of sharing factual information about deer and deer hunting that other hunters could benefit from while afield, and that has been a dominant theme throughout the magazine's history. Besides being informational, the magazine has also been entertaining, controversial and has generated plenty of excitement, all of which made the information more palatable. Some of the best of those same elements can be found in this book.

What helped make the magazine a success is that both Al and Jack were deer fanatics and they understood the thirst for knowledge shared by others like themselves as well as deer hunters at all other levels, including the novice. Their familiarity with all facets of deer and deer hunting aided them in consistently putting together a package of articles and photos hunters could relate to and profit from. Most of the writers who contribute to the magazine are avid deer hunters, too, adding credibility to the magazine and, in turn, to this book.

To me, reading about deer and deer hunting is the next best thing to being out there hunting and observing whitetails, and I sense that you feel the same way. Through the words of others, we get to experience things we might not otherwise have felt or seen. We get to relive precious moments vicariously, temporarily transported in our minds to that time and place the author shares with us.

Like deer hunting itself, words and pictures that depict the pursuit of the whitetail are distractions from our everyday lives. Distractions that enable us to learn, feel and see what it's like to be afield even when we can't be. That's one of the major values of *Deer & Deer Hunting*, both the magazine and the book. What sets the book apart from an issue of the magazine is there is a greater opportunity to learn, to feel, to be transported and to be distracted by a subject that we feel good about.

To avoid possible confusion, it is important to

point out that this book isn't the first one bearing the same name as the magazine. Rob Wegner joined Al and Jack as an editor at the magazine for a number of years, and he wrote three books with the same title, but there are important differences. Rob's first volume was published in 1984 and was subtitled *The Serious Hunter's Guide; Book 2* (1987) was added to the title of the second edition; and *Book 3* was released in 1990.

All the chapters for those books were written by Wegner and most of them were originally published in the magazine. One of the chapters in this volume was written by Rob, but all the others were produced by numerous authors, which sets this book apart from those done by Rob. The newest *Deer & Deer Hunting* is subtitled *A Hunter's Guide To Deer Behavior And Hunting Techniques*.

The publisher of this book is also different. Krause Publications in Iola, Wisconsin, which now publishes *Deer & Deer Hunting* magazine, produced this book. Stackpole Books in Harrisburg, Pennsylvania, published Rob's books.

This newest *Deer & Deer Hunting* won't tell you all you need to know and probably not all you want to know about deer and deer hunting, nor will it answer all your questions. It isn't supposed to. Like a magazine, there's a limit to what can be included in any single book and this one is no exception.

If you ever do pick up a book that claims to tell you everything about the subject, be awfully suspicious. I've read books whose author or publisher were bold enough to make such an exaggeration, or one very similar, and they invariably failed to deliver what they promised. Because so much is now known about deer and deer hunting, and new ideas and information are surfacing constantly, it is impossible to cram everything into one book.

If we're lucky, this will be the first in a series of deer books from Krause Publications, with each future volume exploring new territory. I know that Al considered a lot of material and he spent a lot of time and effort deciding which chapters to include in this book to make it the best possible product. He's good at that, as I mentioned before, and I'm not the only one who thinks so.

While manning booths for *Deer & Deer Hunting* magazine at outdoor shows, I've heard an endless stream of compliments from readers. Most were complimenting the magazine, but in reality they were complimenting Al because a lot of him went into each issue of the magazine. This book is no different.

While selecting the chapters for this book, I'm sure Al reviewed many articles he would have liked to include, but wasn't able to for one reason or another. Perhaps those articles will help make up the contents of another book in the future. But, for now, let's concentrate on the book you are holding in your hands.

The reason this material is in book form is that it is important for you to read and know. It is valuable enough to be given new life so that it can be preserved for posterity and for other deer hunters like you. So that the lessons the words and pictures teach, the experiences they share, the images they create in our minds and the emotions they bring to the surface won't be forgotten.

I think it is impossible to read this book and not become a better deer hunter. This volume should also help you develop a deeper appreciation for whitetails, the role we play in their world and their place in ours. If you've already purchased this book, you made a wise choice. If you haven't, you should!

— Richard P. Smith
Marquette, Michigan

Introduction

In June 1977 I watched the premier issue of *Deer & Deer Hunting* magazine roll off the printing press. By anyone's standards that premier issue was a modest production — 12 pages with a total distribution of 1,500 copies — that more closely resembled a newsletter than a magazine. Now, 16 years and more than 100 issues later, the magazine has a readership numbering in the hundreds of thousands.

As a co-founder of the magazine and its editor from 1977 to 1992, I had the pleasure and satisfaction of watching and participating in the growth and evolution of the magazine. *Deer & Deer Hunting* was the first national magazine devoted exclusively to white-tailed deer and the hunting of them. In hindsight, that was probably a significant factor in the eventual success of the magazine because our staff had virtually no publishing experience. But we did have much experience in the deer woods pursuing whitetails with bows and guns. Thus, the magazine was not the product of a grandiose plan developed by a large publishing house. Instead, the magazine evolved issue-by-issue under the direction of deer hunters striving to acquire and disseminate comprehensive and practical information about deer and deer hunting techniques. In the early years, we made our share of mistakes, but the quality of the magazine steadily improved and the readership constantly increased.

By the conclusion of *Deer & Deer Hunting's* fifth year, the circulation had exceeded 30,000. During those first years, several regular columns were incorporated into the magazine and remain an important part of the magazine. The first regular column, the "Deer Browse" section, appeared for the first time in the sixth issue. "Deer Browse," a collection of short items and photographs reporting incidents of unusual deer behavior and hunting experiences, continues to be one of the most popular aspects of the magazine.

In 1982, two more departments were added: "Letters" and "Gear." The "Letters" section (now titled "Readers Recoil") was added to the magazine in response to increased feedback from the ever-growing number of readers. The feedback was not always complimentary, but as editor I always felt it important to provide the readers with a forum to express their opinions, even when those opinions were critical of the material included in the magazine.

The "Gear" section also became a regular column in the magazine in 1982. This column provides readers with brief descriptions of new products available to deer hunters. "Rue's Views," another column which continues to the present, made its debut in 1983. It incorporates a question and answer format with the magazine's readers asking the questions and Leonard Lee Rue III, a well-known naturalist and wildlife photographer, providing the answers.

As the magazine continued to grow both in size and circulation in the 1980s, it became necessary to obtain editorial material apropos to deer hunters hunting under a variety of conditions in widely scattered geographic regions. In addition to relying more heavily on freelance writers from across the country, the selection of three field editors in the early 1980s provided readers with a continuous flow of diverse information to improve their hunting skills and increase their knowledge of white-tailed deer. Richard P. Smith (Michigan), Charles J. Alsheimer (New York) and Kent Horner (Alabama) have each been providing the readers of *Deer & Deer Hunting* magazine quality material on a regular basis for approximately a decade. Selections from all three of these popular field editors are included in this book.

The magazine's circulation continued to grow in the early and mid-1980s, surpassing 100,000 in 1986. In the following year, *Deer & Deer Hunting's* tenth anniversary year, the magazine was the recipient of the Northeast Section of The Wildlife Society's Certificate of Recognition "for maintaining the highest professional, educational and literary standards while focusing on the deer as a biological species and the art and science of deer hunting." Receiving that award will be remembered as one of the highlights of my tenure as editor of *Deer & Deer Hunting* magazine because it spoke volumes about the many dedicated and hard-working individuals who contributed so much to the magazine's success.

In 1988, the magazine increased its frequency of

publication from six to seven issues per year and modified its production schedule to provide readers with more information at the time of year they wanted it most — just prior to and during the archery and firearms deer hunting seasons. Two years later, in 1990, an eighth issue was added. This issue, the *Deer Hunters Equipment Annual*, is designed to provide information that will aid readers in buying, using and getting the most from their hunting gear.

Also in 1990, *Deer & Deer Hunting* was redesigned from front cover to back cover to make the magazine more visually appealing. At the same time, several more regular columns were added, including an editorial page ("Editors' Stump") and the "Deer Behavior" column.

A major development in 1992 was the acquisition of *Deer & Deer Hunting* magazine by Krause Publications in Iola, Wisconsin. Though the actual acquisition occurred in April of that year, the November 1992 issue was the first produced by Krause. Despite the change in ownership of the magazine, the focus of the magazine's contents remains the white-tailed deer and the hunting of them. Certainly there will be some changes, but that's nothing new. In its first 15 years, the magazine was in a constant state of change — an ongoing effort to better serve the readers and meet their needs.

And by a rather circuitous path that brings us to this book, *Deer & Deer Hunting: A Hunter's Guide To Deer Behavior And Hunting Techniques."* It could be argued that this book was 15 years in the making because it is a collection of articles that were published in *Deer & Deer Hunting* magazine during its first 15 years.

In many ways, I believe the book captures the essence of the magazine. The book is divided into four sections — *Natural History, Hunting Methodology, The Deer Hunt* and *The Deer Hunter* — to reflect the diversity of material published in the pages of the magazine throughout the years. In my years as editor of the magazine, the readers constantly demonstrated a thirst for information about the white-tailed deer as well as how to hunt them. The message they conveyed was that they were interested in anything and everything pertaining to white-tailed deer. This resulted in the publication of a diverse blend of articles dealing with emotional and controversial issues, in-depth discussions of deer biology and behavior, prosaic pieces about the deer hunting experience, the principles and practices of deer management, and detailed examinations of what makes the deer hunter tick. After sifting and sorting through the nearly 600 articles published in the magazine during my stint as editor, I tried to include this same diversity of subject matter in the book. Simultaneously, I attempted to select material written by authors from throughout the country (and Canada) and who have a wide range of backgrounds. They all, however, have one thing in common: Each is an avid and knowledgeable deer hunter.

Readers will note that the design of this book differs considerably from the standard fare at the book store or library. Again, this was a deliberate attempt to capture the essence of the magazine. Readers of the magazine consistently let it be known that the information contained in the articles was of prime importance. But they also made it clear that the overall design of the pages that made up each issue and the liberal use of top-notch photos enhanced the editorial content. I think you will agree that the book's designer, Valerie Smith, succeeded in enhancing each chapter in the book with an appealing design that incorporates the extensive use of color throughout and numerous photos from many of the country's foremost wildlife photographers.

As we neared completion of this book, Valerie and I noticed a final similarity between the book and preparing an issue of the magazine — there were not enough pages to include everything we had originally hoped. But perhaps that's to be expected. Deer hunters continue to thirst for more information about deer and deer hunting and no single volume could ever be large enough to be all-inclusive. In the final analysis, I hope this book is judged for what is included and how the material is presented.

— Al Hofacker
Athelstane, Wisconsin

Acknowledgments

This book bears my name on the cover, but in reality it is the product of the efforts of countless individuals who contributed so much to the success of *Deer & Deer Hunting* magazine. Unfortunately, it would be virtually impossible to mention by name all my dedicated co-workers at the magazine through the years, the many talented freelancers who contributed most of the articles and photos that appeared in the magazine, and all the other people whose diverse talents I relied upon as editor of the magazine from 1977 to 1992, but I am indebted to all of them. And although not all of those people can be mentioned by name, I want to thank the following individuals for their many years of invaluable assistance in producing the magazine and making my years as editor a truly enjoyable experience.

For more than a decade, Faye Cerasoli served as my editorial assistant and always performed her varied and numerous duties in a timely and professional manner. Jill Ganzel-Redlin, the magazine's former art director, deserves much of the credit for transforming *Deer & Deer Hunting* from a modest black-and-white publication to a magazine with a colorful and visually appealing design from front cover to back. Pat Durkin, the magazine's current editor and a more recent addition to the editorial staff, immediately became a valuable asset to the magazine in general and me in particular.

The current publisher of *Deer & Deer Hunting* magazine at Krause Publications, Debbie Knauer, became the magazine's advertising manager in the early 1980s. As the magazine grew, she was joined by sales reps Barb Cramer, Jackie Daniels and Dave Larsen; Connie Boone and Audrey Kohel ably handled the administrative tasks in the advertising department. The proverbial brick wall separating the editorial and advertising departments always contained enough small cracks and holes to facilitate satisfying the advertisers without compromising the editorial content of the magazine, making it a pleasure to work with these competent individuals.

While a magazine is typically judged by its outward appearance and its contents, many others made valuable contributions that were not as readily apparent. John Pagel and Sandy Ness wore many hats in their years of handling the duties associated with magazine fulfillment. Among his other duties, John kept the computers functioning properly and efficiently to ensure that the subscribers received their copies of the magazine. Sandy processed literally hundreds of thousands of subscriptions over the years and resolved more than a few problems relating to subscription fulfillment. Joey Wenzel, who also wore several hats, carried out the somewhat unusual dual role of bookkeeper and receptionist.

Although they were not a part of the magazine's full-time staff, I am indebted to the magazine's long-time field editors: Charles J. Alsheimer, Kent Horner, Leonard Lee Rue III and Richard P. Smith. These four writers/photographers always provided me with first-rate material and consistently met their assigned deadlines, something any editor would appreciate.

Teamwork was always an essential ingredient in the publication of each issue of *Deer & Deer Hunting* magazine. The "team" responsible for taking this book from the idea stage to the printing press involved a smaller cast of characters, but I again had the pleasure of collaborating with a group of talented people. The seed for this book was planted at Krause Publications by Debbie Knauer and she initiated the discussions between me and Pat Klug, the manager of Krause's book division. Debbie also provided valuable feedback as the pages of the book took shape. Mary Sieber, managing editor of the book division, also became involved during the early stages of the book. I want to thank Pat for her vote of confidence in allowing me to select and work with an "out-of-house" designer, Valerie Smith, and for then giving us the freedom to produce a book whose format is quite different from what most would consider "normal" in the field of outdoor publishing. Mary Sieber was especially helpful in answering my many questions and putting out occasional brushfires while the book was being edited and designed.

I especially want to express my gratitude to Valerie Smith, the graphic arts director at Graphic Management Corp. in Green Bay, Wisconsin, and the designer of this book. I asked Valerie to be the designer because I've had the privilege and pleasure of working with her in the past. Among her many credits, she was the designer of the 1991 and 1992 *Deer Hunters Equipment Annual* and assisted in the design of many of the issues *Deer & Deer Hunting* in those same years. More importantly, I wanted Valerie to design "our" book because she is a skilled professional who takes a tremendous amount of pride in her work, and that is always clearly evident in the finished product. I've also found that the pride she takes in her craft is contagious, prompting me to put forth a little extra effort as well whenever we work together.

Finally, I hope everyone who reads this book enjoys it as much as I enjoyed working with the many people who made this book possible.

Contents

Len Rue, Jr.

Brad Herndon

Part One

Natural History

To the beholder, antlers are status symbols of male supremacy. They serve primarily in highly ritualized sparring matches and more serious fighting among bucks, necessary to determine dominance order and male mating privileges in advance of the breeding season.

BONES OF CONTENTION

John J. Ozoga

They're prized by hunters as trophies, by the Orientals for their supposedly potent medicinal properties and by nature lovers as magnificent ornaments carried by one of the world's most graceful creatures. But to the zoologist, says Dr. Richard J. Goss, an authority on antler regeneration, "they are fascinating curiosities that seem to defy the laws of nature." And because of the confusion, differences of opinion and the oftentimes heated debate surrounding almost all aspects of antler biology (deer herd management included), they've become known among scientists as "bones of contention."

Curt Helmick

For in fact, the mature antler is true dead bone, making it quite different from the horns carried by cattle, sheep, goats and bison. Antlers are typically branched, grow outward from the tips and are cast annually. Horns, on the other hand, are actually living bone covered with hard layers of skin and are normally unbranched, permanent structures (except in the pronghorn antelope) that grow from the base.

In his book, *Antlers: Regeneration, Function, and Evolution* (1983), Goss refers to antlers as ". . . an extravagance of nature, rivaled only by such other biological luxuries as flowers, butterfly wings and peacock tails." So highly improbable are antlers, says Goss, "that if they had not evolved in the first place, they would never have been conceived even in the wildest fantasies of the most imaginative biologists."

Only members of the deer family (Cervidae) grow antlers. Of the several dozen major deer species living in the world today, only the musk deer of eastern Asia and the tiny Chinese water deer do not grow antlers. As secondary sex characteristics, only the males carry them, except in reindeer and caribou, where both sexes grow them. In white-tailed deer, one female among every few thousand also grows antlers, generally due to some type of hormonal imbalance. Does can also be experimentally induced to grow antlers when injected with testosterone, a male sex hormone.

To the beholder, antlers are status symbols of male supremacy — adornments that evolved hand in hand with certain aspects of deer breeding behavior. They serve primarily in highly ritualized sparring matches and more serious fighting among bucks, necessary to decide dominance order and male mating privileges in advance of the breeding season.

No two antlers are exactly alike, although their similarities from side to side, or even from one animal to the next, are oftentimes striking. An individual buck commonly grows one antler containing more tines than the other and its branches may differ in length or grow out at variable angles. Such differences make antlered bucks distinctive and permit deer to readily distinguish one buck from another, based upon antler features alone.

Large antlers are showy structures that permit bucks to display and advertise themselves, to attract prospective mates and to intimidate rival males. Although sometimes used as lethal weapons for defense against predators, antlers certainly did not evolve mainly for that purpose.

One thing that makes antlers so unique, and of interest to scientists from varied disciplines, is that they regenerate themselves. That's something no other mammalian appendage can do.

The cycle of antler growth, hardening, casting (dropping off) and regrowth is controlled by the endocrine system and involves a complex interplay between the hypothalamus, pituitary gland and testes in response to seasonal changes in amount of daylight, or photoperiod. The cycle follows the seasonal, rhythmic rise and fall in circulating blood levels of testosterone, a hormone produced principally by the male's testes. Captive bucks exposed to artificially shortened seasonal light cycles have produced and cast as many as four complete sets of antlers in a single year.

In the northern latitudes, white-tailed deer grow

Richard P. Smith

The live antler is richly supplied with sensory nerves and even the delicate velvet hairs may serve as touch-sensitive feelers that warn of a pending collision.

antlers in spring and summer, when testosterone production is at its lowest annual level. The antlers harden, the velvet dries, and antlers are polished in autumn when the amount of daylight decreases just prior to the breeding season. At the same time, rising testosterone output stimulates fighting among bucks. The dead antler falls off in winter, after completion of breeding, as testosterone concentrations diminish.

Because deer living near the equator experience only slight seasonal changes in the amount of daylight, they lack the photoperiod cues and, thus, the seasonal aspects of reproduction displayed by their northern cousins. In the tropics, does may breed and give birth, and bucks may carry hardened antlers, at any time of the year.

Castration of the adult buck causes old antlers to be cast prematurely and permits new antler growth (even during the "wrong" season) but prevents final antler maturation. The result is growth of permanently viable antlers. In the absence of testosterone, the antler can neither harden nor shed velvet, it adds new tissue each year, and sometimes gives rise to tumorous growths that achieve monstrous proportions — a condition superficially resembling cancer.

Skeletal injury, or direct injury to the tender growing antler, can also produce antler abnormalities, but these should not be confused with malformations caused by poor nutrition, old age or genetics. Generally speaking, genetically or nutritionally controlled antler abnormalities show on both beams, whereas a one-sided oddity more likely signifies some type of injury.

Nonetheless, the live antler is richly supplied with sensory nerves and even the delicate velvet hairs may serve as touch-sensitive feelers that warn of a pending collision. As an added safeguard, bucks seem to possess special senses that permit them to judge the size and shape of their antlers. Even large-antlered bucks can move rapidly through dense forest cover and surprisingly few show signs of velvet antler damage.

Many antler peculiarities such as rack shape, tine length and configuration, and other specific features are unquestionably hereditary. Numerous examples exist of captive bucks reproducing successive antler sets very similar in appearance year after year. The racks tend to get a little larger and may add an extra point here and there with advancing age, but otherwise closely resemble one another. Keep in mind, however, that only the important antler features are strictly coded in genes. Other less important details are generally left to chance.

One perplexing observation is what scientists refer to as "contralateral effects:" an injury to one side of the buck's body results in antler deformity on the opposite side. For example, if a buck breaks its right hind leg, it more than likely will grow a short left-side antler. This

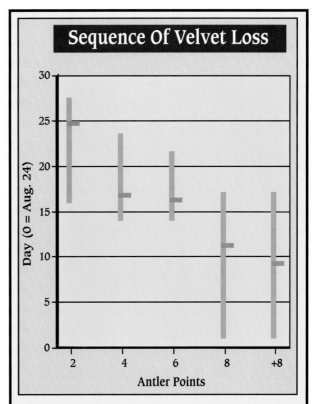

This graph illustrates the sequence of velvet loss by bucks with antlers ranging from two to more than eight points as observed by deer researcher David H. Hirth on the Welder Wildlife Refuge in Texas. Hirth observed a total of 393 bucks from August 24 (Day 0) through September 23 (Day 30). Although there was significant overlap of the dates of velvet loss by bucks with antlers of various sizes, Hirth's observations, reported in a 1977 issue of *The Southwestern Naturalist*, suggest that large-racked bucks lose their velvet earlier in the year than smaller bucks.

In the graph, the range of velvet-loss dates is indicated by the vertical bars and the horizontal bars show the mean velvet-loss dates.

— Al Hofacker

response may prevail for several years. Investigators consider many such reports valid, but lack a sound biological explanation for the phenomenon.

Researchers generally agree that the size of a normal buck's rack varies depending upon the animal's age, his nutritional history and inherited traits. They argue vehemently among themselves, however, as to the relative importance of the various factors.

To complicate matters even more so, behavioral studies indicate that psychological stress can also influence deer physical condition (including antler growth) and reproductive performance. "Crowding stress" due to overpopulation and frequent conflict among deer can be costly to the animal. It can disrupt certain basic physiological functions in deer and even suppress antler growth in young bucks when nourishing foods are plentiful.

> *To the beholder, antlers are status symbols of male supremacy — adornments that go hand in hand with certain aspects of deer breeding behavior.*

As an example, a special study conducted by the Michigan Department of Natural Resources in a one-square-mile, fenced-in area at the Cusino Wildlife Research Station in Upper Michigan revealed that when deer density surpassed 100 deer per square-mile, social stress caused delayed breeding, lower than normal fawning rates among young does and high newborn fawn losses (63 percent) among first-time mothers. As an added surprise, an unusually high 22 percent of the yearling (1.5 years old) bucks grew short, sub-legal (less than three inches long) spike antlers, despite their large body size as the result of being supplementally fed unlimited amounts of high-quality artificial feed year-round.

The male hormone testosterone (or lack of it) appears to be the magical link involved in the poor

antler growth noticed among well-fed but density-stressed bucks. This hormone is critically important throughout the antler cycle and is absolutely essential for proper development of a buck's first set of antlers.

Before any deer can grow antlers, it must first grow pedicles, or stumps, on which antlers form. This is an intriguing process that requires a certain threshold level of testosterone.

Pedicles first show as a pair of cowlicks in the forehead pelage of very young fawns, where they can be felt as small bony lumps beneath the skin. They usually don't become pronounced "nubbins" until the fawn is about four to five months old, at which time increased output of testosterone stimulates the laying down of additional bone at the pedicle sites.

In the absence of testosterone, or the presence of the female hormone estrogen, no pedicles form and antlers fail to develop later. Buck fawns born late in the season, those poorly nourished during summer and autumn, or those subjected to severe social (psychological) stress, tend to grow small pedicles (or none at all) due either to a deficiency in testosterone production or because of a hormonal imbalance that blocks its effects. Remember, antler size is largely a function of pedicle diameter. Bigger antler "buds" (pedicles) give rise to longer antlers with more points.

A buck fawn that experiences a serious physiological setback early in life, for whatever reason, will invariably form small pedicles, as well as undersized antlers a year later (when 1.5 years old), regardless of what other superior genetic traits for large antlers he may possess.

In sharp contrast, some physically superior buck fawns mature faster than normal. Whereas most bucks carry their first antlers when 1.5 years old, some well-developed fawns grow, polish and shed small "button" (infant) antlers less than one-half inch long — thus undergoing one complete antler cycle prior to nine months of age.

Buck fawns that grow "infant" antlers in effect carry their second sets of antlers as yearlings. In fact, they then commonly sport eight-point racks, instead of the spikes or forks more common for bucks their age, and closely resemble 2.5-year-olds, which is a rather clear sign of an advanced rate of maturity.

These "super" bucks tend to achieve large, maximum body and antler size when relatively young — perhaps at 4.5 years of age — instead of when 5.5 or 6.5 years old, as is more common.

However, in order to accomplish such a fantastic growth rate, as well as maximal pedicle formation and final "infant" antler mineralization, excellent nutrition during early life is absolutely essential — a simple, but highly important, fact that cannot be overemphasized.

The growing antler may elongate at the astounding rate of more than one-half inch per day, making it one of the fastest growing structures in the animal kingdom. Furthermore, because body growth takes precedence over antler growth, any deficiency in dietary energy, protein, calcium, phosphorus or certain vitamins during spring and summer can have strong negative effects on subsequent antler length, mass and number of points among young growing bucks, in particular. (Nutritional shortages during winter have less overall impact upon antler size.)

Because whitetails are selective feeders, an expanding deer herd can drastically reduce or even eliminate preferred herbaceous forage that is readily digestible and rich in protein. At the same time, other plants may increase either because they're less palatable, resistant to grazing, or both. Thus, severely overgrazed range may not exhibit the stark, overused appearance one would expect. Even so, the land's nutritional base and capacity to naturally support healthy deer — including bucks with sizeable antlers — steadily declines with continued overuse. For this reason, wildlife managers closely monitor antler size among 1.5-year-old bucks, because the information provides a good indicator of the deer herd's general health status.

Unfortunately, as one nutrient component decreases in availability so do others. No "quick-fix" solution,

Len Rue, Jr.

Generally speaking, genetically or nutritionally controlled antler abnormalities show on both beams, whereas a one-sided oddity more likely signifies some type of injury.

such as providing vitamin/mineral supplements, will remedy the more chronic problem of inadequate protein and low caloric content in the deer's diet.

There are only two logical solutions to the poor nutrition/small antler dilemma. One is to reduce deer numbers to more closely match the capacity of the natural habitat to favorably support them. The other is to improve the habitat by cutting, burning, planting, fertilizing, or by whatever means is necessary to restore the land's inherent capacity to support healthy deer. Most times, favorable results are not likely to be achieved unless both measures are undertaken.

Research conducted with penned deer rather convincingly shows that genetics can also exert a strong influence on antler and body size. Small, poorly antlered yearling bucks, when permitted to breed, typically sired small male fawns that also eventually grew short antlers. Superior-antlered yearling bucks more commonly fathered large, well-antlered sons. However, researchers also found that mothers play an important role in antler genetics. Some does con-

Leonard Lee Rue III

All too often, a spike-buck is nothing more than a stressed young animal, not necessarily one of inferior genetic ancestry.

sistently reared well-antlered sons, while others more commonly raised small ones with poor antlers.

Antler-genetic researchers suggest that inbreeding may be an important factor in reducing antler quality among whitetails in certain sections of the country. In turn, they raise the question: Would intensified selective harvesting of inferior (spike) bucks help to remove inferior genes and improve the population's overall genetic composition and ultimately increase antler quality?

Other well-meaning individuals suggest introducing "new bloodlines" — genetically superior bucks — as a means of upgrading antler quality.

On the surface, these schemes have a great deal of appeal. In reality, neither approach is likely to succeed nor are they necessary if deer herds and their habitat are properly managed. Furthermore, given proper herd management, whitetails possess built-in behavioral protection against inbreeding because yearling bucks disperse from two to 20 miles to a new range before breeding.

Even promoters of the inferior buck harvest concept acknowledge that increased harvesting of "spikehorns" will not improve antler quality wherever poor nutrition, harsh climate, excessive buck harvest or adverse social circumstances interfere with proper antler growth. All too often, a spike-buck is nothing more than a stressed young animal, not necessarily one of inferior genetic ancestry. Remember, females may carry inferior antler genes, too, and inferior bucks may disperse into new areas, making complete elimination of inferior antler genes via selective harvesting next to impossible to accomplish.

Contrary to popular belief, translocating big-bodied, large-antlered "races" of deer to small-bodied ones to increase antler size won't work either. Within relatively few generations, the new "bloodline" assumes the hereditary traits of the local population.

By now you probably recognize one rather important generalization: antler size and body size normally go together. That is, a "big" buck tends to carry a "big" rack, whereas a small-bodied buck with a huge set of antlers is about as rare as hen's teeth.

This relationship has special significance because, from an evolutionary standpoint, all bucks compete to individually produce as many offspring as possible.

A buck's dominance rank and, therefore, his chances of being a breeder, depends highly upon his body size and physical strength. The size of the buck's antlers, which serve as important display and fighting organs, and his aggressiveness, which is determined by the amount of testosterone coursing through his veins, are also important factors leading to attainment of high dominance rank. All of these determinants tend to increase with a buck's age and peak when he's between 4.5 and 8.5 years old.

Study evidence also suggests that the experienced breeder-buck's elaborate courtship behavior — which includes scent-marking in the form of rubs and scrapes — may even permit does to solicit attention from preferred and presumably physically superior mates. If so, such behavior in itself would assure genetic fitness and favor perpetuation of superior antler traits.

> **Antler-genetic researchers suggest that inbreeding may be an important factor in reducing antler quality among whitetails in certain sections of the country.**

Yearling bucks, by comparison, are very energetic and capable breeders when pressed into service due to a shortage (over-harvest) of mature bucks. However, these young warriors lack courtship finesse, fail to form a strict pre-rut dominance hierarchy, and all of them seem to do some of the breeding in the absence of mature sires. Above all, their "seek-and-chase" style of courtship eliminates any chances for mate selection.

Proponents of the spike-harvest idea frequently point to the "culling" type of big game management practiced in Europe, for support. In Europe, wildlife managers insist that hunters heavily harvest the young, old and physically unfit animals — an admirable system which closely mimics natural predator-induced mortality.

Oftentimes overlooked, however, is that selective harvesting in this manner involves much more than "weeding out" undesirable animals. Most importantly, European managers strive to maximize the herd's reproductive performance by retaining well-nourished populations, in balance with range carrying capacity, that are comprised chiefly of thrifty, highly productive, prime-age animals — the so-called population's social governors. This system emphasizes the value of maintaining social order to minimize tension and strife among animals. It also favors selective mating by superior males which assures genetic fitness (and high-quality antlers) within the population.

Today, in the near absence of effective large predators, such balance and harmony can be accomplished only by concerted selective harvesting by hunters. Usually this means heavy cropping of surplus young antlerless deer and giving some protection to prime-age individuals when necessary. Healthy bucks with "good racks" are a natural and obvious byproduct of such management, as are a goodly number of "trophy-class" racks, because more physically fit males are permitted to achieve maturity.

Needless to say, European big game management contrasts sharply with that practiced in North America. Years of buck over-exploitation and years of doe over-protection here have greatly altered the structure of deer populations in many areas. Antlered bucks, regardless of their age, are routinely hunted so intensely that few survive the annual harvest in many sectors. Ironically, at the same time, because of the stigma associated with shooting a "small deer," American hunters shy away from cropping fawns, which occur in greatest abundance. On northern range, in particular, excessive harvesting of antlered bucks, on the one hand, is accompanied by frequent and heavy winter mortality of young antlerless deer, on the other.

Because of our fanatical quest for those "bones of contention," we American deer hunters traditionally fail to play responsible predator roles, which leads to wanton waste of a valuable resource and inevitably contributes to a scarcity of high-quality antlered bucks — the very thing we most diligently seek.

Editor's Note: "Bones Of Contention" was originally published in the October 1987 issue of Deer & Deer Hunting *magazine.*

Romancing

Why should we deny it? We love big deer sporting memorable headgear. Typical or atypical, eight points or thirty, perfect or flawed, ivory or stained, we love them all.

Bill Kinney

The Antler

Joseph L. Arnette

Romancing The Antler

The long crevasse sliced through a massive bulge of rock just to the south of eastern Utah's Book Cliffs. In outward appearance, it resembled the multitude of other splits and fissures that cut up the land into an arid moonscape. Yet, this particular crevasse differed greatly from those around it. Wedged neatly along its V-shape, from five to 10 feet down, were more than 30 of the finest mule deer racks I ever saw. All but eight or nine of the antlers were record-class, and at least a half-dozen were truly enormous. Those bleached and weathered bones represented the stuff of dreams.

Few people knew of the antlers, and only the oldest among them remembered the hunter who lived by the crevasse, the man who shot those magnificent deer. I consider myself fortunate that they shared the unique collection with me. I don't expect to see anything like it again.

As long as sportsmen can be awestruck by the sight of a magnificent buck, deer and deer hunting have a chance at survival. That we care about deer may prove to be all that matters; why we care about them may become secondary.

The most extraordinary thing about the antlers, however, was not their number or size or age, but that they were there at all. The hunter had to backpack the heads over terrain where every step was a challenge in survival, where bare subsistence was a study in energy conservation. Why did he bother with the antlers? Why didn't he leave them where they fell, forgotten, and concentrate on the venison that kept him alive? The man's reason was ageless: there is more to a buck than meat. The crevasse was a backcountry trophy room and the racks in it served a personal, esthetic purpose. The hunter wanted his antlers at home, where he could look at them, to marvel and remember. So would I. So would most of us.

And why wouldn't we? Antlers, especially great ones, are the fabric of myth and fascination, of memory and November visions woven into an elegant tapestry. Even the most experienced hunters see magic in deer antlers, a special quality as deep and basic as the wilderness itself. To find that magic, to touch it if we can, is the woof and warp of deer hunting.

A buck, like lesser human royalty, wears the symbol of his majesty on his head. His crown is an advertisement of himself, but contrary to the human variety, there is only truth in this advertising. His antlers show what he is, his strength and vigor, nothing more or less. He displays the antlers for judgment by both mate and rival. Because antlers are so fundamentally honest, hunters too can take a buck's measure through his rack. By it, we can rate his beauty, worth and desirability. And, to no small extent, we can rate ourselves by our skill at bringing him home to our own crevasse.

The very sight of big antlers strikes a nerve untouchable by any other view. We have been entranced by these remarkable growths of bone since our hairy ancestors swarmed out of the trees and evolved the wits to hunt the deer that carried them. It is not difficult to conjure up an image of primitive man fidgeting around a fire, chipping at flint, and pondering strategies for killing a heavy-racked buck.

There is little doubt that antlers were important to our forebears in a number of ways. Throughout man's history, antlers have been used for everything from tools and weapons to finery. But there was more to them than pure function, as demonstrated by rock paintings that portray antlers as much larger than their deer owners. Whether these monumental racks represented what hunters hoped to kill or were records of success remains unknown. Perhaps oversized antlers served hunters in the same fashion as they did deer, announcing to all who passed that here was "mucho hombre" and competitors had best stay out of his territory. Or, like us, antiquity's hunter may have been something of a sporting liar.

Whatever the reasons for the art, clearly the antlers

were meaningful objects even to hunters who lived or died by their competence at bringing home food. Antlers symbolized a great deal more than an ability to keep stomachs full. As anthropologists point out, if meat was the main issue why draw antlers at all, let alone such disproportionate racks. Obviously, antlers were big medicine in their own right.

Not much changed over the millennia. Today's sportsmen may praise the superior table quality of a doe or spike, but few would pass up a rocking-chair buck for toothsome eating. Old saws such as, "You can't eat horns," or "Better an empty wall than an empty freezer," begin their annual rounds with the first shot of deer season. But I suspect these are smoke screens, alibis for tagging the first legal deer that comes along. No, this attraction is now, and always has been, something far beyond a yen for 50 pounds of tender venison. Deer hunters have a love affair with antlers, a massive and incurable romance out of the very core of our minds. And the bigger the racks, the greater our passion.

Why we possess this infatuation with antlers is unknown and, in all likelihood, will remain that way. The underlying reasons seem too deeply buried within us to be brought to the surface by rational explanation. By nature, we seek definitions of the world around us and attempt to unravel our relationships with its inhabitants. But the thread that ties us to antlers, like that of hunting as a sport, has twisted itself into a basically unanswerable question. For most of us, however, that doesn't change a thing. Our "antler affair" is little more than a topic for deer-camp chatter and late-night ponderings alongside ranks of malty dead soldiers. We would rather spend our time hunting big-racked deer than analyzing our reasons for doing so. We prefer enjoying a fine set of antlers to cerebrating at length about why we enjoy them. Perhaps this is as it should be. As long as sportsmen can be awestruck by the sight of a magnificent buck, deer and deer hunting have a chance at survival. That we care about deer may prove to be all that matters; why we care about them may become secondary.

On the other hand, a strong case can be made that it is indeed important to consider our motivations, particularly our romance with "horn" hunting. Given today's bitter anti-hunting climate, possibly each of us could better serve ourselves and deer by seriously thinking about why we pursue them, why antlers are so meaningful. Not a clinical breakdown, not an attempt to resolve the questions, just a hard look at what compels us into the big-buck woods and what we can derive from being there.

Social scientists may be close to the mark in saying that at the heart of modern hunting (which is epitomized by deer hunting) is a deep-seated urge to revert, at least temporarily, to an older, freer world; that we have a need to be out stalking in the fading tracks of our primitive ancestor, man the hunter. It is probably true that genuine deer hunting represents an effort to project ourselves away from "unnatural," everyday circumstances and deal directly with uncluttered nature. Deer hunting is the only means avail-

Ian McMurchy

Deer hunters have a love affair with antlers, a massive and incurable romance out of the very core of our minds. And the bigger the racks, the greater our passion.

able to us to commune personally with a wild heritage that is shrinking and easily lost. It is the one clear path left us to continually rediscover a part of ourselves and our relationship with the natural world.

Speculations of this sort are difficult to fault, and there is probably no legitimate reason to try. There is nothing wrong with admitting that the civilized world cannot fill every need of our lives. Where is the problem in confessing that we require something more vital and enduring than golf, pizza and endless "M.A.S.H." reruns? Why shouldn't we acknowledge that the blandishments of a microchip society come to nothing compared to an eight-point buck and a week in the November woods? To pursue a fine deer honestly and take it fairly on its own ground is to accomplish something fundamental, to touch the essence of all that is wild and free in the deer and in ourselves, to capture timeless moments that many will never know. Without these "primitive urges," we would be lesser men in a diminished world.

Deer hunting has been called a contest between man and deer. That's arguable, but if it is a contest, it is one which includes man, deer and nature equally — a total package. We do not hunt simply to win. We do not chase deer, kill them, eat them, slap their antlers on the wall, then forget the whole episode. We hunt deer to possess the package — sights, smells, thoughts, every sensation of being part of a deeper world — or we do not hunt them at all. And the threads that bind our package are antlers. It is as natural as deer hunting itself that we plan seasons around antlers and, if we succeed, we use them to keep the experience complete. What better way to tie up the details of a hunt than with the rack of a savvy whitetail? These incredible bones summarize the complexities of our deer hunting perceptions and fulfillments, our anticipations and disappointments.

In an essay entitled, "Goose Music," Aldo Leopold

Bill Vaznis

Deer hunting is the only means available to us to commune personally with a wild heritage that is shrinking and easily lost. It is the one clear path left us to continually rediscover a part of ourselves and our relationship with the natural world.

wrote that, "Poets sing and hunters scale the mountains primarily for one and the same reason — to thrill to beauty. Critics write and hunters outwit their game primarily for one and the same reason — to reduce that beauty to possession." And antlers are the lasting material feature of that beauty which we can retain. They are both the symbol and the reality of our entire deer hunting package. At a glance, a touch if we choose, we can scale the mountains again, relive the days and moments with deer, and retrieve

Even the most experienced hunters see magic in deer antlers, a special quality as deep and basic as the wilderness itself.

the primeval sense of having hunted them well. A trophy room, an artist's cave, a remote crevasse are calendars of hunting experiences that antlers have fixed in time. In each, the beauty has been thrilled to, possessed and held; only the style differs.

All deer are beautiful. All deer are important regardless of their sex or size. No hunter worth the name actually believes that, "It ain't a deer without decent horns." If we are honest, however, most of us will admit to the merest twinge of discontent when we bring home a doe or young buck. These deer are of no less value, but a fine buck and the difficulty in taking him is the yardstick of hunting challenge and achievement. We may not consistently shoot rack bucks, few of us do, but who doesn't plan each hunt

around that hope? Who among us thrashes in his sleeping bag the night before deer season dreaming of a yearling doe? Has any deer hunter ever lied a six-pointer down to a fork? We occasionally kick truth out on its treacherous behind but never in that direction. Why should we deny it? We love big deer sporting memorable headgear. Typical or atypical, eight points or 30, perfect or flawed, ivory or stained, we love them all. At its roots, deer hunting means antlers and what they represent.

Now, is this bad? Is our love affair with antlers immoral? Is it, as some T.V. celebrities proclaim, a demonstration of Neolithic machismo? No, I don't think so. But if these accusations were true, we would be in good and plentiful company — about a half-million years worth of deer hunters.

Across much of this country, deer, especially whitetails, are the wildest of creatures and the most prized of game animals. They are the embodiment of freedom and beauty, of mystery and craft. And at the top of this wild hierarchy is the gargantuan, heavy-racked buck. Of course, we place these deer at the zenith of our hunting experience; to do anything else would be pointless. We hunt to possess the total beauty of a well-antlered deer and to return that beauty to our crevasse, to marvel and remember.

"My heart's in the highlands, a-chasing the deer," wrote Robert Burns in a minor 18th century poem. We don't know if Burns was scaling mountains and outwitting game, but he certainly was thrilling to beauty. And I'd wager a custom .30-06 that if his heart was a-chasing the deer, his mind was romancing the antler.

Editor's Note: "Romancing The Antler" was originally published in the December 1985 issue of Deer & Deer Hunting *magazine.*

How Deer Communicate

Valerius Geist

Deer do not have language in the strictest sense of the word, but they do tell one another plenty just the same. They communicate with signs and gestures of the body, with some sounds, with puffs of odor and now and again with tactile stimuli.

Len Rue, Jr.

How Deer Communicate

Have you ever watched deer and wondered what, if anything, they told one another? Sagas and fairy tales tell of a few chosen people like Sigurd the Dragon Slayer who, after burning his fingers on the dragon's heart he roasted, suddenly understood the language of the animals. In all cases that was a blessing, for without a knowledge of the animal's language, the hero would have succumbed sooner.

Deer do not have language in our saga's sense, but they do tell one another plenty just the same, much of it in a subtle manner easily missed by the uninitiated observer. They communicate with signs and gestures of the body, with some sounds, with puffs of odor and now and again with tactile stimuli. They thus use exclusively what scientists label, in bloated technical language, "nonverbal communication" and which adds zest, emphasis and life to our conversations. Since we are visually oriented animals bound to daylight hours, we can only get a glimmering of what scent may mean to deer or how one signals at night. Most of my previous deer research centered on mule deer, but their social signals are very similar to those of whitetails, as one expects from such close relatives.

To watch deer for communicative signals, the observer must unglue his eyes from the animal's head. We love watching heads! All my students must first learn to systematically watch the entire animal — its tail, its glands, its hair, its posture. They must also watch for details, such as the closure of an eye, the position of the ears, the actions of the lips, nostrils and tongue, and the orientation of one animal to another. The student must also note where deer sniff and lick. In short, one must observe systematically and in detail.

The most difficult situation to understand, because of the subtlety of signals, is that of a group of feeding does. The observer must note less what the deer do than what they don't do. They do not look into one another's faces. That is one important rule. If the observer knows who ranks above whom, he soon notices that the subordinate deer avoid looking at the faces of dominants and when resting assume an orientation so as not to look at the dominant deer.

Among bucks, at short range, the dominants avoid looking at the subordinates (but not when inspecting a subordinate at long range). The subordinate buck, however, does look — even stares — at the dominant. Consequently, a dominant buck moving toward a subordinate acts as if looking aside, while the subordinate evading the dominant looks at the dominant buck.

A courting buck will close his eye on the side facing the female and avert his head if she glances at him. Females may look with interest towards an unfamiliar, courting buck until he gets within 50 to 60 feet, at which point he is likely to squint. The female then turns hesitantly, lowers her head and feeds, avoiding eye contact. In sparring matches, friendly

Richard P. Smith

Does, as well as bucks without antlers, will use their flailing front legs as weapons. Rising up on the hind legs serves as a threat. If the threat is not heeded by the opponent, flailing commences.

engagements between bucks of unequal rank, the partners avert eyes upon breaking antler contact. They stand, pausing, as if looking past one another.

Eye contact, of course, is pointedly made by a big buck about to rush a small one to chase him away from an estrous female. Any attacking deer about to strike another deer with its front legs faces the opponent and looks at him squarely. Bucks attacking from a dominance display will not do that, but suddenly drop the display and plunge into the opponent, giving him as little time as possible to defend himself.

So, in a peacefully grazing doe group the first point of etiquette is to not look at each other's face. The second one, most noticeable in grazing whitetails and least conspicuous in mule deer, is to move past one another at close range in a submissive or appeasement posture. This posture consists of head down, low to the ground as if about to feed and, in whitetails, a noticeable crouching while passing another deer. In mule deer, the head-low posture will suffice; mulies dispense with the crouch. A white-tailed doe, taking a shortcut through a dispersed mule deer group may travel so low to the ground that she almost appears like a snake in the grass. That's an extreme appeasement posture. Black-tailed deer exhibit an intermediate behavior.

The grazing deer thus maintain the peace by letting each other know that they are appeasing, that they pose no threat; it is as if they smile at one another but use the whole body to do it. It can also be compared to courtesy and upon seeing enough of it, one realizes that deer are very courteous — in the correct sense of courtesy. That is, after all, a form of appeasement in human society, a highly formalized set of activities of symbolic submission. Among mule deer, a mature buck itching for a sparring match with a smaller one may turn to appeasement to encourage the subordinate to spar. To someone uninitiated in the finer points of deer behavior, that can be a most confusing situation.

Another form of appeasement displayed by deer, and found also in other ruminants, is grazing. That may sound strange, but that's how grazing is used — be it by a courting subordinate who suddenly sees a dominant, be it by a smaller deer avoiding a larger one, be it by a larger buck diligently following a smaller one and periodically soliciting a sparring match, or a larger buck approached by a smaller one with whom he will ultimately spar.

When one looks, just looks, at a group of feeding deer, uninitiated in the niceties of deer language, one does not notice these things. Stick with it and you will begin to see the patterns. It may take some time, though, because we do not readily detect subtle signals. By the way, there is no such thing as an unpredictable animal, only uninformed or careless observers.

> *Grazing deer maintain the peace by letting each other know that they are appeasing, that they pose no threat. It is as if they smile at one another but use the whole body to do it.*

Let's examine the behavior most difficult for us to grasp — the very dangerous dominance displays of bucks, dangerous that is if the buck is held in captivity and you stand close to the fence. I know of one zoo warden who was killed and two others who were seriously wounded due to a lack of understanding dominance displays. That need not be!

A buck approaching another buck in dominance display normally is testing the mettle of an opponent he knows none too well, but whom he rates as inferior. To do this the buck approaches indirectly — never walking directly at the opponent. This indirect, tangential approach confuses us, or at least fails to arouse suspicion that something very dangerous has begun. Worse still, the approaching buck averts his head, as if ignoring whoever he is approaching. That type of behavior fools the uninitiated completely because we expect something attacking us to do so directly. A buck attacking from a dominance display will most likely do so when we are not looking; he will exploit any weakness to his own end. One cannot predict the timing of an attack, but one can predict that a displaying buck is likely to attack. The full-fledged dominance display includes erected body hair, ears folded back, tail somewhat erect in mule deer, quite highly raised in blacktails and curled downward in whitetails. The buck approaches in a stiff walk, the mule deer being the slowest and stiffest in his approach.

A subordinate buck will avoid displaying to a larger one. He will depress his body hair, depress his tail and crouch slightly with a depressed back. He will keep his distance, feed, circle to the dominant's rear and occasionally crouch down and attempt to sniff the dominant's hocks. He will test the wind moving from the dominant to him and keep his distance. From a distance the dominant will look dark because he erects his hair, and the evading subordinate will look lighter in color because he depresses his hair.

If the dominant buck succeeds in moving a subordinate, he may stop and horn shrubs, urinate on the tarsal brushes growing from his hocks (urine-rub) and snort in a peculiar fashion. He will quickly whip up his head and grunt while inhaling, then expel the air with a hiss through closed nostrils. The more excited a displaying buck becomes, the more likely are his tarsal brushes and his preorbital glands to be wide open. He may, while following a subordinate, reinforce his actions by periodically stopping to horn brush, snort or urine-rub.

Much more rarely, the approaching buck will find an opponent who is ready to resist. If so, the addressed buck comes in full dominance display toward the original aggressor. The bucks, looking away from one another, circle one another. Their movements become slower and stiffer as they close the gap. At this stage, they sink lower and lower to the ground, moving forward on crooked legs. Then the hair is raised maximally. They glance at one another, heads averted. Suddenly one bolts. The other jumps up, performing a hard rut-snort after the departing opponent. Escalation can work to frighten off one of the rivals. Sometimes one or both rut-snort with no effect, sometimes the bucks get closer and closer, slower and slower, lower and lower and in a

split second, much too fast for human eyes to follow, they clash into each other's antlers. The bucks strain mightily, low over the ground; they spin around one another, twisting necks as if to rotate the opponent onto his back; they may drive each other's head downward so that the antlers dig deeply into the soil, temporarily immobilizing each other. One of the bucks suddenly pulls the opponent backward, tipping him completely off balance, throwing him through the air. This locking and pulling is a trick mule deer use and so far I know of no other deer to use it.

> *The full-fledged dominance display of the white-tailed buck includes erected body hair, ears folded back, and then the tail curled downward.*

The fighters may push each other about until one suddenly disengages, turns and flees, closely followed by a poking, gouging dominant whose antlers pierce the haunches and croup of the departing loser. The dominant follows the loser a hundred feet or so on the run, coughing loudly and slapping the ground loudly with his hooves. These fights are spectacular, usually brief and very rare. They are also very damaging. However, deer wounds appear to heal fast. Nevertheless, examination of tanned hides indicates that 20 to 40 antler scars per year are added to a buck's body.

Dominance displays represent a test and a challenge, and are common enough to be seen by someone who spends even a limited amount of time watching rutting deer. The point of these displays is to raise anxiety in opponents and make them move off so that the physical cost of fighting can be avoided. While dominance displays by bucks occur commonly, escalation to a full-fledged fight is rare, very rare in fact. I have not seen more than three fights in any one rutting season and none in some. Dominance displays, including the approach at a tangent in the typical posture, urinating on hocks, rut-snorting and horning are the typical behavior of the large or of dominant bucks towards subordinates. Some of these displays, however, occur even when a large buck is alone.

In mule deer, large bucks of high status periodically go on excursions, testing if potential challengers are about. You might say they go looking for trouble. They travel at a measured walk, frequently stopping to scan the countryside with their ears. Now and again such a buck stops to horn loudly on a bush, then cups the ears forward and listens. What he listens for is an answer in kind. That is, other large bucks may respond to the sound of horning with a few strokes of their antlers on a bush. If that happens, one can see the instant flare-up of the body hair on the challenging buck and then, walking stiffly, he proceeds to plod in the general direction of the reply. The two bucks do not approach directly, but at a tangent, as if to miss one another. While out of sight of each other, the bucks whack bushes for a few strokes so one can follow their progress very nicely. When they meet, as with all displaying bucks, they appear to ignore one another. They look past the rival as if he were not present, begin horning a bush vigorously, terminating this with urination on the hocks. Once in sight, the challenge may proceed in any of the ways described above.

Unlike white-tailed bucks, mule deer bucks do not scrape and scrapes found in the vicinity of rutting mule deer have been placed there by white-tailed deer. Where big mule deer bucks roam in numbers, however, white-tailed bucks stay away. Mule deer are dominant over whitetails of equal size, although large whitetails do dominate small mule deer. The marking behavior of mule deer consists of urinating on their large tarsal glands, so much so that they become very soggy in the large, dominant bucks. Females and small bucks, after urinating on their hocks, during which time the hocks are pinched together and the tarsal brushes rubbed against one another, lick the tarsals extensively. They act as if attempting to remove the scent they just deposited. Not so the big

bucks. Their hind legs become matted with urine and they smell quite noticeably, even to human noses. Also, the larger the buck, the more frequently he urinates on his tarsal glands. This phenomenon is common in other animal species as well: The most dominant marks himself and becomes the most showy, smelly and loud individual.

The source of tarsal odor in mule and white-tailed bucks is lactones found in the buck's urine, which are selectively absorbed onto specialized, fat-covered hairs in the tarsal brushes. Yearling males that are not rutting and females have the same pattern of lactone concentrations (there are 26 lactones), but adult bucks have a different pattern. It thus appears that sexually inactive males may smell like females.

In the presence of a dominant buck, a subordinate buck will not urinate on his hocks. Rather, he will urinate in a deep squat, just like a female. It's another way for an observer to recognize the relative dominance ranks of bucks.

The mule deer exhibits a greater propensity than whitetails to horn shrubs, poles and tree trunks. Occasionally, mule deer bucks lick and nibble on the damaged bark. They do not grasp branches in their mouth and pull them. Horning may be directed at another buck, it may be done by lone bucks, it may be done as a signal and it may be done apparently for its own sake. It has to be a brave buck to horn and make a racket. I have seen defeated bucks gingerly horn, jump back in fright at the first loud clatter and then work themselves into a horning frenzy. Horning by large males is terminated by copious hock rubbing.

A brief glimpse into the mind of a deer was provided some time ago by the large glass doors of a church in a little town in a national park. Here deer and people coexisted peacefully for decades and deer rutted in the town among the houses, parking lots, workshops and picnic sites. I used to check out the deer briefly each morning and noticed that a buck I knew from previous years had arrived for the rut. He walked stiffly past the church, his reflection clearly visible in the large glass door. The buck suddenly saw this stiff-walking "stranger." He never flinched but walked on. Three paces past the door he paused and looked towards the church. Then carefully and gingerly he retraced his steps and peeked around the door's edge — seeing, of course, his image peering back at him. He withdrew his head and stood quietly for half a minute or so. Then he stepped closer and peeked around again. This time he faced his image and bobbed his antlers at it. The image bobbed back. He lowered his head gently and carefully stepped forward until his tines touched the glass. He poked only twice, then withdrew and ignored the image in the door from then on. To be noted is that he would not flinch or "lose face" at the sudden appearance of another large buck. His peeking around the corner revealed that he was quite interested in the stranger. The gentle bobbing of antlers is the sparring invitation, a very important behavior of mule deer bucks, but he identified the fake by the false tactile signals his antler tips registered when touching and scraping along the glass panels. "Keeping face" is a very important principle in animal behavior; large males will not respond to

threats by smaller ones and the loser of an encounter — even though both bucks display — may be identified quite readily. He is the one who glances most frequently at the opponent and tips his antlers towards him. He is the one most ready to catch the sudden attack; he is insecure.

Large bucks guarding does in heat skip all niceties of display when a yearling buck approaches. Such bucks are rushed by the big buck without great ceremony; rivals larger than yearlings are all approached in display, at least initially, before being rushed. Rushes that connect can leave ghastly wounds in junior bucks.

Females can, and occasionally do, display like males, but much more likely they will attack after a threat. The threat is something different from displays: It's an indication of the weapons a deer is about to use. Since does and bucks without antlers use their flailing front legs as weapons, their threat is

Len Rue, Jr.

At short range, dominant bucks avoid looking at a subordinate. The subordinate buck, however, does look — even stares — at the dominant.

an attention movement to rise up and clobber the opponent. This threat is accentuated by the deer dropping its ears and staring directly at its intended victim. Humans have no great problem learning what that behavior means. At least a deer about to strike them is addressing them and moving in menacingly. In the much more dangerous dominance displays of the males, the human observer does not realize that the display is intended for him because the displaying buck averts his eyes and does not move directly towards the observer.

Dominance displays, threats, attacks, combat, marking and submission are but part of deer social behavior. There are also the complex sparring behaviors of mule and white-tailed deer, as well as the courtship activities. But of that, we shall hear another time.

Editor's Note: "How Deer Communicate" was originally published in the August 1986 issue of Deer & Deer Hunting *magazine.*

It appears that deer are fair weather creatures that prefer clear skies, low wind velocity, and no precipitation.

DEER ON THE MOVE

Scott Hygnstrom

How does weather affect your hunt? Where do deer go when the temperature dips below freezing, or when the rain pours down? How does a howling wind or a scorching sun affect daily deer movements? To what extent does hunting pressure affect deer activity? Which hunting methods produce the best opportunities for seeing deer and how does the terrain being hunted relate to the number of deer that hunters observe? Hunters have asked these questions repeatedly through the years, but we still know little about how these many variables influence deer movements and, therefore, hunting results.

In 1977, readers of *Deer & Deer Hunting* magazine embarked on a research project attempting to answer these questions, and to set aside some of the old wives' tales pertaining to deer activities. The project began when Al Hofacker, the magazine's editor, designed standardized data sheets that readers could use, on a voluntary basis, to record their deer hunting activities. The data sheets facilitated the recording of

variables such as time of day, hours afield, weapon, hunting method, terrain, air temperature, cloud cover, wind direction and velocity, precipitation, snow cover, number of deer sighted, and the direction of deer movement.

After two years of data collection by bow, gun and camera hunters, some apparent patterns in deer activity began to emerge. Hofacker learned, however, that tabulating by hand the large quantity of hunter observations was a time-consuming, tedious task. He also noted that a large sample size (hours afield and deer sightings) was required to formulate meaningful conclusions regarding the effect of the many variables on deer activity.

When these problems surfaced, *Deer & Deer Hunting* magazine and the University of Wisconsin — Stevens Point initiated a cooperative research project in August 1980.

The objectives of the project were to (1) continue collecting data for an additional two years; (2) evalu-

Len Rue, Jr.

Whether it be for the sport of outwitting a buck or the esteem of collecting a trophy, most hunters admit they desire to see antlers. In this study, bow hunters observed bucks nearly three times more frequently than the gun hunters.

ate the data sheets and test their reliability; (3) develop a computer program to store, retrieve, and analyze the information collected; and (4) determine which variables most directly influence deer activity patterns and deer hunting results.

The Data

My first objective was to tabulate what participating hunters observed while afield. For this, I computerized the 33,027 hours of observations recorded on the data sheets. The data could then be recalled and complex statistical analyses produced.

During their combined total of 33,027 hours afield, the hunters sighted 10,121 deer. By doing a little arithmetic, we learn that hunters, on the average, see approximately one deer for every three hours of hunting time. If you consistently sight more deer, consider yourself fortunate. Many hunters sit for hours on end without seeing any deer.

The sex/age ratio of deer can provide a great deal of information about the productivity and survivability of deer. Of the 10,121 deer observed (Figure 1), hunters most frequently sighted does (41.4 percent of the total deer sightings), followed by fawns (21.9 percent), deer of uncertain sex or age (21.7 percent) and bucks (14.9 percent). These ratios are not consistent with other sex/age ratios found in the scientific literature (Roseberry and Klimstra 1974, Hirth 1977, Dapson et al. 1979, McCullough 1979).

In 1974, John L. Roseberry and W. D. Klimstra reported on the harvest of white-tailed deer during a 10-day controlled hunt held on Crab Orchard National Wildlife Refuge in southern Illinois. For this controlled hunt, "all hunters were requested not to be selective but to attempt to take the first deer that presented a good shot." The hunters harvested 1,109 whitetails consisting of 39.0 percent does, 33.1 percent fawns, and 27.9 percent bucks. The researchers believed the harvest represented the pre-hunt sex/age composition of the herd, but also pointed out that the hunt occurred on a portion of the refuge previously closed to hunting. Such an area could easily produce a deer herd with a different sex/age ratio than a similar area with an annual deer harvest.

Between 1965 and 1971, Richard W. Dapson and other researchers collected more than 5,000 white-tailed deer from two contiguous areas in South Carolina. They categorized one of the study areas as "swamp" and the other as "uplands." They found, as have other researchers, that "a greater proportion of young does bred in the uplands than in the swamps" and that young does produced a higher percentage of male fawns than did the older does.

Quite obviously then, a combination of factors can alter sex/age ratios, even in areas quite close to one another. While most other studies of sex/age ratios focus on areas of limited size, in this project I tabulated observations from a large geographic area made over a period of four years.

Although hunters from many parts of the country submitted data sheets for analysis, a large percentage (45.7) of the total hours of observation took place in Wisconsin. Other states that were well represented include Pennsylvania (11.2 percent), Michigan (7.5 percent), New York (6.0 percent) and Iowa (5.2 percent). Hunters from 23 other states contributed the remaining 24.3 percent of the total hours.

As expected, hunters recorded the majority of data in the months of September, October, and November

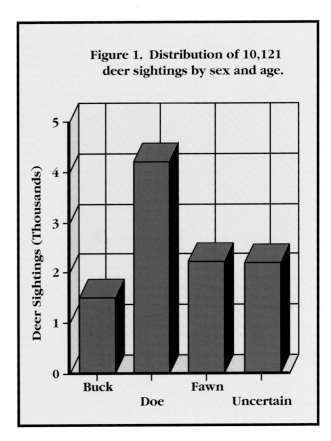

Figure 1. Distribution of 10,121 deer sightings by sex and age.

(Figure 2). This is no surprise, since relatively few hunters visit their deer hunting grounds at other times of the year. One compounding factor with data collected in the autumn months concerns the effect of the rut on deer movements. Since this study took into account only physical factors (temperature, wind, precipitation, terrain, etc.), all conclusions must be considered with the rut in mind.

Deer hunters collected the data and made this study possible. For this study to be accepted in the scientific community, however, the reliability of hunters as data collectors had to be tested. I conducted hunter reliability surveys on the opening days of the Wisconsin deer archery season in 1980 and 1981, in cooperation with Kim Mello, Fish and Wildlife Biologist at the Fort McCoy Military Reservation.

One hundred forty-two bow hunters consented to fill out the same data sheets used to collect the data for this project. These hunters estimated weather conditions experienced while hunting and I instrumentally monitored air temperature, cloud cover, wind velocity and direction, precipitation and snow cover

every half hour. By statistically analyzing the data, I found that hunter estimates matched my own weather recordings for all variables except wind direction. This difference might be expected considering the variety of topography and vegetation at Fort McCoy. Knowing that hunters can accurately record weather conditions, I feel more secure about my findings.

How Weather Affects Deer Movements

One of the main objectives in this study was to compare the weather variables on a nationwide, annual basis to determine if any one variable overrides all others in its influence on deer movements. For example, is temperature more important than wind, precipitation or cloud cover in dictating when and where deer move? I used many multivariate statistical analyses to determine if any overall relationships existed. The sample sizes were more than adequate and the statistical tests were appropriate, but I

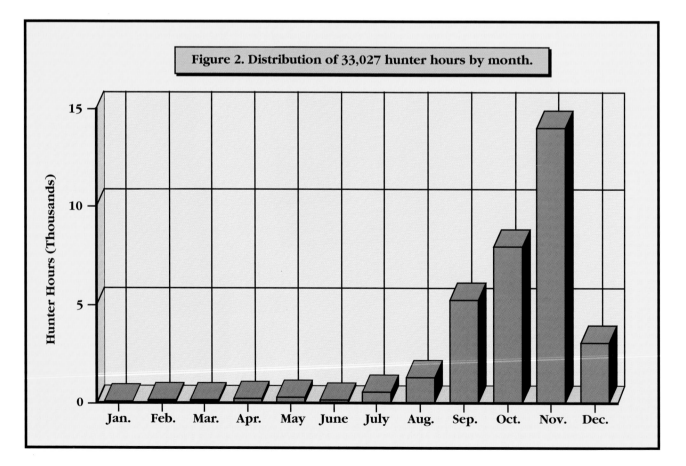

Figure 2. Distribution of 33,027 hunter hours by month.

found no overriding variables affecting deer movements. Clearly, all weather variables were equally important in affecting deer movements. To further study deer-weather relationships, I found it necessary to examine each weather variable individually.

Wind has been noted as an important factor affecting deer movements in a variety of ways. Several observers of deer behavior report that whitetails become nervous and wary during times of high winds (Hardin 1974, James 1976, Rue 1978). Leonard Lee Rue III, in *The Deer Of North America* (1978), remarks that "high winds make deer extremely nervous, because the clashing of the wind-lashed trees and branches covers almost all sounds and the eddying and reversal of air currents makes scenting almost impossible. With the whole world in motion, deer are almost panicked." W.R. James (1976), while attempting automobile census counts of white-tailed deer, also observed a rise in the wariness of deer. At the same time, however, he reports that deer activity increased during periods of high winds.

Studies conducted in Michigan (Ozoga 1968, Ozoga and Gysel 1972, Verme 1973) indicate that deer apparently seek shelter from winter winds in the Lake States region. John J. Ozoga and Leslie Gysel monitored deer activity within a Michigan deeryard to determine the effects of weather and snow condition on deer use of protective cover. Their data showed "an increase in deer activity within the heavily sheltered site during periods of low temperature or high air chill" which "probably indicates a shelter-seeking response by deer." In an earlier study of microclimate variations in a conifer swamp deeryard, Ozoga learned that a densely stocked, mature swamp exhibited warmer temperatures and lower wind flow than other, more open portions of the yard. Based on the available evidence, it appears that deer actively seek shelter from high winds during the winter months in the northern portions of their range.

While deer may seek shelter from the wind in the winter, at other times they may take advantage of the wind. Deer sometimes rest on ridges in full wind to escape annoying insects or let the breezes cool them on hot summer days (Taylor 1956).

In this study, deer activity decreased as wind velocity increased. Calm and light winds produced an increase in deer sightings while moderate, gusty and strong winds reduced sightings (Table 1).

Interestingly, buck movements deviated from the overall pattern. Observers witnessed decreased buck movements during calm winds and increased movement during strong winds (Table 2). I dare not venture to explain why bucks move when they do, but this inconsistency should be of some interest to the deer hunter.

In reviewing the scientific literature, I found no studies dealing with the effects of wind direction on deer movements. Where the wind blows one's scent has always been an important consideration in developing hunting strategies. Deer certainly take advantage of the wind and its airborne aromas, but do they actively utilize it? Might the direction of the wind dictate the direction of deer travel?

Unfortunately, the participants in my hunter reliability survey did not accurately estimate wind direction. As noted earlier, this was quite likely due to local topography affecting wind movement. Another

Table 1. Observed and expected deer sightings (all deer) for differing wind velocity.

Wind Velocity	% Of Total Hours	Observed Deer	Expected Deer
Calm	8.2	877	810
Light	44.9	4,943	4,437
Moderate	28.1	2,548	2,777
Gusty	12.2	977	1,206
Strong	6.6	537	652

Expected Deer = % of Total Hours x Total Deer Observed

Table 2. Observed and expected buck sightings for differing wind velocity.

Wind Velocity	% Of Total Hours	Observed Bucks	Expected Bucks
Calm	8.2	105	120
Light	44.9	769	658
Moderate	28.1	361	412
Gusty	12.2	128	179
Strong	6.6	103	97

Expected Deer = % of Total Hours x Total Bucks Observed

consideration is that the hunters used in the survey were not necessarily readers of *Deer & Deer Hunting* magazine. They were resident bow hunters from southwestern Wisconsin. Those readers who collected the 33,000 hours of data are a devoted lot, likely more reliable in estimating weather conditions than the general bow hunting public.

> ***Participants in this study sighted proportionately more deer during times of clear skies than under partly cloudy or overcast conditions. And, bucks also appeared partial to clear skies.***

In comparing the direction of travel for deer and the associated wind directions, a very interesting relationship developed. Deer moved directly into the wind (for all eight compass points) proportionately more often than they moved directly with, perpendicular to, or quartering with or away from the wind. This movement pattern appears to be selective and reflects a behavioral defense mechanism in deer.

Deer hunters commonly debate the effect of sky conditions on deer movement. Like hunters, researchers disagree on the relationship between cloud cover and deer activity patterns. Donald R. Progulske and Donald C. Duerre (1964), for example, studied the feasibility of using spotlight counts of deer to estimate deer populations in South Dakota. Although they reported decreased activity during cloudy nights, they cautioned that "cloud cover was particularly difficult to analyze because some counts were conducted on clear, dark nights; thus the correlation is somewhat meaningless."

H.C. Hahn, Jr. (1949), while censusing deer in the Edwards Plateau of Texas, also noted decreased activity with increasing cloud cover. Other researchers, however, state that deer activity increases when cloud cover increases. For example, G.G. Montgomery (1963) studied the nocturnal movements

and the activity rhythms of white-tailed deer in Pennsylvania. In the study area, deer fed primarily on field crops and bedded in nearby forested terrain. Montgomery experienced increased deer activity with increased cloud cover.

For this study, hunters collected data only during daylight hours and, therefore, analysis of the data compares daytime deer activity with the various weather conditions. I found that participants in this study sighted proportionately more deer during times of clear skies than under partly cloudy or overcast conditions (Table 3). Bucks also appeared partial to clear skies (Table 4). A statistical test of the buck sightings, however, revealed that increased buck sightings on clear days possibly occurred due to chance. Nevertheless, deer generally become more active under fair sky conditions.

How many deer hunters hunt in the rain? I frequently read articles describing the virtues of hunting in the rain, but what are the deer doing while it rains, snows, sleets or hails? Researchers generally agree that during periods of rain, deer activity decreases (Progulske and Duerre 1964, Tibbs 1967, Hawkins and Klimstra 1970, Michael 1970). The results of this

Table 3. Observed and expected deer sightings (all deer) for varying cloud cover.

Cloud Cover	% Of Total Hours	Observed Deer	Expected Deer
Clear	41.9	4,451	4,217
Partly Cloudy	21.9	2,112	2,204
Overcast	36.2	3,411	3,643

Expected Deer = % of Total Hours x Total Deer Observed

Table 4. Observed and expected buck sightings for varying cloud cover.

Cloud Cover	% Of Total Hours	Observed Bucks	Expected Bucks
Clear	41.9	655	630
Partly Cloudy	21.9	324	330
Overcast	36.2	525	544

Expected Deer = % of Total Hours x Total Bucks Observed

study reinforce the findings of previous researchers.

Data from this study show that deer sightings decreased not only while rain fell, but also markedly decreased during periods of fog, hail, sleet and snow. Deer sightings were proportionately higher during periods of no precipitation (Table 5). Buck sightings also followed this pattern of increased activity at times of no precipitation (Table 6). An important factor to consider is that as precipitation increases, the hunter's visibility decreases. Some or all of the discrepancies in deer sightings may reflect an inability to see deer rather than reduced deer movements.

It appears that deer are fair weather creatures that prefer clear skies, low wind velocity and no precipitation. I can't think of better conditions for deer hunting either, but more questions remain.

▨ Bow Season Vs. Gun Season ▨

For years, the opening day of the deer season has perplexed many hunters. They scouted their favorite areas for weeks in advance of the season to learn where and when deer move. For some unknown reason, the deer apparently vacated these same areas when the season opened.

More than 40 years ago (1948), Larry Koller remarked that "with hunters tramping through almost all available cover and feeding grounds throughout the day, deer will be constantly on the move from one hide-out to another, breaking their normal routine sufficiently that no rules of conduct apply." More recently, a number of popular magazine articles addressed the topic of hunting pressure (Brauer and Hofacker 1978, Steinke 1979, Taylor 1980, Weiss 1982), but little has been said about it in the scientific field. Al Hofacker reported from a 1977 deer hunt survey that 25.0 percent of the gun hunters experienced heavy hunting pressure during their outings, and approximately 40 percent experienced moderate pressure. These figures must be seriously considered when hunting or researching whitetails, due to the implications of hunting pressure on natural deer movements.

For the purposes of this study, participants filled out data sheets on which they recorded the type of weapon used: bow, gun, camera, and none. Bow hunters spent a combined total of 16,800.2 hours in the field while the gun hunters logged 10,237.2 hours (Table 7). By comparing the number of deer seen with the amount of time spent afield, we learn that bow hunters observed 35.14 deer per 100 hours while gun hunters saw 17.59 deer per 100 hours. (Note: "Deer" refers to bucks, does, fawns, and deer whose identity is uncertain. "Bucks" specifically refers to adult male deer.) During bow season, therefore, hunters saw twice as many deer per hour as during gun season.

Whether it be for the sport of outwitting a buck or the esteem of collecting a trophy, most hunters admit they desire to see antlers. In this study, bow hunters observed 5.45 bucks per 100 hours compared to 1.94 buck sightings per 100 hours by gun hunters. Bow hunters saw nearly three times the number of bucks per hour as did gun hunters! These figures comprise the first of a number of results which indicate that bow hunting may affect natural deer activity less than gun hunting.

The amount of time available for hunting is an

Table 5. Observed and expected deer sightings (all deer) for varying precipitation.

Type Of Precipitation	% Of Total Hours	Observed Deer	Expected Deer
None	82.6	8,588	8,358
Fog	1.8	99	180
Rain	10.5	919	1,060
Snow	5.2	515	523

Expected Deer = % of Total Hours x Total Deer Observed
Snow includes snow (4.9%), sleet (0.2%) and hail (0.1%)

Table 6. Observed and expected buck sightings for varying precipitation.

Type Of Precipitation	% Of Total Hours	Observed Bucks	Expected Bucks
None	82.6	1,265	1,246
Fog	1.8	16	27
Rain	10.5	159	158
Snow	5.2	69	78

Expected Deer = % of Total Hours x Total Bucks Observed
Snow includes snow (4.9%), sleet (0.2%) and hail (0.1%)

important factor for all of us, especially in this work-a-day world. It pays to be efficient, even in the sport of deer hunting. Bow hunters, on the average, spent 2.85 hours afield each outing compared to 5.68 hours for the gun hunter (Table 7). Even when we consider the differences in season lengths, it appears that bow hunters are far more efficient in seeing deer than gun hunters.

Average distances between hunters and the deer they observed also differed for the two types of hunting seasons. The average sighting distances for bow and gun hunters were 41.08 and 50.85 yards respectively. For bow hunters, 65.9 percent of the deer sighted were within 50 yards while 52.4 percent were within 50 yards of the gun hunters.

Considering the amount of time spent hunting, the number of deer seen, and the distances of these sightings, the data show a marked difference in the nature of bow and gun hunting seasons. High hunter densities, characteristic of gun seasons, affect natural deer movements and make deer less predictable, more wary and, in general, more difficult to observe.

If you really want to see deer, however, the data

suggest you never carry a weapon into the woods. Participants in this study who photographed or simply observed deer saw a combined 40.30 deer per 100 hours and 6.58 bucks per 100 hours; far more than either gun or bow hunters observed! The majority of the time spent photographing and simply observing took place when no hunting season was in progress, however. These results further reinforce the idea that hunting pressure affects deer movements.

Because of the vast differences in bow, gun, and no weapon observations, I will address them separately. The following sections regarding Hunting Methods and Terrain will deal only with data collected from September to January 1977-1981 to simplify the discussions and lend consistency to the conclusions.

Hunting Methods

The selection of the most effective hunting method has led to many heated debates in deer camp. Many knowledgeable authors have presented their opinions, which often conflict. In 1979 Michael Wallschlaeger

Table 7. Hunting time and deer sightings while afield with various weapons.

Weapon	Total Hours	Average Hours	Deer Per 100 Hours	Rank	Bucks Per 100 Hours	Rank	Average Distance
Bow	16,800.2	2.85	35.14	3	5.45	3	41.08
Gun	10,237.2	5.68	17.59	4	1.94	4	50.85
Camera	2,019.0	2.36	42.35	1	7.28	1	51.91
None	3,966.5	2.55	39.25	2	6.23	2	55.19

Table 8. Bow hunting time and deer sightings using various hunting methods.

Hunting Method	Total Hours	Average Hours	Deer Per 100 Hours	Rank	Bucks Per 100 Hours	Rank	Average Distance
Still Hunt	2,281.5	3.38	29.63	4	4.30	4	49.47
Tree Stand	11,289.2	2.70	37.03	2	5.96	1	39.00
Ground Stand	1,818.5	3.33	30.02	3	4.40	3	41.19
Deer Drive	302.5	3.21	26.12	5	3.31	5	42.18
Scouting	988.5	2.46	40.67	1	4.55	2	48.02

wrote, in *Deer & Deer Hunting* magazine, of the many benefits and detriments of tree stands. In a 1978 article, Jack Brauer and Al Hofacker discussed the challenging method of still hunting. Many others have written on stand hunting, deer drives, stalking, and rattling up bucks (Cartier 1976, Hofacker 1980, Mattis 1980, Harrison 1981, Mattis 1982). Though information from this study may not apply to your situation, there appear to be some obvious trends concerning which hunting methods are most effective in producing deer sightings.

Deer hunters involved in this study recorded their method of hunting on data sheets as either Still Hunt, Tree Stand, Ground Stand, Deer Drive, or Scouting. Of the 32,325.5 hours of hunting time logged, by far the most effective method for seeing deer was tree stand hunting. Bow hunters used tree stands 67.6 percent (11,289.2 hours) of the time and observed 37.03 deer per 100 hours (rank #2 for bow hunting methods) and their 5.96 bucks per 100 hours ranked first among bow hunting methods (Table 8). Gun hunters showed less enthusiasm for climbing trees and logged 2,122.0 hours (20.9 percent of their hunting time) in tree stands. Ironically, those gun hunters were very successful in seeing deer, with 20.31 deer (rank #2 for gun hunting methods) and 2.54 bucks (rank #2) sighted per 100 hours (Table 9).

From an elevated position, such as a tree stand, a bow hunter transmits fewer danger cues (movement, noise, odor) to deer and thus becomes less detectable. Deer often came within a few yards of the tree stand hunter, with the average sighting distance being 39.00 yards. This sighting distance ranked first among all hunting methods (Table 8). Of all bow hunting sightings, 41.4 percent were within a range of 30 yards.

From an elevated position, the hunter's ability to see usually increases. This aids him in detecting deer early and enables him to adjust for a suitable shot. Gun hunter sighting distances from tree stands averaged 53.30 yards and ranked high among other hunting methods (Table 9). By evaluating the number of deer sighted and the average sighting distances, hunting from a tree stand proved to be very effective.

Deer drives are very popular among some larger hunting groups, especially late in the season after hunting pressure affects natural deer movements. George Mattis, in his book titled *Whitetail: Fundamentals and Fine Points for the Hunter* (1980), details a number of small and large group strategies for driving deer and discusses conditions in which driving may be an effective, if not the only, way to hunt deer. Driving deer, however, has changed. Mattis states, "The drive today is not the drive made earlier in the century, for the modern whitetail refuses to be pushed ahead of a line of men." In *The Modern Deer Hunter* (1976), John Cartier comments on learned behavior and how experienced deer avoid drives.

Returning to the data from this study, it appears that deer driving is a rather ineffective hunting method. Gun hunters spent 7.5 percent (766.5 hours) of their time driving (Table 9). While making drives, they sighted 18.40 deer per 100 hours (rank #3) and their 1.04 buck sightings per 100 hours ranked fifth among the various hunting methods. These sightings are appreciably lower than for other methods and may be due to learned behavior by deer or time of the season. Bow hunters rarely use drives (1.8 percent, 302.5 hours). Sightings of 26.12 deer and 3.31 bucks per 100 hours both ranked fifth when compared to other bow hunting methods and might reflect why bow

Table 9. Gun hunting time and deer sightings using various hunting methods.

Hunting Method	Total Hours	Average Hours	Deer Per 100 Hours	Rank	Bucks Per 100 Hours	Rank	Average Distance
Still Hunt	2,448.0	6.39	15.65	5	1.72	4	46.95
Tree Stand	2,122.0	4.92	20.31	2	2.54	2	53.30
Ground Stand	4,456.2	5.97	16.74	4	1.76	3	49.42
Deer Drive	766.5	5.44	18.40	3	1.04	5	51.42
Scouting	271.5	3.72	26.89	1	5.16	1	64.03

hunters conduct deer drives less frequently than gun hunters.

The success of deer drives depends highly upon the size and coordination of the group. Other important factors that must be considered include topography, vegetation, field history, hunter experience, safety and ethics.

Two age-old methods, still hunting and ground stand hunting, remain popular among the hunting legions. Unfortunately, in this study they were only moderately effective in producing deer sightings.

George Mattis, a master of the art of still hunting, stated most accurately that "true still hunting is a happy combination of trail watching and walking, with more use of the eyes than the feet." (Mattis 1980). To effectively still hunt, one must exercise all his hunting knowledge and skills. Often regarded as the most difficult method of hunting whitetails, it is likely to be the most rewarding for the successful hunter.

Contrary to the belief that still hunting is a dying art, this study revealed that both gun hunters (2,448.0 hours, 24.1 percent) and bow hunters (2,281.5 hours, 13.7 percent) frequently still hunt (Tables 8 and 9). Popular literature and scientific research agree that still hunting is a very difficult and challenging method for producing venison. As T.S. Van Dyke observed more than 100 years ago, "With whatever proficiency in still hunting any mortal ever reaches, with all the advantages of snow, ground, wind, and sun in his favor, many a deer will, in the very climax of triumphant assurance, slip through his fingers like the thread of a beautiful dream."

The use of a ground stand has always been a popular method of deer hunting. In this study, it was the most preferred method of gun hunters. Nearly half (4,456.2 hours) of their total time was spent on the ground, hoping that deer would pass or be "pushed" within shooting range. Bow hunters also used ground stands, but to a lesser degree (1,818.5 hours, 10.9 percent).

A number of authors (Cartier 1976, Mattis 1980) discuss stand hunting and its considerations. George Harrison, in an interesting article written for *Sports Afield* in 1981, included comments by famed deer biologists R. Larry Marchinton, Bill Severinghaus and Louis J. Verme, all of whom recommended stand hunting as the most productive method of deer hunting.

In this study, the ground stand, although not the most productive method, was relatively consistent (rank #3) in producing deer and buck sightings for gun and bow hunters. Gun hunters observed 16.74 deer and 1.76 bucks per 100 hours, while bow hunters reported more success by seeing 30.02 deer and 4.40 bucks per 100 hours. Though not as productive as other hunting methods, many deer hunters still use ground stands because they do provide numerous opportunities to see deer.

Tree stand hunting appeared to be the most effective hunting method in this study. Hunters using tree stands saw more deer and at closer ranges than those who still hunted, conducted deer drives, or used ground stands. Surprisingly, scouting during any season produced the highest number of deer and buck sightings per 100 hours (Tables 7, 8 and 9). It is difficult to explain this difference, but it seems we might have another addition to Murphy's Law: The less you act like a deer hunter, the more deer you will see!

Table 10. Bow hunting time and deer sightings while hunting various types of terrain.

Terrain Hunted	Total Hours	Average Hours	Deer Per 100 Hours	Rank	Bucks Per 100 Hours	Rank	Average Distance
Edge Of Field	3,703.7	2.55	39.15	2	4.37	5	44.32
Conifer Forest	1,353.5	3.60	27.78	5	4.43	4	43.10
Hardwood Forest	7,491.0	2.95	33.92	3	6.55	1	40.86
Softwood Forest	2,549.0	3.35	32.95	4	4.71	2	37.68
Swamp	1,600.5	2.44	40.99	1	4.56	3	39.16

Terrain

Deer activity depends highly upon habitat. The placement of life requisites (food, water, shelter, etc.) within an animal's home range dictates daily movements. By thoroughly knowing your hunting area, you can gain an understanding of local deer movements and, ultimately, you will observe deer at close range.

In this study, I looked for any overriding effects that terrain might exert on deer movements. Hunters recorded the hunting terrain as Edge of Field, Conifer Forest, Hardwood Forest, Softwood Forest or Swamp, but I noted some confusion between the terms Conifer Forest and Softwood Forest. For the purposes of this study, Conifer Forests represented areas dominated by coniferous species (spruce, pine, fir, hemlock, etc.) while Softwood Forests were areas of broadleaved, deciduous, softwood trees (aspen, willow, etc.).

Differences between bow and gun hunting methods were readily apparent when analyzing Hunting Methods data. In examining the influence of terrain on deer activity, however, things are far less clear. For example, swamps ranked first for deer sightings by bow hunters (Table 10), but fifth for gun hunters (Table 11). Similarly, on field edges, sightings of bucks ranked first for gun hunters but fifth for bow hunters. A quick look at Tables 10 and 11 gives you an idea of the broad overlap regarding deer and buck sightings in different terrains.

Sightings, in general, for bow and gun hunters were highest on field edges and in hardwood forests. Of all 16,697.7 bow hunter hours, 3,703.7 (22.2 percent) were spent on field edges, producing an average of 39.15 deer and 4.37 buck sightings per 100 hours. Deer sightings from field edges ranked relatively high (rank #2) among terrain types, but buck sightings were quite low (rank #5). These statistics most likely reflect buck behavior and their reluctance to fully expose themselves in open fields during legal hunting hours.

Field edges produced many sightings for gun hunters, ranking first in both deer (19.77 deer per 100 hours) and buck sightings (2.77 bucks per 100 hours). It is interesting to note that only 14.8 percent of the 9,787.2 gun hunting hours were spent overlooking field edges. Considering the good visibility and increased shooting range associated with edges, it is surprising that gun hunters don't spend more of their time there.

Habitat use by whitetails has also been a popular subject in the scientific community. A number of studies have been made and a wide range of methods used to learn more about deer habitat. In the past 15 years, the scientific literature frequently included one observation regarding deer habitat: Deer use is highly associated with "edges." Keith McCaffery conducted two research projects in northern Wisconsin dealing with the use of forest openings by deer. In newly constructed openings, he found deer numbers to be 40 times greater than the expected average of adjacent range! Two other articles in the *Journal of Wildlife Management* (Kohn and Mooty 1971, Kearney and Gilbert 1976) noted the high frequency of edge use by deer in the summer and discussed the importance of maintaining forest openings for food production.

Wildlife professionals consider the white-tailed deer an "edge species." "Edge" is the close association of different habitat types. Animals thrive there because of the presence of diversified food and cover-producing plants. Deer, feeding in a forest opening, can easily slip into the protective cover of the woods when danger

Table 11. Gun hunting time and deer sightings while hunting various types of terrain.

Terrain Hunted	Total Hours	Average Hours	Deer Per 100 Hours	Rank	Bucks Per 100 Hours	Rank	Average Distance
Edge Of Field	1,446.5	5.06	19.77	1	2.77	1	61.13
Conifer Forest	1,377.5	5.58	17.93	3	2.40	2	48.42
Hardwood Forest	3,254.2	5.13	19.48	2	2.30	3	48.40
Softwood Forest	1,674.5	5.64	17.74	4	1.55	4	54.93
Swamp	2,034.5	7.48	13.37	5	1.03	5	44.15

approaches. It wasn't surprising that participants in this study did so well when hunting on field edges.

When one thinks of deer hunting, pictures often come to mind: Colorful oak ridges and acorn-fattened does; vast bottomlands of maple and ash, where bucks grow old and develop large antlers. It seems there is a tradition in deer hunting and hardwood forests. Indeed, hardwood forests were by far the most popular areas, with bow hunters logging 44.9 percent (7,491.0 hours) and gun hunters 33.2 percent (3,254.2 hours) of their time in this type of terrain. Deer and buck sightings were relatively high for both types of hunters, although all but one of the four categories analyzed fell short of the average number of deer observations on field edges (Tables 10 and 11). Bow hunter buck sightings ranked highest in hardwood forests (6.55 bucks per 100 hours).

In another study by McCaffery (1976), deer trail counts were used as an index to determine populations and habitat use by deer in northern Wisconsin. He found the greatest abundance of deer trails in areas of intolerant (sun-loving) forest types such as aspen, jack pine, red pine, pin oak, and upland brush and grasses. Trail abundance was lowest in a hardwood, tolerant forest type (sugar maple).

In Minnesota, Kohn (1971) also found high deer use of softwood stands (aspen) in the summer. Kearney and Gilbert (1976) reported the most highly used forest type in Canada, from October through April, to be deciduous softwoods and mixed coniferous forests.

It is interesting to note that the scientific literature and the results of this study are in direct opposition. The literature says that softwood forests are the place to be. Our results show hunters quite successful in hardwood forests and consistently unsuccessful in softwoods! While hunting in softwoods, bow and gun hunters ranked fourth in all categories except bow-buck sightings (rank #2). It is surprising that softwoods ranked so poorly in this study. They are highly productive and often considered prime habitat for game animals. Possibly there is some bias present in the data due to the frequent close association of softwoods and field edges.

Coniferous forests ranked as the least popular terrain among bow hunters (rank #5, 1,353.5 hours) and gun hunters (rank #5, 1,377.5 hours). Similarly, they produced low sightings of deer and bucks, with the exception of gun hunters who observed 2.40 bucks per 100 hours (rank #2). Coniferous forests are typically areas of low productivity due to the effects of shading and acidic soils. Still, there are always exceptions to the rules.

Something must be said about swamps. Gun hunters spent a good share of their time there (2,034.5 hours, 20.8 percent), perhaps to catch a glimpse of the mythical "swamp buck." Unfortunately, they were relatively unsuccessful in seeing deer (13.37 deer per 100 hours, rank #5) or bucks (1.03 bucks per 100 hours, rank #5). It is possible that a majority of the swamp hunting occurred late in the season, after deer are pushed into swamps and become particularly wary. Limited visibility is likely to be an inhibiting factor, too, as reflected by the low average sighting distance of 44.15 yards (rank #5). Although bow hunters spent little time in swamps (1,600.5 hours, rank #4), they were very successful in seeing deer (40.99 deer per 100 hours, rank #1).

A great deal of research has been done on swamps in the Lake States. Ozoga (1968) and Rongstad and Tester (1969) reported on the marked increase in conifer swamp use by deer from November through February. This yarding behavior is important, as deer seek out the limited protective cover of swamps during the stressful winter period. Larson et al. (1978) reported on a project in southcentral Wisconsin in which deer traditionally moved into a large tamarack swamp shortly after the opening day of the deer-gun season. This movement was reasoned to be an avoidance of hunters, since the swamp was heavily posted and had very little hunting pressure.

In summary, results from this study show that your best chance of seeing deer might occur while bow hunting from a tree stand on a field edge or in a hardwood forest. This is not a sure-fire method for harvesting a deer, but rather a statement of results formulated from the data collected by hunters participating in this study. Perhaps you'll consider this information when preparing for future hunting expeditions.

Editor's Note: This chapter was originally published as two articles in Deer & Deer Hunting *magazine: "The Effect of Environmental Conditions on Deer Movements" (October 1982) and "Deer on the Move" (February 1983).*

Brauer, J. and A. Hofacker. 1978. "Still Hunting: Scouting Tool and Hunting Technique." *Deer & Deer Hunting* 1(6):12-14.

Brauer, J. and A. Hofacker. 1978. "Coping with Human Pressure." *Deer & Deer Hunting* 2(2):7-10.

Cartier, J.O. 1976. *The Modern Deer Hunter*. Funk & Wagnalls. 310 pages.

Dapson, R.W., P.R. Ramsey, M.A. Smith, and D.A. Urbston. 1979. "Demographic Differences in Contiguous Populations of White-tailed Deer." *Journal of Wildlife Management* 43:889-898.

Hahn, H.C. Jr. 1949. "A Method of Censusing Deer and its Application in the Edwards Plateau of Texas." Texas Fish, Game and Oyster Commission. Job Completion Report, P-R Project 25R. 24 pages.

Hardin, J.W. 1974. "Behavior, Socio-biology and Reproductive Life History of the Florida Key Deer (Odocoileus virginianus clavium)." Ph.D. Dissertation. Southern Illinois University, Carbondale. 226 pages.

Harrison, G. 1981. "Take a Stand for Deer." *Sports Afield* 186(4):63-65, 153-154.

Hawkins, R.E. and W.D. Klimstra. 1970. "Deer Trapping Correlated with Weather Factors." *Transactions of the Illinois State Academy of Science* 63:198-201.

Hirth, D.H. 1977. "Social Behavior of White-tailed Deer in Relation to Habitat." *Wildlife Monograph No. 53*. The Wildlife Society. 55 pages.

Hofacker, A. 1978. "Results from the 1977 Deer Hunt Survey." *Deer & Deer Hunting* 1(6):9-11.

Hofacker, A. 1980. "The most Popular Hunting Method." *Deer & Deer Hunting* 4(1):24-28.

James, W.R. III. 1976. "The Relationships of Selected Weather Parameters with Automobile Census Counts of White-tailed Deer (Odocoileus virginianus) on Crab Orchard National Wildlife Refuge." M.S. Thesis. Southern Illinois University, Carbondale. 49 pages.

Kearney, S.R. and F.F. Gilbert. 1976. "Habitat Use by White-tailed Deer and Moose on Sympatric Range." *Journal of Wildlife Management* 40:645-657.

Kohn, B.E. and J.J. Mooty. 1971. "Summer Habitat of White-tailed Deer in North Central Minnesota." *Journal of Wildlife Management* 35:476-487.

Koller, L.R. 1948. *Shots at Whitetails*. Alfred A. Knopf. 359 pages.

Larson, T.J., O.J. Rongstad and F.W. Terbilcox. 1978. "Movement and Habitat Use of White-tailed Deer in Southcentral Wisconsin. *Journal of Wildlife Management* 42:113-117.

Mattis, G. 1980. *Whitetail: Fundamentals and Fine Points for the Hunter*. Van Nostrand Reinhold Co. 248 pages.

Mattis, G. 1982. "The Persevering Solo Hunter." *Deer & Deer Hunting* 5(4):22-25.

McCaffery, K.R. 1976. "Deer Trail Counts as an Index to Populations and Habitat Use." *Journal of Wildlife Management* 40:308-316.

McCaffery, K.R., J.E. Ashbrenner and J.C. Moulton. 1980. "Forest Opening Construction and Impacts in Northern Wisconsin." Wisconsin Department of Natural Resources. Technical Bulletin 120. 40 pages.

McCaffery, K.R. and W.A. Creed. 1969. "Significance of Forest Openings to Deer in Northern Wisconsin. Wisconsin Department of Natural Resources. Technical Bulletin 44. 104 pages.

McCullough, D.R. 1979. *The George Reserve Deer Herd: Population Ecology of a K-Selected Species*. University of Michigan Press. 271 pages.

Michael, E.D. 1970. "Activity Patterns of White-tailed Deer in South Texas. *Texas Journal of Science* 21:417-428.

Montgomery, G.G. 1963. "Nocturnal Movements and Activity Rhythms of White-tailed Deer." *Journal of Wildlife Management* 27:422-427.

Ozoga, J.J. 1968. "Variations in Microclimate in a Conifer Swamp Deeryard in Northern Michigan." *Journal of Wildlife Management* 32:574-585.

Ozoga, J.J. and L.W. Gysel. 1972. "Response of White-tailed Deer to Winter Weather." *Journal of Wildlife Management* 36:892-896.

Progulske, D.R. and D.L. Duerre. 1964. "Factors Influencing Spotlighting Counts of Deer." *Journal of Wildlife Management* 28:27-34.

Rongstad, O.J. and J.R. Tester. 1969. "Movements and Habitat Use of White-tailed Deer in Minnesota." *Journal of Wildlife Management* 33:366-379.

Roseberry, J.L. and W.D. Klimstra. 1974. "Differential Vulnerability During a Controlled Deer Harvest." *Journal of Wildlife Management* 38:499-507.

Rue, L.L. III. 1978. *The Deer of North America*. Outdoor Life/Crown Publishers. 463 pages.

Steinke, T. 1979. "Hunting Under Pressure." *Deer & Deer Hunting* 3(2):31-32.

Taylor, J.S. 1980. "Where Do You Stand on Whitetails?" *Deer & Deer Hunting* 4(2):8-11.

Taylor, W.P. (Ed.). 1956. *The Deer of North America*. Stackpole Books. 620 pages.

Tibbs, A.L. 1967. "Summer Behavior of White-tailed Deer and the Effects of Weather." M.S. Thesis. Pennsylvania State University, University Park. 93 pages.

Van Dyke, T.S. 1882. *The Still-Hunter*. Fords, Howard & Hulbert. 390 pages.

Verme, L.J. 1973. "Movements of White-tailed Deer in Upper Michigan." *Journal of Wildlife Management* 37:545-552.

Wallschlaeger, M. 1979. "Tree Stands: Helpful or Detrimental?" *Deer & Deer Hunting* 2(4):17-20.

Weiss, J. 1982. "Where the Bucks Go." *Outdoor Life* 170(2):46, 87-88.

Mother Nature in her infinite wisdom "plots and schemes" to replenish the earth with her creatures. The female of the species plays a major, even if subtle, part.

William S. Lea

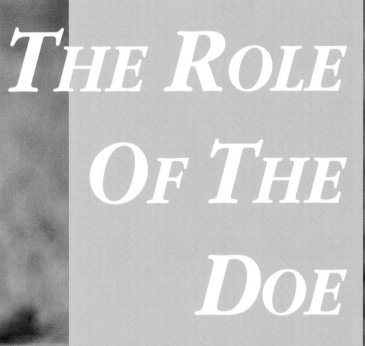

THE ROLE OF THE DOE

Kent Horner

*S*ocial order in a white-tailed deer population centers around the activities of the doe. Bucks fight for her sexuality and fawns depend upon her for milk. For the deer family, the doe is definitely the "goody-wagon" tripping through the forests; she brings good things for the ol' man and the kids.

THE ROLE OF THE DOE

The doe performs well in nature's plan, too. Over eons of time, survival of the species is of utmost importance, more important than the survival of individual animals. And, to enhance the survival of the herd, the doe plays out her biological role as well as the buck. It's analogous to a dance. "It takes two to tango," and there's not going to be a gala affair without the girls present. Nature bases species survival solely upon gendered activities — sex. And, in the long run, both sexes play equally important roles.

In the case of deer, evolution adapted them to survive predominantly in temperate zones. To accomplish this, a fawn's survival of its first winter must be maximized. Mother Nature seemingly has a sense of fair play and makes adjustments accordingly. Nature, thus, makes it highly improbable for deer to breed in cold climates except in the fall and early winter.

Instinctive maternal behavior like spacing newborn fawns apart from each other at birth has significant survival advantages.

Because of an approximately 200-day gestation period, fawns are then dropped at the time of optimum vegetative growth. Consequently, feeding first on the doe's milk and then later munching on succulent plants, the fawn gains weight quickly before the harshness of its first winter begins. Breeding and subsequent fawning, then, are geared to the seasons. Were it otherwise, deer survival in cold climates would be difficult since they are mainly vegetative browsers. Furthermore, any newborn browser would be at a critical disadvantage during its first winter.

To bring this seasonal breeding to fruition, it is mandatory that a period of infertility be incorporated into the deer's annual life cycle. That's done in the case of the buck, not the doe. Deer are hormonal animals; their seasonal activities are geared to their endocrine systems. The buck, as it turns out, is incapable of breeding except during a few months in late fall and early winter.

That one important restriction assures that the fawns will be dropped seven months later during the bounty of spring. Unlike the doe, who goes through her estrous cycles and produces fertile female sex cells every month except while pregnant, the buck has a very low sperm count except during the rut and is incapable of breeding for much of the year.

Since temperate-world deer can breed only during a few months each year, the act is greatly heightened. During the rut, glandular secretions deposited by both the buck and the doe are important communication signals helping to assure fertilization of the doe. Consequently, the pheromones produced by the doe during her estrous cycle become strong sexual stimulants for the buck.

From the hunter's standpoint, pheromone-based sexual lures are excellent lures to use while hunting during the rut. It is a fact of deer existence that, during the rut, the buck becomes much more interested in breeding than in any of his other physiological functions. The urge to breed is even stronger than that of eating and resting.

Also during the rut, sexual stimuli from the doe cause tremendous psychic pressures within the buck. Thus, during their estrous cycles, when does deliberately seek out the bucks' scrapes, the does greatly enhance breeding potential and subsequent fawn production.

In social orders, females of most animal species, by their nature, are more gregarious than males. The doe is no exception. Whereas the buck, especially during the rut, remains a loner that solitarily roams the woods, the doe is strongly matriarchal. The matriarchal doe is usually the first deer along the trail as she guides her entourage through the forest. This bit of knowledge can be helpful to the hunter who hears deer coming while on his stand. In short, the buck may be lagging behind and hoping that the doe has courtship on her mind.

The buck, however, could care less about coddling his young offspring; he's too interested in trying to start another family by maintaining his dominant status. If he succeeds, he gets to breed more — a simple but true dictum in nature.

Young fawns that at birth imprint visually and by scent upon their mother maintain this social dependence for several months. The yearling buck, however, is the first family member to leave the maternal influence. After leaving, the young buck roams freely until he establishes a new home range.

The maternal drive of female care and possessiveness toward her offspring is nature's method of promoting species survival. During spring and summer, for instance, when the fawns are suckling, the doe is the more dominant figure in the deer family. Bucks with sensitive, velvet-covered antlers cater to the actions of the doe. During summer, it is common to observe the doe physically kicking the buck as she bosses the daily activities within the herd.

This domineering attitude of the doe changes, though, during the breeding season when the buck is at his dominant height. During the rutting season, penned, sexually frustrated bucks bearing hardened antlers have been known to gore a doe to death. Thus, both sexes execute their authoritative roles in promoting species survival.

Charles J. Alsheimer

The maternal drive of female care and possessiveness toward her offspring is nature's method of promoting species survival.

THE ROLE OF THE DOE

The death of individual deer is relatively unimportant when viewed in the context of species survival. However, by following their internal, physiological drives, overall deer survival is assured over time. Furthermore, does are indirectly the restrainers on deer territory, even for the bucks. It has been well established that, with few exceptions, white-tailed deer typically live within a home range with a radius of 1.5-miles or less. And, even though yearling bucks may disperse when first leaving the social order controlled by the doe, the young buck soon settles into his own relatively small home range.

Following nature's plan, though, no sexually healthy buck lives completely isolated from the doe population for long. So, a buck naturally chooses a home range at least proximal to does. More directly, a doe in estrus may alter the home range boundaries for the buck during the rutting season. While performing her sylvan shenanigans, a doe becomes a free-floating "breeding territory" as bucks follow her in hot pursuit. Consequently, home range boundaries for a buck are more prone to change during the breeding season than at any other time after the original establishment of his home range.

Usually bucks feel more secure within their home range as they work it against predators. Sprinting and hiding within familiar terrain, the buck can more successfully evade potential captors. For species survival, however, progeny production always comes before individual safety. Thus, a buck willingly lets his guard down somewhat during the rut as he chases does. For the deer hunter, the buck's diminished caution provides an added advantage as the buck becomes more mobile during the day. While rutting, the buck is physiologically motivated more by the sexual drive than by feeding, resting or sticking strictly to his home range. So, indirectly, the doe stimulates deer activity even though, on the surface, it may not be that obvious.

Moreover, the doe is a population regulator. Ultimately, the number of fertile does is the limiting factor for population growth. There can be no more fawns produced than there are fertile female sex cells within the reproductive system of the does. For this reason, sound wildlife management practices limiting the number of does is often of primary importance.

The driving sexual force within any deer herd is to overpopulate its habitat. Deer populations always tend to multiply to the point of depleting the food supply. Should wildlife management practices fail to regulate the number of does, nature soon steps in

Curt Helmick

When deer herds are in balance with the habitat's carrying capacity, adult does typically give birth to twin fawns and triplets are not uncommon.

and reduces the herd through starvation and disease.

The reluctance of hunters to harvest does can become, ultimately, a self-defeating act in deer perpetuation. Should that be the case, the end result is poor management and a subsequently reduced herd.

Does not only set the population parameters, they also carry one-half of the genetic traits passed on to future progeny. Over evolutionary time, the doe is instrumental in governing adaptive factors that promote the survival of future deer generations, too.

Young fawns that at birth imprint visually and by scent upon their mother maintain this social dependence for several months.

Amazingly, the white-tailed deer, a large animal, has the unique ability to survive close to man. In so doing, a premium is placed upon the evasion of danger. Consequently, inherited traits such as speed, deception, camouflage, size, immunity to disease and tolerance of harsh weather are important survival traits that the doe helps pass on to her progeny.

Whereas for bucks, herd survival value is placed on strength, stamina and a large set of antlers, good maternal characteristics are called for in the doe. For instance, milk production, stealth, scenting ability and a healthy endocrine system are critical survival traits.

Also, instinctive maternal behavior like spacing newborn twin fawns apart from each other at birth has significant survival advantages. The survival value, of course, would be that if a predator kills one fawn, it might not find the other fawn.

Does also have the physiological ability to govern the number of fawns, even after conception. For example, following breeding, a doe on a starvation diet may form only one fetus from a potential set of twins. At birth, then, the doe can provide enough milk for survival of one fawn. Had twins been born, both youngsters might have died from malnutrition.

Wildlife biologists have also found that does on a starvation diet produce more male fawns than female fawns. The survival benefit, supposedly, is that males, as yearling bucks, will disperse and leave the starvation zone. Biologists have also demonstrated that does bred late in their estrous cycle will produce a preponderance of male fawns. This often happens under intense "bucks-only" hunting conditions.

Under this severe selection pressure, the breeding population of bucks is often drastically reduced. This being the case, does often are not bred during their first estrous cycle simply because there are too few bucks available to service all the receptive does.

Although the exact biological mechanism has not been fully explained yet, wildlife scientists have shown that does bred later, in their second or third estrous cycle, produce a greater percentage of male progeny. The end result, of course, is that the breeding population of bucks will increase the next generation.

Thus, Mother Nature in her infinite wisdom "plots and schemes" to replenish the earth with her creatures. And, as is stated in so many of Man's early writings, the female of the species plays a major, even if subtle, part. Thus ... the role of the doe.

Editor's Note: "The Role of the Doe" was originally published in the February 1984 issue of Deer & Deer Hunting *magazine.*

Charles J. Alsheimer

Understanding
— *Scrapes & Rubs* —

Rich Waite

Before choosing to hunt a particular scrape or rub line, it's important to know why deer made them in the first place. Understanding what influences rubbing and scraping provides valuable insights into deer behavior.

Rubs and scrapes made by white-tailed deer serve as visible evidence that deer, particularly bucks, have been in the area. It is this physical evidence that many hunters use each year to fill their freezers with tasty venison.

But before choosing to hunt a particular scrape or rub line, it's important to know why deer made them in the first place. By understanding what influences rubbing and scraping, hunters gain insights that help decipher the deer woods.

Two important factors are deer density and herd structure. These elements can cause differences in rutting behavior and, thus, cause changes in the frequency of scrapes and rubs. In most cases, as deer densities increase, so do the number of scrapes and rubs in an area. It seems that high densities of deer promote extensive scraping by white-tailed bucks 12 to 23 days before any successful breeding takes place. Apparently, certain pheromones produced by does during this time trigger early sexual activity in bucks. The appearance of early scrapes signals the start of the pre-rut. This "silent" estrus, as it's called, is thought to help promote synchronization between the male and female breeding cycles. However, seasonal changes in food quality and abundance can alter pheromone production in white-tailed does and

Mark S. Werner

Bucks that have taken part in previous ruts produce significantly more scrapes than younger males. The limb above the scrape is marked with the buck's saliva, or glandular secretions from his forehead glands.

can, thus, affect the timing of this "silent" estrus. Also, seasons with poor forage may delay actual breeding activity and force delayed conceptions. So be aware that the exact timing of the "silent" estrus can vary from year to year and, thus, affect the timing of the first scrapes.

Rubs are also generally found in greater numbers when deer densities are high. But, like scrapes, they seem most abundant in herds with good populations of mature bucks. However, even in herds that contain mostly young bucks, rubs will still be made. In such instances, though, rubs will generally be fewer in number and made on smaller trees. It's important to realize that both rubs and scrapes serve as visual and olfactory signposts, as well as dominance symbols, and play key roles in the overall reproductive success of the white-tailed deer.

It has been proven repeatedly that mature, dominant bucks make most of the scrapes and rubs in an area. Therefore, in areas with lots of deer but few mature bucks, one should expect to find few breeding scrapes. The key word here is "breeding." That's because even in high-density areas with few mature bucks, a flurry of buck scraping activity will still occur 12 to 23 days before the peak of the rut. The difference is that the bucks making the scrapes will be juveniles or, at least, not yet "socially" mature bucks. Again, these scrapes will signal the start of the pre-rut, but will not be made when does are receptive. They are made to synchronize breeding so that both the bucks and the does will be "ready" when the time to breed arrives. Remember, though, that you'll likely find fewer scrapes used for actual breeding because of few mature bucks. That can be expected for rubs as well.

According to a study by T.L. Kile and R.L. Marchinton, antler rubs serve as visual and olfactory signals through which males mark areas and establish dominance in preparation for the breeding season.

Marchinton, T.G. Sawyer and K. Miller also found that rubs serve as a type of "scent communication post" that can alter the physiological status of does so they will be ready to breed when the bucks are. Apparently, odor that's rubbed onto the tree to produce this reaction in does comes from the sudoriferous glands on the buck's forehead. These glands become more active as the rut nears.

Breeding scrapes are made to intimidate rival

males and to attract females for breeding. Some believe that most scrapes are made by dominant bucks. However, Miller and his associates suggest that high dominance rank may not be as important as the buck's physical and behavioral maturity. They also say that bucks that have taken part in previous breeding seasons produce significantly more scrapes than younger males.

Scrapes also play a role in scent communication. Nearly all scrapes are made beneath some type of overhead vegetation. This is usually a single limb that is one to two yards off the ground. This limb is marked with the buck's saliva or glandular secretions from his forehead glands. The scrape itself consists of a pawed-out depression in the soil that the buck urinates on. Does have also been observed making scrapes and urinating on them. But it's rare for a doe to make a scrape, and they've never been observed, to my knowledge, scent-marking an overhead limb.

White-tailed bucks have preferences for scrape sites. Good scrape sites are those with concentrated deer activity, open understory vegetation, relatively level ground, a suitable overhead limb, and moderately dry and easily exposed soil. The ground should not be water-logged or excessively rocky or sod-covered. Michigan researcher John Ozoga has found that, given favorable circumstances, white-tailed deer can be induced to scrape beneath human-positioned overhead limbs. This probably isn't news to serious deer hunters. Mock scrapes have been used by some hunters for quite a few years. But it's important to realize the significance of this fact. Not only can hunters benefit from placing a stand near natural scrapes, but they can also make their own scrapes where it's most convenient to hunt.

If you decide to try mock scrapes, you need to first look for areas that meet the above criteria. If the site lacks a suitable overhead limb, you'll need to place one. Find a limb that's one to three yards long, and about an eighth- to quarter-inch thick at its terminal end or tips. Next, you'll need to suspend the limb horizontally with brown twine, not nails, so that its tip is about 45 inches above the ground. Once in place, it should bow slightly downward. Many hunters prefer to place the branch's tips directly over a deer trail, providing the trail is in a suitable area. Many hunters who make mock scrapes say the next step is to expose the soil beneath the limb. Ozoga says this may not be necessary, however. In fact, he found deer do not show a significantly greater scraping response to mock scrapes with exposed soil. He thinks deer may be induced to scrape just by the sight or accidental bumping of the overhead limb.

This, then, is a judgment call. If you feel more confident by exposing the soil in your mock scrape, it won't hurt anything. If you expose the soil, use

Table 1. Frequency of white-tailed deer pawing artificial and natural scrapes in a 252-hectare enclosure near Shingleton in Michigan's Upper Peninsula from October 8 through November 12, 1987.

| | Artificial Scrapes | | | | Natural Scrapes | | | |
| | Overhead Limb Only | | Overhead Limb And Bare Soil | | Old | | New | |
Week	n	No. Pawed	n	No. Pawed	n	No. Pawed	n	No. Pawed
October 8-15	20	2	20	0	20	2	7	7
October 16-22	20	3	20	4	20	6	20	15
October 23-29	20	5	20	10	20	8	30	12
Oct. 30 - Nov. 5	20	2	20	3	20	10	48	23
November 6-12	20	5	20	8	20	9	51	7

Adapted from John J. Ozoga, 1989. "Induced Scraping Activity in White-tailed Deer." *Journal of Wildlife Management* 53(4):877-880.

either a stick, antler or small garden tool. Loosen the soil with your tool and make a circular depression that's about 18 inches in diameter, but don't go down more than a half-inch or so. Then shake a little leaf litter or similar debris over all but the center one inch of soil. Lightly covering the exposed soil makes it easier to tell if a buck has worked the scrape. I think it also encourages the buck to scrape it out cleanly. The next step most hunters take is to place some kind of scent onto the soil and overhead limb.

It has long been thought that you can't make an effective mock scrape without scents. However, Ozoga found that applying scents to encourage deer to use artificial scrapes is not warranted. He also thinks that elaborate attempts to minimize human odor when checking and making mock scrapes is probably not necessary. He said a properly positioned overhead limb serves as a strong visual trigger, and is all that's necessary to make an effective mock scrape. However, I encourage hunters to keep human scent near mock scrapes to a minimum. Maybe a little human scent won't hurt anything, but it definitely won't help, either.

Mock scrapes can be made before you find the first pre-rut natural scrapes. In fact, an early mock scrape may trigger earlier-than-usual scraping and rubbing by bucks. I have a feeling that using scents on these early mock scrapes helps "prime" the bucks for the upcoming rut. For best results, however, I'd suggest not making mock scrapes earlier than one month before the peak of the rut. Anytime sooner is probably too unnatural. The most active scraping activity occurs about two weeks before the peak of the rut. After this, scraping by bucks and scrape visitation by all deer decreases daily. And, nearly 80 percent of all scrapes are made before the time the first female conceives, Ozoga reports. He also found that only 35 percent of all scrapes were visited by any deer during a 24-hour period at the height of the rut. This should tell us something about where not to hunt during the peak of the rut.

Ozoga found that scrapes made the previous year are likely to be used again. He reports that 65 percent of the scrapes made the previous autumn were reopened the next year. He also found that 95 percent of these old scrapes contained deer tracks throughout the year. Thus, even if old scrapes aren't reopened the next breeding season, there is still a

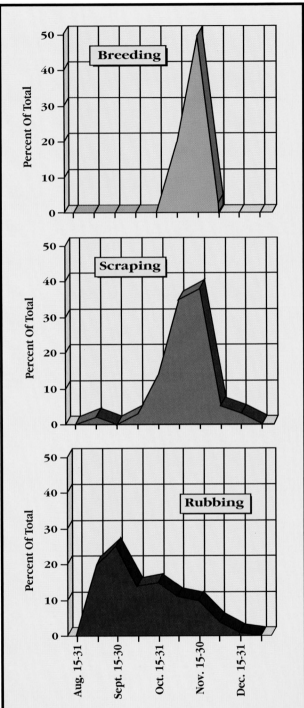

Figure 1. The frequency of rubbing, scraping and breeding activity of white-tailed deer in the Georgia Piedmont during two-week periods from August 15 through January 14.

Graph data from T.L. Kile and R.L. Marchinton, 1977. "White-tailed Deer Rubs and Scrapes: Spacial, Temporal and Physical Characteristics and Social Role." American Midland Naturalist, 97(2):263.

good chance deer are visiting the scrapes. It's been suggested that deer use the overhead branch in these old scrapes all year to scent-mark their home ranges. Thus, look for old scrapes when scouting. They are good locations for an early mock scrape.

> *A Michigan researcher found that 95 percent of old scrapes contained deer tracks throughout the year. Thus, even if old scrapes aren't reopened the next breeding season, there is still a good chance deer are visiting them.*

Since it's believed that a main purpose of scrapes is to attract a receptive doe, one might expect breeding does to methodically walk from scrape to scrape during the peak of the rut. However, this is not the case. Unlike bucks, does don't exhibit a search strategy for finding a mate. Instead, they limit movement during the peak of the rut, spending most of their time in the core areas of their home ranges. This helps explain why scrape visitation by all deer reaches a low point at the peak of the rut. It seems that by staying in one small area instead of roaming the countryside, does increase their breeding chances. This may make you wonder why bucks go through the hassle of making scrapes. Well, remember that scrapes are made for a variety of reasons. They serve a much more complex role than simply bringing the sexes together for breeding. And, indeed, the role scrapes play in attracting breeding females may be somewhat overrated.

All this information should tell you to focus on areas most frequented by does during the peak of the rut. You'll likely have more success than sitting over a scrape. If you know the core areas of one or more does, get in there. That's where the bucks will be looking for mates.

Deer rubs and scrapes play key roles in the life cycle of the whitetail and need to be understood by anyone interested in increasing their knowledge of deer. To be a consistently successful deer hunter, you need to be as familiar as possible with deer behavior.

Editor's Note: "Understanding Scrapes And Rubs" was originally published in the October 1992 issue of Deer & Deer Hunting *magazine.*

Must They Starve?

Nancy Lee Brownell

What could be the adaptive value of going into a winter deeryard where many deer are doomed to starve, and even the survivors are weakened and suffer terrible privations? There must be some overwhelming benefit from yarding to counterbalance the heavy death toll.

Bill Kinney

As a child, I liked to ride to the end of the road and observe the deer that gathered in the winter, flitting among the dark, overhanging hemlocks of their traditional deeryard along the creek banks. To my young eyes, it seemed a cold and cheerless place. As I grew older and realized that each winter many deer actually starved to death in the yards, I wondered all the more why, year after year, they came back to a place where all the browse within reach had long ago been eaten. It seemed to show a sad lack of intelligence for the survivors of each winter's ordeal to return annually to the scene of such devastation.

> *The only time of year when whitetails gather into what might be considered a herd is in the winter yard. Deer come into the yard singly or in small groups, often from widely scattered summer ranges.*

When I began some serious reading on the subject of behavioral ecology, I encountered the concept of "adaptive value," or the way in which an animal's behavior increases its chances of survival as a species. Again I thought of the curious behavior of white-tailed deer in the wintertime. I wondered what could be the adaptive value of going into a winter yard where many deer were doomed to starve, and even the survivors were weakened and suffered terrible privations? There must be some overwhelming benefit from yarding to counterbalance the heavy death toll, but I didn't know what the benefit might be.

Nothing I learned in my college years as a wildlife management major, or in my five years of working for a state fish and wildlife agency, addressed my questions about yarding by white-tailed deer from a behavioral point of view or explored the mechanisms by which such an apparently stupid habit was

perpetuated. Intrigued, I turned to the accumulated literature of the last half a century in search of an answer to the question: If winter yarding behavior leads to starvation, what powerful selective pressures are at work to override the obviously nonadaptive starvation? In other words, what benefits do the deer obtain from going into deeryards that are so vital they are worth the cost in dead and debilitated deer?

First, let's look at what constitutes a deeryard. The classic deeryard, as described by deer researchers from the 1930s through the 1950s, is the protected lowland of big conifers. C.W. Severinghaus and E.L. Cheatum describe such areas in "Life and Times of the White-tailed Deer," a chapter in Walter P. Taylor's *The Deer of North America* (1956). They also picture deer, after heavy snowstorms, lying in "dens" underneath the low-hanging evergreen branches where they are insulated from the cold and protected from the wind. Contrary to my childish impressions of cold and gloom, such places offer deer a fair degree of comfort.

The number of scientific papers describing winter concentrations of deer in coniferous lowlands or evergreen swamps attests to the fact that deeryards are common throughout the whitetail's range in the northern United States and the forested parts of Canada. Not all deer winter in such areas, however, even in the northern states. Wildlife biologist Nathaniel R. Dickinson reports that in the southern tier of New York, where conifers are scarce, deer often gather for the winter on steep, south-facing slopes. In northern New York's Adirondack Mountains, they commonly yard in coniferous valleys or swamps, but sometimes use exposed south slopes, as do the deer of Vermont. On the other hand, in northeastern Minnesota whitetails live in extensive forest, much of it wilderness, and winter in traditional coniferous lowland deeryards. Both types of wintering areas provide conditions that reduce the amount of energy a deer must use — snow depths are less than in the surrounding summer habitat and the wintering areas are warmer.

Since deer winter in a variety of habitats, many biologists prefer to use the term "winter concentration area" rather than "yard." "Deeryard" carries with it certain unfortunate connotations, among them well-defined boundaries, very restricted movement, and an ingrained response of deer to the changing seasons which brings them, willy-nilly, to the same spot each fall. But many winter concentration areas do not fit this stereotype and deer are not automatons. Deeryards vary, and so does the animal's behavior.

Not all deer populations concentrate in winter. In fact, according to David Hirth's *Wildlife Monograph No. 53* (1977) — "Social Behavior of White-tailed Deer in Relation to Habitat" — the deer in Texas may actually range over a larger area in winter than they do in the summer. Most populations of northern whitetails do go into some sort of wintering area where their movements become more restricted than in the summer. Yarding appears to be an adaptation that helps them survive in harsh climates. As you go farther north, to the limits of their distribution, the deer's yarding behavior becomes more pronounced and the yards more closely resemble those described in the earlier literature than those in milder climates. Also, severe winters tend to encourage yarding while open winters allow the deer to remain spread out

over much of their summer range, or to concentrate in a number of small areas of winter habitat in or near their summer range, rather than to move to a large winter yard.

Many biologists have studied the whitetail's winter habitat and looked at the factors which cause deer to move into their winter yards. Severinghaus and Cheatum suggested that snow depth is the most important factor, and most research since that time confirms their findings. Wind chill may also be important. Deer often move into wintering areas before the arrival of deep snow, however, and may pass up patches of good winter cover close to their summer range to travel several miles and winter in a distant yard. In addition to the environmental factors, there is apparently an important behavioral component, whether inborn or learned, which makes them seek their traditional deeryards.

When discussing deer populations and management, biologists refer to the deer "herd," but the

Richard P. Smith

What benefits do the deer obtain from going into deeryards that are so vital they are worth the cost in dead and debilitated deer?

whitetail is not a herd animal in the same sense as the red deer of Scotland, whose "life and times" are so ably chronicled by F. Fraser Darling in *A Herd of Red Deer* (1937) and by T.H. Clutton-Brock and his associates in *Red Deer: Behavior and Ecology of Two Sexes* (1982). Whitetails prefer woodland and brushy habitats, unlike the open moors favored by the gregarious red deer. Skulking through the brush or scattered over a broad, mountainous forest, deer are hard to monitor; most observations have been done at feeding stations or along lake shores and roads. Indirect observations, using track counts or browse sign, and more recent research with radio telemetry has revealed much about the whitetail's behavior and social structure, but the big picture must be pieced together from research papers contributing facts like the pieces of a jigsaw puzzle.

White-tailed deer live solitary lives, or move about in small groups. In the summer an old doe, her yearling daughter and her newborn fawn or fawns form a family group; sometimes two or three generations of does and their fawns remain together. Bucks may be solitary or join small groups of other bucks in the non-breeding season. They are seldom part of a family group once they reach maturity. Bonds between the buck and doe are short-lived, lasting only five or six days at the time the doe is in heat, but bucks are found in mixed-sex groups at many times of the year outside the breeding season.

The only time of year when whitetails gather into what might be considered a herd is in the winter yard. Deer come into the yard singly or in small groups, often from widely scattered summer ranges. Within a few days a hierarchy is established among them so that they become not just a chance aggregation of individuals but a structured social group. In some cases, several small "herds" exist within what appears to be a large, continuous deeryard.

The details of this social hierarchy, while interesting, are outside the scope of this chapter. What is important is the fact that the structure exists, for social interaction of the individuals in a species is an important factor in the adaptation of the species to its environment. We are concerned not with the survival of individuals, but with the survival of the species. Variation in behavior among individuals is necessary, for it is upon such variation that selection works in

order to evolve the behavior pattern best adapted to the environment in which the species lives. If members of a species do not interact with one another, and act only as individuals, their experiences will not contribute to the collective knowledge or "culture" of the species. There will be no tradition. Deer do show a capacity to learn, and fawns learn a great deal from their mothers, so learned behavior certainly influences their adaptation to a changing environment.

Biologists have done innumerable studies of the white-tailed deer, its habitat, social structure and behavior. But very few of these studies examine the adaptive significance of winter yarding behavior from an evolutionary standpoint, or attempt to explain how such behavior is perpetuated over the years. Two of the most interesting studies on the subject are the doctoral research done by George Mattfeld at Huntington Forest in New York's Adirondacks, and the work of Michael Nelson and L. David Mech in the wilderness of northeastern Minnesota. Mattfeld, in his 1974 doctoral dissertation, approaches the question of why deer move to winter yards from the point of view of energetics — yarding saves energy, thus increases the chance that yarding deer will survive to produce young the following spring. Nelson and Mech, in their *Wildlife Monograph No. 77* (1981), "Deer Social Organization and Wolf Predation in Northeastern Minnesota," favor the hypothesis that predation by wolves is the selection factor which led to the development of traditional yards, and encourages deer to return each year.

The idea that deer save energy by yarding is not original with George Mattfeld, but he builds upon the observations of earlier researchers such as Severinghaus and Cheatum, and D.F. Behrend who did research at Huntington Forest in the 1960s, to approach the subject quantitatively. His data support the idea that deer do not move into the wintering areas out of stupidity or slavish adherence to set behavior patterns; they go there because it is the place in which they have the best chance to survive the winter.

Mattfeld fitted a captive deer with a mask to measure the animal's oxygen consumption, an indication of energy used when the deer was resting, walking, running or driven through deep snow and over bare ground. He found that when a deer sinks into snow

10 to 16 inches deep, walking or running used much more energy than the same activity on bare ground. In very deep snow, more than 40 inches deep, the deer changes to a gait and speed which conserve energy, moving one plunge at a time, progressing slowly. Given a choice, deer avoid deep snow. In deep snow they become vulnerable to predators such as wolves, mountain lions or bobcats, but Mattfeld feels that energetics is a greater factor than predation in determining the survival value of a deer's winter behavior and habitat choice.

Deer appear to reduce their metabolic rates in winter, so that at rest they burn fewer calories. They

Deeryards are an adaptation against the rigors of severe winters, whether through predation or energetics, or a combination of the two. But the behavior is not necessarily coded genetically — the behavior of an individual or a group of deer is based to a large extent on learning.

survive not on the food which they find but on the fat reserves they built up prior to the onset of winter. Combating the deep snow and the exposure to wind and cold in the open hardwoods, they are less likely to make it through the winter than they are lying among the protective evergreens of the traditional lowland wintering areas. Looked at from this point of view, it does not seem quite as stupid for them to leave areas in which food is plentiful and move to areas which may or may not contain much browse. The relative food supply in open hardwoods and

winter yards is debatable anyway. Mattfeld's analysis indicated that clumps of witchhobble, a favorite winter deer food in his study area, occurred nine times as often along the deer trails in winter concentration areas as they did in the open hardwoods.

However, on their migration to large deeryards in which they congregate from as far as 25 miles away, many deer pass up small areas of thick evergreen cover which seem equally as good as that in the yard. Nelson and Mech present a very good case for wolf predation as the determining factor in the development of this tradition among deer. Not only do deer create a trail system in the yard, which makes it easier for them to move about and escape an attacking wolf, but in a large group there are many eyes to look out for wolves and each deer can be less vigilant. Since deer scatter when chased, the group may serve to confuse the wolves somewhat so that each deer is less likely to be caught.

Perhaps even more significant is the relationship of the traditional deeryards to the wolf packs' territories. Around a winter yard, two or more wolf packs may compete for the hunting rights to the deer herd. The dominant, or alpha, wolves of each pack may actually fight each other, sometimes to the death. This strife among wolves makes them less effective as predators upon deer, wasting their time and energy competing among themselves rather than spending it to catch and kill deer. Also, many of the deer in the yard have come from miles away, moving out of the territories of other wolf packs which could have surrounded and killed them as small, isolated bands or individuals. In the 1960s, after a series of mild winters in Nelson and Mech's study area, deer that might formerly have moved to their traditional winter yard stayed on or near their summer range in small, scattered groups. Of those that stayed in such groups many, if not all, were killed by the wolves; only those that joined the larger herd in the traditional winter yard survived.

The two hypotheses, Mattfeld's or Nelson and Mech's, are not incompatible. In fact, it seems likely that both energetics and predation could be factors in developing and maintaining deer yarding behavior. In the Minnesota wilderness, wolves are important. At one time wolves inhabited northern New York as well. Now, the wolves are gone, but the behavior that

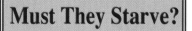

developed in response to the wolves is still favored by the energy savings that yarding represents.

In northern New York, deer behavior varies more than in northeastern Minnesota. In winters with little

> *The congregation of deer in winter yards, which may seem to be a rather stupid habit on the part of the deer, might actually be a necessary adaptation for survival of the species, especially in the most inhospitable portions of its northern range.*

snow and few days when the temperature does not rise above zero degrees, deer in the Adirondacks can survive in many scattered locations, including more open hardwoods and mixed forests. There are no wolves to contend with. In severe winters, the deer that remain isolated and in more open locations are less likely to survive because they use up their energy reserves battling deep snow and cold winds.

Deeryards are an adaptation against the rigors of severe winters, whether through predation or energetics, or a combination of the two, but the behavior is not necessarily coded genetically — the behavior of an individual or a group of deer is based to a large extent on learning. Fawns come to the yard with their mothers and thus learn where to go in the winter. If there is a series of open winters, the deer will learn new places to go and the traditional yard may even be abandoned or moved to a new location.

That deer respond to changing habitat conditions is illustrated in Mattfeld's research. He compares deer in Huntington Forest, where logging created a variety of habitat types, to those on the neighboring Santanoni Preserve where the habitat is more uniform, perhaps similar to the wilderness described by Nelson and Mech in Minnesota but without the wolves. On Huntington Forest, yarding behavior is more varied than it is on the Santanoni Preserve or in the Minnesota wilderness where the habitat is more uniform.

I did not find a clear-cut answer to my original question on the adaptive value of yarding to the white-tailed deer. The situation is too complex for simple explanations. Considering the deeryard from a sociobiological point of view sheds some light on the puzzling behavior of whitetails, but neither the energetics hypothesis put forth by Mattfeld nor the predation model outlined by Nelson and Mech has been proven. It may be that neither is really subject to proof. Both hypotheses suggest likely ways in which what at first seems to be a rather stupid habit on the part of the deer might actually be a necessary adaptation for survival of the species, especially in the most inhospitable portions of its northern range.

Editor's Note: "Must They Starve?" was originally published in the April 1985 issue of Deer & Deer Hunting *magazine. "A Winter Loss" (facing page) was orginally published in the February 1985 issue.*

A Winter Loss

George Hartman

Almost like a sleeping dog, the deer lies on its side, neck outstretched, as I approach. Last night's inch of fluffy snow, on top of the 20 crusted inches already on the ground, makes my approach a silent one. Silence, however, is unnecessary. The deer, a fawn, is dead.

The ratty look of its face indicates starvation. The heavy winter coat softens the deer's body contours, but by running my mittened hand over its back I feel the bony thinness of severe malnutrition. After cutting through the thin ham with my hand ax, I break the femur. Instead of solid, white, fatty marrow, I find it to be thin, red and jelly-like — a condition which confirms starvation.

In spite of the near-zero temperature, the animal is only partially frozen. Death came only a few hours earlier. Opening the body cavity and cutting the paunch, I find that the fawn's last meal consisted of stems of tag alder, hazel and a few red pine needles — all "stuffer" foods.

I write up my field notes. As I am about to leave, I see the fawn's footprints in the snow fluff. Backtracking the prints only a hundred feet or so, I find several places where the fawn fell. Here it browsed on a badly chewed small red pine, there on hazel, and near the swamp edge it fed quite extensively on tag alder. I look for better deer food species: red maple, jack pine, aspen and cherry. They are here but mostly above browse height. I observe that the lower branches of these trees, and even those of the starvation species, show a heavy browse line to a height deer can reach. The finger-thick aspen stubs show that their diets, this winter, consisted more of wood than of nutritious barks and buds. The best winter deer foods in this locale — wintergreen, swamp dewberry, cranberry, blueberry and a number of other ground cover plants — have long been sealed under the crusted snow. A few futile pawings show at the base of larger trees where adult deer tried, but failed, to uncover the ground cover plants. Tracks of a larger deer join the fawn in the tag alder. Scuff and fall marks, a gob of deer hair show where it knocked the fawn down. No mercy here.

I return to the carcass and sit down on a nearby fallen tree to rest, smoke and think. This is my first starved deer find of the season. I will find more, as it is only mid-February. March is the bad month and deer can be lost in April, too. Even after the snow is gone, some of the stressed animals will die. They are just too far gone to recover.

I review the factors involved and, of course, search for a solution. Basic problems include too many deer and the long, harsh winter. High deer populations are the result of favorable winters and human efforts such as eliminating predators, establishing refuges, holding conservative deer seasons, logging and burning of mature forests, creating forest openings and introducing farm crops.

I look at the dead fawn. For a moment I visualize it as a beautiful summer-spotted fawn — and then as it was in its gray October coat. I think of the November hunting season when we shot deer by the thousands. Then, most, but not all, of the deer shot die quickly. True, there are crippling losses, and that also makes me sad. I ponder a bit about more humane solutions than hunting, but can find none. It is hard to accept the idea that all living creatures must die.

I adjust my snowshoe bindings and as I hike to the car, I find some solace in the knowledge that most of our bullet-killed deer die quickly. Deer hunting represents a better alternative than starvation any day.

March is the bad month and deer can be lost in April, too. Even after the snow is gone, some of the stressed animals will die. They are just too far gone to recover.

Charles J. Alsheimer

Part Two
Hunting
Methodology

Charles J. Alsheimer

Not Just To Kill

Al Cornell

Most people have heard about things of beauty and intrigue in the woods. Hunters know they exist because they are there to see them. And because they have seen, they care.

If you're never there, you'll never know that squirrels visit some hollow stumps because they are natural cisterns.

. . . Or that a drumming grouse may stop after a couple beats if it started at the same time as a nearby rival.

. . . Or that autumn's fawns may eat large Caesar's mushrooms in such big bites that you can watch the lump go down their throats.

. . . Or that chickadees may sip sap off the tips of icicles on maple branches.

Many people who watched "Crocodile Dundee" have never carried a knife. Most who hunt have made decisions to shoot or to pass. Some can detail the vital area of a deer from various angles and can place their shots with deadly precision. A few scout the deer woods in March.

Many people who enjoy prime rib have never forked silage. Most who flip venison butterfly chops in the skillet have examined acorns. Some can tell you that red-oak acorns taste more bitter than white-oak acorns. A few know that tender green oak sprouts may be heavily browsed by deer during the summer.

Many people who eat buttered bread have never churned cream. Most who watch sunrises from a tree stand have sensed the increase and wane of nature's larder. Some have followed deer tracks in the snow and observed which shrubs and saplings were browsed. A few have seen a starving deer stare at them indifferently.

Many people who smell the roses have never handled the fertilizer. Most who have squeezed the trigger have felt their heart pounding. Some have pondered the life and death cycle of nature. A few have shed a tear.

I recently visited a part of the country where much of nature's enchantment had succumbed to structures and implements of humanity. I scanned a large magazine rack in a busy mall. Nature and hunting magazines sat obscurely in a corner.

From human clusters of suburbia a voice asserts that hunters are an evil force at work against nature and wildlife. This voice falls as bizarre gibberish upon the ears of those who have paid for the nation's wildlife programs and fought to maintain a place for wildlife. Those who have paid for land purchases and

By definition, killing an animal is a goal of hunting. Beyond definitions, the experience of hunting bonds the hunter to the creation.

Bill Vaznis

striven to help game and non-game species are appalled that their motives and mission could be so misunderstood.

Most of our current population have never seen wind and rain unfasten autumn's maple and aspen leaves. They have never watched a buck materialize in late-blooming asters. They have never seen a squirrel strip bark from a red cedar or a grouse peck buds in an old apple orchard. Lack of association causes lack of understanding. Lack of understanding causes misdirected energy.

> ## Many people who smell the roses have never handled the fertilizer.

The positive interactions of humanity and nature stem from active participation. Bird watching and hiking contribute to a concern for ecosystems. But no other catalyst has bound as large a sector of humanity to the woods and fields as hunting. Historically, people hunted from necessity. Recently, recreation has become a primary motive to hunt. Be it societies of the past or individuals of the present, hunters demonstrate a great affinity to the untamed and to nature.

In times when we were less flush, economic motives often caused our ties to the deer woods. Ginseng could buy shoes to protect our feet. Once soled, we would go afield to secure meat, fruits and mushrooms. Those outings made impressions that are still evidenced in today's lifestyles. Yet, not all inspiration came of necessity. The one who sat on the knob in the evening, watching for the doe and her fawns, and saw the first stars shortly after the early owl challenge, probably hunts today.

The future of much wildlife, and of hunting, depends on a bond formed between our children and the deer woods. If a lifestyle persuades youngsters that the cinema and the coliseum are Earth's most beautiful and entertaining spots, wildlife will lose an important edge in its struggle for a place to exist. Our children need a tie to things fascinating and wonderful. A tie can cause them to be involved for a lifetime. In turn they will be motivated to involve their children.

Hunting can bind the love for nature in the mind of a youth. So, too, I suppose, can other outdoor activities. Yet none other is equal in time-honored and tradition-bound impact.

If mankind ever engraves polished granite for the last Nimrod, the woodlands themselves will mourn and worry.

Editor's Note: "Not Just To Kill" was originally published in the August 1991 issue of Deer & Deer Hunting *magazine.*

Charles J. Alsheimer

Human Scent And Deer Hunting

Tim Lewis

When we look at the total picture of how scents give us away, the prospect of encountering unalarmed deer seems hopeless. Fortunately, some factors are in our favor.

We all know about the whitetail's phenomenal ability to detect odors, but exactly what is this sense? How does it work? How can we overcome it? And what about our scent trail? What is it? Do rubber boots really eliminate it?

The sense of smell is called olfaction, and the nasal cavity's olfactory tissue is the only place in the body where nerve cells are exposed. The exposed portion of a nerve cell is called a receptor site, and each is specific for one type of odor.

Human Scent And Deer Hunting

A chemical — gasoline, for instance — releases molecules into the air. If some attach to the appropriate receptor sites, we smell gasoline. Each receptor can only signal yes or no, so how strongly we smell the gasoline depends on how many gasoline receptors get triggered.

Other receptor sites are unaffected by gasoline. That's why we are able to detect a heavily perfumed woman even while we pump gas. This also explains why cover scents are not the hunter's total solution to human scent problems.

While a hunter's nose contains about five million receptor sites, a deer's nose contains hundreds of millions. In addition, deer have more kinds of receptor sites so they can smell things that seem odorless to us. Deer pinpoint a scent's origin through slight differences in the number of triggered receptor sites

Bill Vaznis

Eliminating odor completely is impossible, but understanding how scent is dispersed and how it's detected allows us to reduce it.

from one side of the nasal cavity to the other, and by temperature changes within the nose. The deer's nose also has something called a vomero-nasal organ. This organ is believed to detect chemical molecules in water, which may explain how deer detect submerged acorns.

You probably have heard deer sniff while searching for acorns. Most olfactory receptor sites are on the upper lining of the nasal cavity and around thin bones that increase the surface area of the nasal lining. When a deer breathes normally, most air flows to the back of its nose, bypassing this region. Some olfaction occurs, of course, but deer improve odor detection significantly when they inhale sharply. This causes the air to lift and directly contact the receptive surfaces. Try it yourself. Flare your nostrils and sniff deeply and quickly. The coolness you feel in the nose's upper portion proves the air flow took a different route. This explains why deer sniff when they first encounter a scent, whether searching for acorns or pinpointing danger.

Odors are chemicals that evaporate into the air and then trigger the deer's receptor cells. Deer become aware of us by detecting chemicals evaporating directly from our bodies or clothing, or by detecting those we leave behind on our trail.

Minimizing Human Odors

To minimize direct odors, stay clean and wear clean clothing. As you know, soaps, shampoos and detergents make us clean but increase our odor level by leaving a residue of perfumes and other chemicals. These gradually evaporate and disperse evidence of our presence into the air. Soaps for hunters are available, but ordinary unscented soaps and shampoos also work well, providing you rinse thoroughly. Hunters use many techniques to clean their clothes, ranging from unscented detergents or baking soda to washing or drying with leaves and wood scents.

Even when clean, we emit identifiable odors from our skin, mouth, throat and lungs. The greater the amount of skin we keep covered, the less odor we release to the wind. Thick, windproof cloth provides a better barrier between our skin and the air than a T-shirt. However, if we wear so much clothing that we sweat, we'll release more moisture even though we have little exposed skin. Moisture carries many smelly chemicals from our body, plus many more released by bacteria on our skin. Therefore, we should cover as much of our body as possible without inducing perspiration. The proper amount of clothing will vary with the temperature and chill factor, and whether we still-hunt or stand-hunt. Most stand hunters carry their outer layers of clothing in a backpack and put them on when they arrive at their stand to avoid building up an odor-rich sweat.

What about our breath? A simple review of our bodies' chemistry is in order. Blood coursing along our intestinal walls picks up nutrients, gases and digestive byproducts. While these move through the body, our blood also picks up metabolic wastes and carbon dioxide, our "waste" gas. When the blood enters our lungs, it absorbs oxygen and releases the other gases. When we exhale, food odors and digestive byproducts, including intestinal gas, enter the air. Some — such as garlic, onions and alcohol — are so strong that we smell them. Others are less noticeable to us, yet deer detect them easily. This is why many hunters caution against spicy foods or alcohol a few days before hunting. Chlorophyll tablets might minimize these odors, but they cannot be totally eliminated. Exhaled air is usually warmer than the air it contacts, and should rise if winds don't push it downward. One offsetting factor is that air is propelled downward as it leaves our nose.

Mouth odors are also a concern because a great volume of air passes through the mouth before being released to the wind. These odors can be reduced by regularly and thoroughly flossing our teeth, and brushing our teeth and tongue. Strong-smelling mouthwashes may disguise mouth odors to you, but they may be alarming to deer.

When we smell a dead animal, rotting seaweed or pond vegetation, we are actually smelling microscopic creatures called bacteria. Bacteria are everywhere, including on and in us, and are responsible for most smells associated with the mouth, intestinal gas and perspiration. They also grow in areas like hat bands. Therefore, hats should be washed or replaced occasionally.

What about equipment? Are the arrows or bowstrings waxed with a scented wax? Are the broadhead blades coated with a smelly rust inhibitor? Has the backpack been sweat-soaked for several seasons? Do tree stand lubricants and paints give off telltale vapors? How about the gun's cleaning and lubricating agents?

That covers most direct odors we release, but what about indirect smells? How do they occur and how do they affect our hunting?

Problems with Scent Trails

My first buck came to me because of my indirect scent. He had passed out of range to the north and angled southwest after he encountered my scent track on a path to my stand. The smell alarmed him and he stood still a long time. He then moved back toward the area he had come from, but he cut the angle, thereby walking within range of my stand.

Unfortunately, our scent trails don't always work to our advantage. Several times I've seen deer change directions after they reached a place I had earlier walked. Who knows how often this occurs at points on trails beyond our view.

Deer become aware of us by detecting chemicals evaporating directly from our bodies or clothing, or by detecting those we leave behind on our trail.

What is this scent trail we leave? Will rubber soles stop it?

Many hunters think a scent trail results when their boot soles touch the ground. In truth, this accounts for only a small portion of it. Most deer that cross my trails sniff the leaves, twigs and branches that hang along my path.

Five vehicles release scent: body moisture, skin oils, shed-skin cells and hair, clothes-borne chemicals, and chemicals carried by our boots.

Body moisture and skin oils that touch leaves, branches and other obstacles remain behind to slowly emit chemicals. Laboratory tests have found that smears from our fingers or the back of our hands release detectable odors for more than three weeks. How long they remain in the woods is difficult to say because that depends on wind, temperature, humidity, rain and other factors.

To minimize these scents, keep skin contact to a minimum. Cover as much of your skin as possible, and try to wiggle between and under limbs and bushes without touching them. Hands are the worst culprits. Not only do they carry moisture and oils, but also a host of other chemicals because of all the items they touch: car keys, gasoline pumps, camp stoves, greasy hamburgers and countless others.

While our bodies look nearly the same every day, they're actually changing constantly. Blood cells, bone cells and skin cells, those microscopic units that

Dressing for the hunt may involve a trade off. Clean, odorless clothing that covers as much skin as possible can keep scent release to a minimum. Wearing too much clothing, however, causes an increase in perspiration and results in increased human scent.

compose our bodies, are continually replaced. As older skin cells die, they are pushed outward by those developing below them. Dead cells form a protective, dry layer. They can be thick in our palms and soles. They can be thinner and less noticeable elsewhere. This outer layer of skin has no blood supply

A variable wind is particularly troublesome because it deposits scent in several or all directions.

because it is dead and requires no nourishment. If you rub a fingernail firmly along your arm you'll see a roughened white trail and maybe some loose, white, powdery material. These are thousands of dead skin cells.

As more cells are pushed outward, the oldest, topmost layer is shed. As a result, we release hundreds of thousands of these cells every day. They are odor-rich because in their dry state they absorb body moisture, skin oils, soaps and anything else they contact.

Another factor in skin odor is bacteria, which are of interest for two reasons. Bacteria produce many of the most pungent odors. Also, their presence led to research on skin-particle shedding. NASA wanted to keep its lunar capsules germfree so as not to expose the moon to new life forms — not even bacteria. Hospitals had the same desire for operating rooms. These groups discovered how difficult it is to control the release of bacteria-rich skin particles. Surgical studies named these particles "scurf" and discovered simple clothing did little to control their release. The hands and face shed large amounts as people walk or stand, and copious volumes from the arms and legs fall out of sleeve ends and pants cuffs. The skin's entire surface has to be contained. Sleeves and pants have to be tied shut or slipped into gloves or boots.

We can apply some of these findings to hunting, but once again we encounter a trade-off. The more clothing we wear, the more we sweat. This magnifies our total scent and leaves more body moisture along the trail. Again, we must balance things depending on the weather and our activity level.

Interestingly, bathing reduces bacteria concentrations, skin oil, butyric acid and other components of sweat, but it increases scurf release because it removes the oils that trap skin particles and hinder their release into the air. Regardless, bathing reduces scent.

Scurf is also shed while hunting from a tree stand. The wind carries it from the hunter and it settles slowly to the underbrush and forest floor. A variable wind is particularly troublesome because it deposits scent in several or all directions. An animal entering this contaminated zone may become alert, feed nervously and quickly, or even bolt despite the fact it is upwind. How often has the effect of disseminated scurf been attributed to a sixth sense? We can only wonder.

Clothing is the fourth cause of the scent trail. If you ever look at your drier's lint collector, you'll see fine bits of clothes that were released by friction and air blowing around them. As we walk, these forces are in action. Our pants legs rub together and our clothes scrape against bushes and shrubs. Trace fibers remain behind and can carry scents. To reduce this scent carrier, wear clean clothes laundered in unscented detergents and try to avoid contact with obstructions. Knee-high rubber boots are helpful because it's nearly impossible not to touch the grasses, ferns and other plant life close to the ground.

Earlier this year I saw the effectiveness of the boots and scent transfer from clothing. Sixty yards away on the trail to my stand was a thick clump of waist-high briars. As I walked through, it was impossible to avoid contact with my pants. Between there and my stand, however, no vegetation exceeded the height of my rubber boots. After 45 minutes on stand, a six-point buck walked by about 15 yards away and

Len Rue, Jr.

While a hunter's nose contains about five million receptor sites, a deer's nose contains hundreds of millions. Deer also have more kinds of receptor sites so they can smell things that seem odorless to us.

headed into the pasture along my path. He showed no sign of alarm until he entered the briar patch. He then stopped abruptly, sniffing and looking around. He took a few steps and stopped again. This time he turned and followed the trail back to the edge of the woods.

Boots are the last vehicle of scent transfer. Rubber absorbs chemical messengers less well than leather or fabric. Therefore, it's less likely to distribute them on your trail. As the prior incident emphasizes, knee-high rubber boots work well for hunting. Keeping them away from chemicals also reduces the amount of scent they carry. That's why so many hunters do not wear their boots except in the woods. The pavement at gas stations and the floors at stores and restaurants are steeped with unnatural scents. If those scents are picked up by our everyday shoes and then transferred to our accelerator, brake and clutch pedals, our hunting boots pick them up, too.

One way to reduce your scent trail is to walk in flowing water. Still water holds skin oils and scurf on the surface, but flowing water almost eliminates it. I once saw an otter swim along a small creek that passed my stand. I watched with interest as it moved along the creek's many branches and divisions. Maybe an hour later another otter came along the same route. It was traveling much faster. At every fork it ran along the edge sniffing. If it didn't encounter the first otter's scent, it tried the other branch. This demonstrates that some chemical messengers are left at the water's edge, even in flowing water.

Scent Dispersal

Some environmental factors must be considered when discussing scents, whether they come directly from our bodies or from our scent trail. Even without wind, odors spread somewhat by diffusion and air turbulence caused by our movements. Diffusion is easily illustrated by opening a bottle of ammonia in

Len Rue, Jr.

Many hunters think a scent trail results when their boot soles touch the ground. In truth, this accounts for only a small portion of the hunter's scent trail.

the corner of a room. Despite the lack of wind, the smell soon spreads to the opposite side.

Wind spreads chemical messages and scurf through the air. The stronger the wind, the more thinly our scent is spread. Therefore, it's more difficult to detect. Uneven terrain, hills, dips, forest edges and ponds all create turbulence. That's why the wind direction at one place may not be the same as the wind's prevailing direction.

Heat makes more chemicals evaporate, thereby increasing the amount of scent. Archers usually hunt the earlier, warmer season, which means they have more scent concerns, particularly because of the bow's limited range.

Humidity is the amount of moisture in the air. The greater the humidity, the less odor the air can absorb. However, a deer's nose functions better with humid air.

Surprisingly, rain and dew may increase the amount of scent. When skin oils are on a leaf or scurf particle, only the topmost portion is exposed to the air, and it easily evaporates. Dew or rain wetting the leaf allows the skin oil to float up and form a thin, broad film, like gasoline on a puddle. This increases the surface area and, therefore, increases evaporation. Bacteria in the soil break down our scent fairly rapidly, so a prolonged rain that carries scent into the earth will wash away much of our scent trail.

When we look at the total picture of how scents give us away, the prospect of encountering unalarmed deer seems hopeless. Fortunately, some factors are in our favor. Warm air rises, so much of our scent travels upward, away from the deer's nostrils. Cold weather results in less chemical evaporation, which means less scent. At the same time, this renders the deer's nasal

lining less sensitive because of heavy moisture condensation. Used properly, wind can be an ally that blows our chemical traces away. Another point is that many chemicals are more pungent than our own in competing for the deer's attention.

Archers usually hunt the earlier, warmer season, which means they have more scent concerns, particularly because of the bow's limited range.

Eliminating odor completely is impossible, but understanding how scent is dispersed and how it's detected allows us to reduce it significantly. Is it worth the trouble? That may depend. Someone hunting a hiking trail or portion of a farm where deer are accustomed to human scent doesn't need to be as concerned. On the other hand, woods-wise deer that encounter your scent too often may become very cautious. Reducing your scent and scent trail always improves your chances in the deer woods.

Editor's Note: "Human Scent And Deer Hunting" was originally published in the September 1991 of Deer & Deer Hunting *magazine.*

Charles J. Alsheimer

Interpreting The Rut

Charles J. Alsheimer

Bucks are able to breed from the time they shed their velvet, but until the does come into estrus a buck's life is little more than days of wandering about the forest in utter frustration.

Learning the many aspects of the rut and how to hunt it can be fascinating. Today, deer hunters have a decided advantage on the hunters of yesteryear. Deer hunting seminars, videos and printed literature abound. Fortunately, the mass communications industry has not been able to provide a quick fix to becoming a successful deer hunter. It still requires a sound background of what I call white-tailed woodsmanship — a keen knowledge of the animal and its environment.

Over the years I've been asked a multitude of questions about how to hunt the rut. These questions ranged from how to hunt the weather fronts to how to locate a primary scrape. From these dialogues has come a feeling that hunting the rut almost has a certain mystique about it. Hunters often appear to be trying to find the one secret formula for success. As a result, they sometimes become easy targets for hunting gear manufacturers.

Everything from ultra cam bows to super-hot, doe-in-estrus buck lures confront hunters from every direction. Though the hardware may help them score on a buck, nothing can replace getting in the woods and learning through experience. Therefore, learning what to expect from a whitetail during the magical days of November can help make one a more successful deer hunter.

Rutting Behavior Of Deer

It is important to realize that a white-tailed buck is not the same animal in November as he was in August or will be in February. From a physical standpoint, a buck enters the month of November as a magnificent specimen. Also, at this time a buck's hormone production reaches its highest annual level with its thyroid, adrenal and testicular glands at peak activity. This, coupled with the does coming into estrus, causes the rut. With bucks appearing to be "wired tight," all kinds of predictable and unpredictable things occur during this time.

During most of the year, a buck confines his activity to a relatively small area. But during the rut, this changes and often drastically. In the northern farm belt, a buck's rutting range may approximate three square miles. In country with big timber, however, like Maine and New York's Adirondacks, a buck may

cover 15 square miles in his pursuit of does. The important thing to remember is that the buck you observed frequently in late August and early September may move out of the area as the rut approaches.

> *It is important to search out early scrapes and pay close attention to them because some will become breeding scrapes during the peak of the rut.*

Where he went is not always easy to determine, but it's safe to say that his sex glands kicked into high gear and he's on the move. The number of does in an area also plays a big part in where the bucks are. Concentrations of does will eventually mean concentrations of bucks as the rut approaches and then reaches its peak.

The role of the doe cannot be underestimated, for she creates the peak of the rut. Bucks are able to breed from the time they shed their velvet, but until the does come into estrus a buck's life is little more than days of roaming the forest in utter frustration.

Pinpointing the peak of the rut is something all deer hunters wish they had a handle on. Several factors play a role in determining the peak. The length of daylight hours represents the key factor, but sudden cold snaps and the number of serviceable does in an area also influence rutting activities. During unseasonably warm Novembers, deer hunters often speculate that the rut is running late. This is not so. What actually happens during warm November weather is that the breeding and related activities take place during the cool of the night rather than during daylight hours. Photoperiodism determines the time of the year in which the rut takes place and temperature determines at what time of day the activity occurs.

Though the actual peak is impossible to pinpoint from year to year, an approximate date is possible for northern whitetails. Many scientific studies have shown that at the 45th parallel the peak of the whitetail's rut occurs around November 15 each year. Knowing this can be beneficial to the hunter while pre-season scouting and can help determine strategy as the rut approaches. From a statistical standpoint, the most popular study, by L.W. Jackson and W.T. Hesselton of the New York State Department of Environmental Conservation, showed that 63 percent of the does were bred between November 10 and 30, with the peak being November 15.

It is during the pre-rut (one to three weeks prior to the rut's peak) that the white-tailed buck starts to let his guard down. He becomes increasingly more careless as he roams the woodlands. This carelessness shows in the form of the sign he leaves, with rubs and scrapes being the most obvious.

Hunters have long been confused by the part rubs play in the rut. Don't overlook their importance in deciding how to hunt during this time. Contrary to long-standing beliefs, rubs represent more than just random trees and shrubs where a buck chooses to rub his antlers. Generally a buck creates rubs as signposts within his home range. Also, areas containing active scrapes generally have more rubs than other areas. Rubs may also reveal the direction of deer movement and the relative size of the bucks that made them.

When scouting or hunting, examine closely the rubs you find. If most appear on the same side of the tree and in a reasonable line, it will be obvious which way the buck normally travels. These rub lines are carefully laid out along travel routes and often the rubs and scrapes appear where a buck's trail intersects a main trail.

As mentioned earlier, the timing of the rut and its peak are determined primarily by the doe, for without the doe coming into estrus there would be no rut. The healthy, older does normally come into estrus earlier than the younger does and trigger the bucks' rutting activity. Many times I have seen this take place in my pursuit of whitetails. What normally happens is that the doe approaching estrus urinates more often that at other times. Where her estrous urine falls will usually be where a buck makes a scrape. Often these early scrapes appear along well-used deer trails, forest edges or any other place whitetails frequent. This first rut (mid- to late-

October) is often referred to as the false rut and is more a prelude of what's to come. But what this false rut does is trigger the bucks into a bit of a frenzy, a frenzy that will peak sometime in mid-November.

It is important to search out these early scrapes and pay close attention to them because some will become breeding scrapes during the peak of the rut. It is at or near these breeding scrapes that much of the actual breeding occurs. It has been my experience that every breeding scrape has a licking branch over it. The licking branch is a low branch, usually broken at a right angle to the ground, hanging directly over the scrape. Generally these will be live branches, though I have seen bucks frequent the same branches on dead trees year after year.

Charles J. Alsheimer

Contrary to long-standing beliefs, rubs represent more than just random trees and shrubs where a buck chooses to rub his antlers.

When a buck approaches a scrape, he doesn't always paw the ground. He will, however, nuzzle the branch in his mouth and rub his preorbital gland (the gland in the corner of the eye) and sudoriferous gland (the gland at the base of the antlers) on the branch. In this manner, the buck deposits his scent on the overhanging branch. It should also be pointed out that more than one buck and doe may use a scrape. Hot breeding scrapes are like bus stations. Every area has them, but because deer can be very nocturnal, they are not always easy to find.

Scrapes along forest edges and logging roads are usually not very productive. Scrapes found in natural funnels or passageways, where deer frequently move, have the capability of becoming breeding scrapes. If the does coming into estrus use the scrapes, bucks will frequent them more often. Repeated use like this often creates large breeding scrapes. Usually, as the doe comes into estrus, she'll urinate in the scrape, nuzzle the licking branch, move off a short distance and wait for a buck to come by if she doesn't have a buck already in hot pursuit.

To a buck, the doe's estrous urine is very strong and for this reason few mature bucks will ever walk directly into a scrape in broad daylight. Instead, they often pass 40 to 75 yards downwind of the scrape and scent-check it as they pass through the area. Yearling bucks, on the other hand, are often careless and foolhardy and usually walk right into the scrape without taking any precautions.

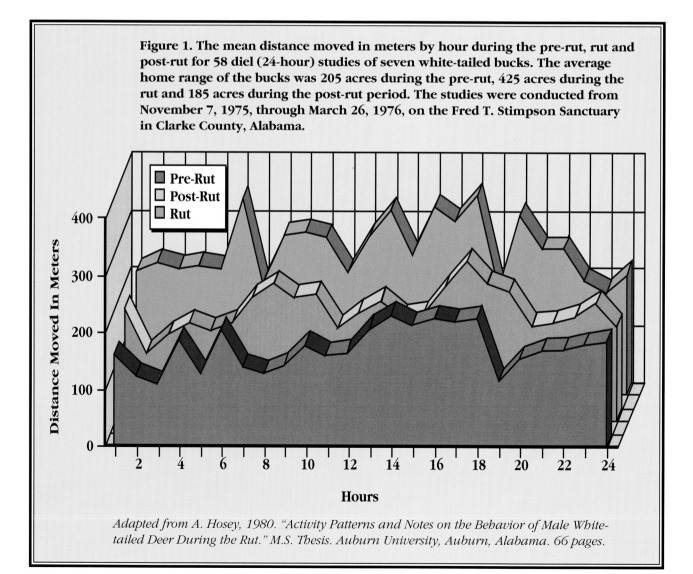

Figure 1. The mean distance moved in meters by hour during the pre-rut, rut and post-rut for 58 diel (24-hour) studies of seven white-tailed bucks. The average home range of the bucks was 205 acres during the pre-rut, 425 acres during the rut and 185 acres during the post-rut period. The studies were conducted from November 7, 1975, through March 26, 1976, on the Fred T. Stimpson Sanctuary in Clarke County, Alabama.

Adapted from A. Hosey, 1980. "Activity Patterns and Notes on the Behavior of Male White-tailed Deer During the Rut." M.S. Thesis. Auburn University, Auburn, Alabama. 66 pages.

Hunting The Rut

A knowledge of thermal currents helps to understand how to hunt whitetails during the rut. Perhaps the best way to explain thermals is that they are slow moving air masses brought on by temperature change. Warm air rises and cool air descends. So, as the sun warms the cool night air in the morning, the thermals move uphill until the cool air is warmed. The opposite occurs in the evening. Thermals are destroyed when there is significant wind velocity. Before the daytime winds start to blow, thermals can pose a tremendous problem to a deer hunter. Thermals are like water and when wind is absent they flow in every direction imaginable. They are not only very frustrating, but they can also ruin a hunt.

Personally, I prefer to hunt when there is a slight breeze and only have to worry about my scent going in one direction. But in reality, the prime hours to be in the woods are the first and last two hours of each day and usually day winds aren't blowing then, so thermals must be taken into account. As a result, the better hunters make it a point to know which way the thermals are moving at all times. Two very successful hunters I know use different methods for determining thermal movements and each works very well. One ties sewing thread on branches around his blind to detect air movement. The other uses a small squeeze bottle filled with unscented talcum powder. By periodically spraying a puff of the powder into the air, thermal currents can be seen.

If more hunters understood thermal currents, their success would undoubtedly increase. All too often hunters fail to check and recheck air movements while deer hunting and end up being unsuccessful because the whitetail spends nearly all its time scent-checking the air.

Another key ingredient to the rut is the weather. Cold snaps and stormy weather set the bucks into a frenzy as mid-November approaches. The best time to be in the woods will be just prior to a weather front moving in, particularly a cold, west one. A whitetail's senses are finely tuned and when the barometric pressure starts to fall they know a weather change is in store. Consequently, they'll be on the move feeding. Hunting these frontal patterns during the peak of the rut increases one's chances for success dramatically. Successful hunters also know that cold, overcast days during the peak of the rut mean the deer will be on the move throughout the day. Days with light drizzle or a few snowflakes are some of the most productive days in November for northern whitetails. Unfortunately, too many hunters exit the woods when the weather is poor. Personally, my choice of optimum hunting conditions during the peak of the rut is a cold, overcast day with little wind. Such days really get my adrenaline pumping because over the years I've seen more big buck activity when these conditions prevail.

Knowing and learning about rubs, scrapes, thermals and weather are all a part of hunting the rut. But the fun comes when you're able to piece all the information together and determine where to ambush the buck you're looking for.

> *It is always a good idea to prepare two stand sites when hunting in the vicinity of a hot scrape. This prepares you to adjust quickly when the wind direction changes.*

When planning your hunting strategy, it's important to know what you want from the hunt. If any buck is your game, then setting your blind 20 yards downwind of the scrape or trail should put you in a position to score. Mature bucks are different, however, and require different methods. Because most mature whitetails rely on their nose more than their other senses, they'll scent-check scrapes from a distance. Therefore, when hunting for such animals, your blind or tree stand should be placed 40 to 75 yards downwind of the scrape.

If you're hunting over a hot scrape, possibly you'll want to erect two stands. Erect one 40 to 75 yards downwind and one 40 to 75 yards upwind. Why? Because, just as sure as the sun rises in the east tomorrow, you'll head for your favorite stand some morning and discover the wind is blowing out of the east instead of the west. When that happens, you can simply move to the other stand instead of wasting a valuable day of hunting time.

If you're a bow hunter, the stand should be 12 to 15 feet high. Higher than 15 feet will give the arrow a poor angle of entry if the buck is within 10 yards when you shoot. And shooting at too steep an angle can cause the arrow to penetrate only one lung instead of both lungs. Also, in most woods being higher than 15 feet causes a problem of too many branches in the way for a clear shot. So, most of the time 12 to 15 feet is a sufficient height if you're hunting on reasonably flat ground.

Ground blinds are totally different than tree stands when it comes to location. Make sure you are far enough downwind from the scrape or trail so the buck doesn't spook if you have to move when he shows up. Too often a hunter erects his ground blind too close to where he expects to see the deer. Also, on damp, still days human scent saturates an area and causes any nearby deer to spook.

Probably the most important thing to remember is never locate your stand or blind in a buck's bedding area. Rather, locate it between his feeding and bedding area. By scouting the area you intend to hunt, you'll be able to determine where the deer are bedding. If you're spooking deer in midday you're probably in the bedding area. Nothing will move a buck out of an area faster than activity in his bedroom. The purpose of using a blind is to take the buck by surprise and if you continually spook him, your chances of successfully hunting him are greatly diminished.

If you expect to ambush that buck of a lifetime, don't put your blind in the bottom of a gully or ravine. You're just kidding yourself if you do. The

Charles J. Alsheimer

The timing of the rut and its peak are determined primarily by the doe, for without the doe coming into estrus, there would be no rut.

wind will change so often in such locations that you'll get dizzy trying to figure out which way it's going to go next. I've seen some outstanding trails crossing streams in the bottom of gullies and been tempted to erect blinds there, but haven't because experience has taught me otherwise.

Hunting rutting whitetails is truly a challenge wherever they are found and requires all the savvy a hunter can muster. It's vitally important to learn as much as possible about the animal and the terrain you will be hunting. Like anything else in life, suc-cess in deer hunting is directly proportional to the time and effort expended. Successful deer hunters are not born nor can they purchase success in a store or through a mail order catalog. No, they are made through trials and experience, and that is the way it should be.

Editor's Note: "Interpreting the Rut" was originally published in the December 1987 issue of Deer & Deer Hunting *magazine.*

Reported Breeding Seasons Of The White-tailed Deer

STATE	BREEDING DATES	PEAK OF THE RUT	RESEARCHER, YEAR
Alabama	Mid-Nov. to Late March	Varies by Region	Lueth, 1967
Arizona		Feb. to Mid-March	O'Connor, 1945
Arkansas	Early Oct. to Mid-Jan.		Donaldson, 1951
Colorado	Oct. to Mid-Dec.		Warren, 1942
Connecticut	Late Sept. to Early Jan.		McDowell, 1966
Florida	Varies by Region		Harlow, 1965
Georgia	Mid-Oct. to Mid-Dec.	November 15-30	Kile, 1977
Iowa		November	Haugen, 1958
Kansas	Nov. 8 to Dec. 20		Anderson, 1964
Kentucky	October to January		Gale & Myers, 1954
Maine	Oct. 20 to Dec. 28	Mid-November	Banasiak, 1961
Massachusetts	Oct. 31 to Jan. 29	November 10-25	Shaw, 1951
Michigan	Oct. 9 to Dec. 5	November 16-22	Haugen 1950
Minnesota	Mid-Sept. into Feb.		Erickson, 1961
Mississippi	Dec. 5 to Feb. 24	December 18-31	Noble, 1960
Missouri	Oct. to Early Dec.		Robb, 1951
Montana	Nov. 7 to Dec. 10		Allen, 1965
Nebraska	Oct. 21 to March 1		Havel, 1963, 1964
New Hampshire		Mid-November	Silver, 1957
New Jersey	Late Oct. to Jan.		Mangold, 1958, 1963
New York	Oct. 28 to Dec. 28	November 10-30	Jackson, 1973
North Carolina	Early Oct. to Early Nov.		Weber, 1966
Ohio	Oct. 22 to Dec. 9		Gilfillan, 1952
Oklahoma		November 2-26	Lindzey, ?
Pennsylvania	Late Oct. to Mid-Dec.	Mid-November	Lang, 1971
South Carolina		Nov. 17 to Dec. 13	Payne, 1966
Tennessee	Oct. 29 to Feb. 9		Lewis 1972
Texas		December 15-24	Illige, 1951
Vermont	Early Nov. to Mid-Dec.		Day, 1964
Virginia	Oct. 1 to Late Nov.		Anonymous, 1948
West Virginia	Oct. 13 to Jan. 11		Chadwick, 1963
Wisconsin	Oct. 1 to Jan. 8	November 10-29	Dahlberg, 1956

The process of learning to still-hunt teaches you to become a better all-around hunter. It presents an opportunity to locate fresh deer sign made during the hunting season. You can apply such knowledge to your in-season hunting efforts, as opposed to post-season observations which only result in predictions for "next year."

Bill Vaznis

Eight Reasons for Still-Hunting

Bill Vaznis

Eight Reasons For Still-Hunting

Sneaking through the woods "Indian Style," commonly known as still-hunting, is a demanding way to bow hunt for deer. Yet, our forefathers of bow hunting chose this method, and they consistently took deer. You, too, can learn to successfully challenge a whitetail's defenses with this technique. Here are eight good reasons to leave your portable tree stand home this season.

Observer Versus Participant

"Frankly, this writer lacks both the infinite patience and courage to face a bitterly cold day on a runway stand. Feet become painfully inanimate lumps of frozen flesh, fingers almost crackle with frost and the entire human frame soon vibrates like a strummed harp. The entire picture is out of tune with the normal theme of deer hunting thrills and pleasure."

— Lawrence R. Koller, 1948
Shots At Whitetails

Anyone who takes a white-tailed deer with a bow and arrow, whether from a portable stand, ground blind, two-man drive or by still-hunting has demonstrated a high degree of woodsmanship and should be proud of this accomplishment. Nonetheless, differences exist between still-hunting and other deer hunting methods.

First, bow hunters who hide high in the branches or conceal themselves in a ground blind often complain of boredom and the inability to remain motionless during the day's hunt. My friends who choose to bushwhack bucks in such passive ways often read a magazine or short novel to help pass the time and keep from fidgeting. One guy habitually wears earphones and listens to stacks of cassettes to "keep from falling asleep" in the woods!

Stationary hunters commonly complain about the lack of stimulating scenery. Sure, they pay attention when a grey fox lopes past or when a red-tailed hawk swoops down on an unsuspecting chipmunk, but such occurrences are infrequent. Stationary hunters often resort to counting pretty red leaves on the forest floor and thinking about what might be for supper that night.

On the other hand, still-hunters spend virtually every minute searching for watchful bucks. With every muscle and every fiber geared for a sudden encounter, these hunters remain alert and captivated all day long. Their hunt begins as soon as they enter the woods and doesn't end until legal shooting hours are over.

Years ago, when I habitually hunted deer from tree stands, I often felt like a spectator at a baseball game. Once seated, I could do little to affect the outcome of the day's events. Patience was my strongest ally back then, and I relied on it heavily as I waited, and waited . . . for the wind to stop blowing, for the sun to rise and, hopefully, for a buck to step into view.

It eventually dawned on me that it was not very enjoyable sitting in the bleachers waiting to be entertained — not when I could be down there on the field playing the game! I learned that a still-hunter could indeed sneak downwind of a deer trail and intercept a buck travelling to a feeding area, or pussyfoot along the edge of a swamp and catch a buck working a scrape line, or even slip into a buck's bedroom and catch him napping.

Still-hunters seem to enjoy more action because they make things happen. Still-hunting is an aggressive sport, and still-hunters are more than mere observers of mother nature's wonderland — they are active participants in the scheme of things.

Keep It Simple

"Any equipment one carries on the hunt should certainly be limited to what is actually needed . . . One can be so burdened with gadgets which might come in handy that he becomes a veritable slave to these accouterments and his hunt suffers because of it."

— George Mattis, 1969
Whitetail: Fundamentals and Fine Points for the Hunter

Have you ever taken a weekend trip and packed every piece of gear you owned "just in case" you might need it along the way? Sure, an extra half-dozen arrows are fine and so is a dry set of clothes and a few munchies, but the list can easily get out of hand.

Not so with still-hunters. There's no need for them to lug cumbersome ladders and noisy stands or tote fanny packs stuffed with wing nuts, bolts, washers, screwdrivers, pliers, ratchet wrenches, safety belt, tree steps, flashlight, sweater, urine bottle, bow hanger, hand warmer, boot warmers, a thermos of coffee, an emergency signaling device and a hundred other pieces of extraneous gear that if somehow left back at camp could cause an acute anxiety attack one-half hour into the hunt.

In addition to my license, knife and binoculars that I always take in the woods with me, I carry a roll of fluorescent orange surveyor's tape, one extra arrow rest (I have a nasty habit of breaking off wire rests in the brush), a small bottle of fox urine and a wad of toilet paper. That's all. I make sure I leave a length of rope, a Coleman lantern with extra gas and mantles and a clean change of "cammies" in the bed of my

Bill Vaznis

With every muscle and every fiber geared for a sudden encounter with a buck, still-hunters remain alert and captivated all day long.

truck. I can do without almost everything else.

The real beauty of still-hunting is the amount of time it allows you to hunt. Years ago, I always had at least two portables squirreled away in various locations, which I used according to the wind, buck sightings, the rut, time of day, etc. I added up the time I spent packing and repacking my "goodies" into a fanny pack, driving back and forth from camp, walking to and from tree stands, finally climbing on board one and then waiting calmly for the area to settle down. I was easily losing 12 hours of hunting time per week. During the rut, that kind of time is precious! Now that I still-hunt almost exclusively, I deer hunt all day long with little or no "wasted" time.

Secret Spot

"The solo hunter must plan his tactics according to weather conditions prevailing, type of terrain he encounters, and the information he gathers from any deer sign observed. In addition to this, he will seek to confine his efforts to such areas that have not been heavily driven or overhunted in recent days."
— George Mattis, 1969
Whitetail: Fundamentals and Fine Points for the Hunter

Here are three good reasons why tree stand hunters should keep their hunting locations a secret to all outsiders: claim jumpers, thieves and saboteurs. Given the opportunity, this rabble will take unfair advantage of your honest efforts and jeopardize both your deer season and your personal safety.

What gives your stand site away to such riffraff? Well, for starters, they look for silhouetted portables, shiny climbing pegs, freshly cut shooting lanes, blazed entrance and exit trails, fluorescent orange yardage markers and a vehicle parked in the same spot night after night. If they are familiar with the terrain and you are not especially careful, you've got problems.

Claim jumpers are lazy hunters who use your equipment when you are not around. And since they're unable to zero in on a buck of their own, the probability of them wounding and losing an animal is high. If they don't shoot at "your" buck, they may still spook him forever from your "secret" spot by contaminating the site with their ground scent or by climbing into the stand when the wind is wrong.

Even a well camouflaged setup can be a target for thieves who specialize in ripping off stands while you're back at camp. Although they may not always be successful (padlocks and steel chains are effective), they may seriously weaken the integrity of your stand while trying to remove it. And ponder this for a moment. In 1988, a New England bow hunter fell from his stand after it was apparently tampered with by local anti-hunters!

Still-hunters can avoid most of those problems because their actions do not draw attention to any particular locale. For example, a good still-hunter rarely hunts the same ridge, apple orchard or creek bottom more than twice a week. And when he does return, he quietly slips along a different path. Why? Deer are quick to pattern hunters and will adjust their travel routes accordingly. And the scent a still-hunter invariably leaves behind can spook a deer long after he's gone. Finally, changes in wind direction, food supplies, hunting pressure and the timing of the rut often call for a different approach to even the hottest of locations.

In-Season Scouting

"In wilderness sections, the still-hunter covers not only the slopes and ridges, looking for resting and bedded deer. The edges of slashings in heavy forests are always favored by feeding deer just after sunup and before sundown. In the heaviest of timber many deer find all their available browse in these slashings — the big timber discourages the growth of small brush and offers little for hungry deer except acorns or beechnuts. Cedar swamps are regular feeding grounds too, and in deer country where high ridges are lacking any swamp ground may be the hideaway of a resting buck. It pays off to spend plenty of time in looking over these spots during the normal daylight feeding hours."

— Lawrence R. Koller, 1948
Shots At Whitetails

Placing stands during the off-season, as most stand hunters do, involves a guessing game. Essentially, you try to anticipate deer movements months before hunting season. But expected patterns of deer movement may not take place. Further, packs of dogs,

jack-lighters, free-roaming trappers, bird hunters, freak weather and even a friendly bow hunter can suddenly ruin a stand location. Many tree stand hunters fail because they do not reposition their stands during the course of the season.

Now, think about this. When is the best time to find a scrape line? After the close of a season? Spring green-up? Not really. The very best time to find one is when it's actually in use during the deer season.

Hunting a scrape line that you found the previous winter could be an exercise in futility — the buck that made the scrapes could be long dead! The same goes for preferred feeding areas, bedding areas, travel corridors and so on. They could be filled with buck sign one year and abandoned the next.

Still-hunting allows a bow hunter to keep his finger on the pulse of deer movement by giving him the opportunity to constantly update his off-season scouting with prime-time, in-season scouting. Locating fresh deer sign is not just a casual "look-see." It involves long hours afield locating the year's first scrapes, unraveling new bedding trails, pinpointing the daily movements of does and fawns, knowing which crops are about to be harvested and where the deer are now feeding — all this regardless of the weather, hunting pressure or the rut. This information allows a still-hunter to see more deer and to be more flexible in his efforts to bag a buck.

More Deer Sightings

"Since it is generally so hard to catch sight of a deer until it is just too late to shoot, and since lying down is a position in which it is generally next to impossible to see one at all, it follows that far brighter prospects of success lie on the side of finding a deer on foot."

— T.S. Van Dyke, 1882
The Still-Hunter

Still-hunters encounter more whitetails than stationary bow hunters do because they search a larger area when bucks are moving about. Of course, on many occasions a still-hunter sees only the flick of an ear or a solitary tine, but that does not diminish the value of the sighting.

To begin with, a glimpse of any buck reinforces your belief that there are indeed bucks in the vicinity.

And although that first buck may have been out of range, your confidence soars because the next critter might just offer you an easy, 20-yard shot.

Close encounters also increase your knowledge of deer behavior. It's one thing to read about deer using the wind to their advantage and quite another to watch a wide-racked buck sniff out a field of does or circle carefully downwind of your position. These firsthand experiences can only help increase your overall success. Seeing plenty of bucks will also help you ward off buck fever when the moment of truth arrives.

Finally, the more bucks you observe the more likely you are to get a handle on the big picture and watch the rut unfold. Last deer season, while still-hunting in New York, Pennsylvania and New Brunswick, I saw more than 50 bucks. I remain amazed at the number of racked deer I caught in the vicinity of — but not in the company of — a mature doe. During the early stages of the rut the big boys seem to lag nearby, just out of sight but not out of touch with her presence. Does seem to be aware of these bystanders, and they can function as both sentinels and as decoys. Next time you see a doe pass you by, keep your eyes peeled to the territory to either side of her — a buck could be dogging her off in the shadows.

Flexibility

"The individual who goes it alone is unfettered by any time limits, appointments, or any of a dozen things that can come up when he is part of a group. Being strictly on his own, he is free to change his tactics or direction of travel to suit the occasion anytime he desires, and he suffers no loss of hunting time in making these changes. Whenever he feels a bit tired, he can rest on some vantage point, and even when he lunches on his cold sandwich he is exposed to deer country under the most favorable hunting conditions."
— George Mattis, 1969
Whitetail: Fundamentals and Fine Points for the Hunter

Len Rue, Jr.

Still hunters can indeed sneak downwind of a deer trail and intercept a buck travelling to a feeding area, or pussyfoot along the edge of a swamp and catch a buck working a scrape line, or even slip into a buck's bedroom and catch him napping.

Eight
Reasons For Still-Hunting

When a hunter fails to fill a tag, it's human nature to minimize the event to some extent by placing the blame on circumstances beyond our control. We often hear: "I didn't see anything all morning long; the wind wasn't right." (He stayed in his stand despite the change in wind direction.) "I passed up a good one yesterday; just a little out of range." (His stand was in the wrong location and he's angry because he couldn't get a shot.)

Archers who take to the trees are often handicapped by their stationary positions, but a bow hunter who "sneaks and peaks" can adapt to almost any situation. In fact, no other method offers such flexibility to the solo deer hunter as still-hunting.

> **Still-hunters can go light, unencumbered with extra gear that tree stand hunters need. Also, still-hunting increases the actual hours you spend hunting, because you don't waste time walking between or repositioning stands.**

What would a still-hunter have done under the above conditions? Well, when the wind changed direction, he would have also changed directions — and continued to hunt. He has learned from past experiences that you must keep the wind in your favor if you have any hopes of tagging a whitetail. And what if a good buck saunters past just out of range? Well, a still-hunter simply goes after him. Putting the moves on a roving buck is darn exciting!

Old-time hunters often claim "the deer hunting's no good when the wind is a whippin', and impossible when them leaves are a cracklin' and a poppin'." Yet, I have tagged a number of bucks under these conditions, including a nine-pointer I caught in his bed one windy morning.

A good still-hunter is unfettered by this "conventional wisdom" and is always looking for a way to improve the odds. Actually, windy days are good days to catch a buck in the brush, and logging roads and power lines are good places to avoid noisy ground clutter.

Double Your Pleasure

"The art of still-hunting deer carries with it nearly the whole art of still-hunting other large American game. As a good and accomplished lawyer has only a few special points of practice to learn in transplanting himself from state to state, so the thorough still-hunter will go from deer to antelope, elk, or other game, already equipped with five-sixths of the knowledge necessary to hunt them. And this very knowledge will, as it does in the case of the lawyer, enable him to learn the rest in one-fourth of the time in which a beginner could do it."
— T.S. Van Dyke, 1882
The Still-Hunter

There are numerous long-term benefits to the sport of still-hunting. For one, it teaches you to become a better all-around hunter. Ironically perhaps, a successful still-hunter could easily become a good tree stand hunter if he chose to use his knowledge of thermals and local topography in that vein.

The ability to slink like a cat and to see deer first are the cornerstones of still-hunting and two other approaches to big game hunting — spot-and-stalk and tracking. All three can be used on eastern deer, while spot-and-stalk is often the method of choice for moose, caribou, mule deer, goats, sheep, western black bear and elk. These critters are not regularly arrowed from elevated platforms.

Two-season hunters can sometimes fill a second tag by combining their early-archery still-hunting with their pre-season scouting for gun season. For example, I am always looking for a good place to slug a buck on my gun tag, and still-hunting with a bow allows me to locate escape routes in preparation for the upcoming firearms opener.

Tracking is another skill that profits from extensive still-hunting experience. Here in the snow belt, picking up a fresh track in the early morning and then following it all day will often lead you to more than one deer, and rifling a buck in this manner is as difficult and exciting as still-hunting a buck with archery equipment.

Sense Of Accomplishment

"But to correct at the onset any misapprehension I will say that, with whatever proficiency in still-hunting any mortal ever reaches, with all the advantages of snow, ground, wind, and sun in his favor, many a deer will, in the very climax of triumphant assurance, slip through his fingers like the thread of a beautiful dream."

— T.S. Van Dyke, 1882
The Still-Hunter

The eighth reason to try still-hunting is the most important one of all — the feeling that sweeps over you after you experience success.

You know it isn't easy, still-hunting a buck with a bow and arrow. It takes time and a lot of hard work, but when you've done it you've done it alone. You earned him. No one drove him past you, and you didn't hide somewhere so you could bushwhack him when his back was turned.

You'll wait for that moment in time when you and the buck meet face-to-face, and you honor him by looking him in the eye and taking him fair and square. There will be no crowds of onlookers to stand up and cheer as if you just hit a home run, and there will be no referee on hand to count the points and add up your score. Oh, there will be some backslapping back at camp and somebody will measure the inside spread for you. But the real reward will take place years later whenever you gaze upon the deer's rack. You'll smile to yourself then and remember that special day in October when you glided like a ghost up to the buck and watched your arrow fly true.

Editor's Note: "Eight Reasons For Still-Hunting" was originally published in the August 1990 issue of Deer & Deer Hunting *magazine.*

The Philosophy

Len Rue, Jr.

Of Waiting

Al Hofacker

The common belief that an undisturbed, wounded deer typically runs a short distance, beds down and dies is, at best, a gross oversimplification of wounded deer behavior. The results of this survey indicate that this type of behavior represents the exception rather than the rule.

◆◆ The Philosophy of Waiting ◆◆

"Some hunters maintain that one should wait for wounded game to lie down before trailing it. They suggest waiting an hour. When we consider the nature of wounds and the game's reaction to them, the entire proposition of waiting is open to question."

— **Francis E. Sell**
***The American Deer Hunter*, 1950**

When Rob Wegner, in the August 1985 issue of *Deer & Deer Hunting* magazine, challenged the "proposition of waiting" before pursuing a wounded deer, readers quickly wrote to criticize the mere suggestion of pursuing wounded deer immediately, or at least very quickly. This response vividly illustrated how controversial the topic of waiting remains among deer hunters.

In his article, "The Myth of the Waiting Game," Wegner traced the beginnings of the philosophy of waiting before trailing a wounded deer. Though some noted deer hunters through the years also questioned the philosophy of waiting, the advocates of immediate pursuit remain in the minority to this day. But the debate continues, often in a very heated manner, and for a good reason.

The reason why the debate concerning waiting versus immediate pursuit remains a controversial subject relates to the absence of factual evidence to support either side. After a comprehensive review of the literature on the related subjects of wounded deer behavior and the advisability of waiting or not waiting, Wegner concluded that no scientific evidence exists to conclusively prove the theory of either the proponents of waiting or the proponents of quick pursuit. Thus, we find that the debate rages on, with both sides of the question relying on unproven theories rather than factual proof.

In this essay I briefly review the history of the philosophy of waiting and the premise upon which the advocates of waiting base their theory: the alleged typical behavior pattern of wounded deer. I then analyze the behavior pattern of wounded deer using data supplied by the readers of *Deer & Deer Hunting* magazine who participated in a survey published in the February 1986 issue of the magazine. Finally, I compare waiting periods of various duration to the success of these deer hunters in recovering wounded deer.

The History And Philosophy Of Waiting

Discussions about the best course of action to take after wounding a deer, whether it be with a gun or bow, appear in nearly every book devoted to the subject of deer hunting, with the philosophy of waiting usually leading off the discussion. The theory that waiting for a period of time (the actual length of the recommended waiting period remains debatable among those who advocate waiting) represents the best course of action probably emanates from our European ancestors. The earliest reference I found regarding the philosophy of waiting appeared in William Scrope's *The Art Of Deer Stalking* (1838). Though Scrope stalked the red deer, similar to North America's wapiti, note the similarity in his description of handling a wounded deer to that of modern-day advocates of waiting:

"The crack of the ball could not be mistaken; it was that particular smack which it makes, distinct from any other, when a deer is stricken. The whole party then lay quietly down in the heather, Peter Fraser being enjoined to examine the herd as they passed up the opposite heights, and keep his eye on the wounded hart. This is always the surest way of recovering him, for if you press him, and he is not hit deadly, he will get forward in the middle of the herd, whilst his wound is fresh, and run with the other deer in such a manner as will most probably occasion you to lose him, but, on the contrary, when he is not urged forward, and sees no one in pursuit of him, his wounded part stiffens, and he seeks ease by slackening his pace, or, if badly wounded, by falling out altogether from the rest of the herd, and, if he is not badly wounded, you must lose him at any rate — at least you will have no better chance with him than with his companions."

The philosophy of waiting evolved and became much more explicit as the years passed, but the recommended waiting period varied considerably from one authority to another. T.S. Van Dyke, in his classic work *The Still-Hunter* (1882), cautioned that "if (the wounded deer) goes off, let him go, and for several hours do nothing to disturb him. If it is near night you had better let him go until next morning." William M. Newsom, in his *White-tailed Deer* (1926), elaborated on the subject by prescribing different waiting periods for different types of wounds. For example, if

you wound the deer in the paunch or intestines, "you will probably have a long chase ahead unless you wait at least two hours for the deer to sicken and lie down." If you wound the deer in the foreleg, Newsom advises that a wait of at least 30 minutes is necessary; if the evidence indicates a lung shot, "you can follow at once."

Despite variations in the recommended waiting period, the proponents almost unanimously agree on the reasons why waiting represents the best strategy after wounding a deer. The philosophy of waiting operates on the premise that wounded deer behave in a predictable pattern. Francis E. Park, Jr., a deer hunter from Maine, summarized the alleged typical behavior of wounded deer succinctly in his *Deer Hunting* (1954). "Leave (the wounded deer) alone, and he will usually not run over a few hundred yards. He will then lie down as soon as he finds some good cover and try to lick his wound. When he lies down, the wound will tend to stiffen up. After a quarter of an hour, the chances are good that he will not be able to get up again." Conversely, if the hunter pursues a wounded deer quickly, he will arouse the deer from its bed before it "stiffens up" and dies. The deer will then run a considerable distance and reduce the hunter's chances of recovering it.

Up to this point, the advocates of waiting and their reasons for doing so pertain to deer hunting with firearms. As bow hunting's popularity increased, bow hunters also adopted the philosophy of waiting as the best strategy for recovering wounded deer. In *Bucks and Bows* (1953), Walter Perry advised bow hunters that "if (a wounded) deer is immediately followed, it will keep on going as long as it has the strength to move. But . . . if it is not followed, it will travel a short distance, lie down and not get up as long as it is not disturbed."

At about the time when bow hunters adopted the philosophy of waiting from the firearms hunters, firearms hunters began to have second thoughts about waiting. Admittedly, they did not alter their views regarding wounded deer behavior, but a new development entered the picture. That new development consisted of the increasing hunting pressure during firearms deer seasons. This led to a change in the recommended strategy for the pursuit of wounded deer, as Frank C. Edminster pointed out in *Hunting Whitetails* (1954). "In heavily hunted country, the hunter who has wounded a deer should pursue it without delay. It may not even pay to stalk it with particular care. The best chance may be to hope that the shot proves deadly in a short time. Then the problem is to get the animal quickly before someone else does." Apparently Edminster, and others, felt a bit uncomfortable with this alteration in trailing strategy. He continues by noting that "to be sure, this is not a very fine picture of sportsmanship or of tracking procedures. When we choose to hunt where lots of others have made the same choice, we have to accept this condition as one of the hazards of the game."

The philosophy of waiting remains basically intact to this day. For example, take this piece of advice from a 1986 issue of a national hunting magazine and compare it to earlier discussions about the advisability of waiting. "After the deer has vanished and you're alone in the woods, you advance to the next and, for most of us, the most difficult step in trailing: You have to wait it out. Give the arrow time to do its deadly work. You cannot rush it. This means staying right there on your stand for a minimum of 30 minutes. Do not move around or make any noise. Don't even look for the arrow yet.

"Even after it is hit, a deer is not fully aware of what has happened. He may not even be alarmed. If not pushed, a bow-shot deer simply retreats to a secure area, beds down and dies. But scare him by making unnecessary sounds from your stand, looking for the arrow or taking up the trail too soon and he may travel miles — often with little or no blood trail."

It's true that modern-day firearms deer hunters are less prone to wait before trailing a wounded deer than are bow hunters, but this relates to the increased hunting pressure in today's deer forests and not a change in attitude regarding the fundamental reason for waiting. The majority of today's deer hunters remain firm in their belief that a wounded deer typically runs off a short distance, lies down and dies if fatally wounded.

In theory, waiting seems logical if we accept the premise that wounded deer behave in the manner described by the advocates of waiting. A potential problem surfaces, however, when one searches for data in the scientific and popular literature to substantiate the behavior pattern of wounded deer. While many hunters think they know how wounded deer behave, no one has ever statistically documented how wounded deer actually behave.

◆◆ *The Philosophy of Waiting* ◆◆

The 1985
Wounded Deer Survey

To obtain data pertaining to deer wounded (whether recovered or not) by firearms and bow hunters, a 60-question "Wounded Deer Survey" was published in the February 1986 issue of *Deer & Deer Hunting.* I designed the reader survey not to quantify how many wounded deer hunters failed to recover, but to gather data necessary to identify and quantify factors which influence, either positively or negatively, the recovery of wounded deer by gun and bow hunters

Readers responded well to the survey and submitted a total of 1,685 completed questionnaires. Since many of the participants hunted deer during both the 1985 firearms and bow seasons, approximately 20 percent of them provided data on two wounded deer — one shot with a firearm and another shot with a bow. Thus, the hunters supplied information for a total of 2,103 wounded deer — 963 gun-shot deer and 1,140 bow-shot deer.

For the purpose of identifying factors which influence the recovery of wounded deer, I needed a method of making comparisons between a large number of factors involved in the recovery of wounded deer. For this purpose, recovery and wounding rates were calculated and used to compare the effect of various factors on the recovery of deer wounded by gun and bow hunters.

When one studies the literature pertaining to the wounding of deer by hunters, he quickly learns that no standard terminology exists. While one researcher categorizes "crippling loss" as all deer wounded by hunters but not recovered, other researchers speak of "unretrieved deer," "illegal in-season losses," "abandoned deer," "crippling mortality," etc. For the sake of clarity and consistency, I itemize and define in Figure 1 the terms used in this chapter. While these definitions may differ slightly from those used by other authors, they should serve to clarify the discussion of the reader survey results.

Wounded Deer Behavior

The premise for waiting before pursuing a wounded deer is based on what the proponents claim to be typical wounded deer behavior and the alterations in

---

Figure 1. Wounded Deer Survey Definitions

Wounded Deer
Any deer the hunter confirmed that he hit. The wound inflicted may range from a superficial cut to an injury which eventually resulted in the death of the deer. "Wounded deer" include both "recovered" and "unrecovered deer."

Recovered Deer
Any deer that dies of a wound or wounds inflicted by a hunter who later finds the dead deer or confirms that another hunter found and claimed the deer. In some cases, deer hunters reported finding the deer after it was beyond salvage. Unless stated otherwise, these deer are also treated as "recovered deer" in this discussion.

Unrecovered Deer
Any deer a hunter wounded but failed to recover. This includes deer that survive after being wounded as well as those that later die as the result of a wound inflicted by a hunter.

Recovery Rate
The percent of all wounded deer that are recovered by the hunter or that he knows were recovered by another hunter. The "recovery rate" is expressed as the number of deer recovered for every 100 wounded. Example: If hunters wound 100 deer and recover 50 of them, the recovery rate equals 50 percent.

Wounding Rate
The number of unrecovered deer expressed as a percentage of the number of recovered deer. Example: If hunters wound 100 deer, recover 50 of them and fail to recover the other 50, the wounding rate equals 100 percent.

Waiting Period
The length of time between when a hunter wounds a deer and when he begins pursuing the wounded deer.

that behavior if the hunter pursues too soon after shooting. Supposedly, wounded deer behavior consists of several components: After the hunter wounds a deer, the deer (1) runs off, (2) runs only a short distance, (3) beds down, (4) "stiffens up" and (5) dies in its bed or weakens to the point where it is unable to arise and the hunter can approach for a finishing shot. Based on this assumption, by waiting the hunter allows time for the deer to "stiffen up" and die a short distance from where he wounded it. Conversely, by pursuing either immediately or too quickly, the hunter increases the likelihood of arousing the wounded deer from its bed before it weakens and dies. Further, proponents of waiting claim that after a wounded deer flees its bed, it usually travels a considerable distance before either bedding again or dying. Thus, the hunter who pursues quickly reduces his chances of recovering mortally wounded deer.

Several of the questions in the "Wounded Deer Survey" allowed deer hunters to provide statistical information describing the behavior of deer they wounded and how long they waited before pursuing wounded deer. An analysis of this data permitted a comparison of actual wounded deer behavior to the theoretical behavior of wounded deer. The data also allowed an analysis of how, if, or to what extent variations in the waiting period influenced the behavior of wounded deer.

An analysis of the data to determine the immediate reaction of a deer after being wounded produced few surprises. The vast majority of gun-shot and bow-shot deer, whether recovered or unrecovered, either dropped dead within sight of the hunter or ran off (see Table 1). This substantiates the first part of the alleged behavior pattern of wounded deer.

The reactions of deer the hunters eventually recovered were quite similar to those of the unrecovered deer. Although the reactions of gun-shot and bow-shot deer varied somewhat, in each category the wounded deer reacted so similarly that it appears doubtful that either gun or bow hunters could consistently and accurately assess the seriousness of the deer's wound based solely upon the deer's initial reaction after being shot.

From the time the hunter shoots until the wounded deer moves out of sight, the hunter can directly observe the behavior of the deer. Typically that behavior amounts to the deer running until it either drops

dead or moves out of sight. After the deer moves out of sight, the determination of its behavior takes place indirectly — usually through the interpretation of signs (blood, hair, tracks, beds) found while trailing the wounded deer. As a result, the analysis of the data relating to the behavior of wounded deer becomes less precise, but provides some interesting insights regarding what happens after a deer leaves the range of the hunter's vision.

The remainder of the discussion of wounded deer behavior pertains exclusively to bow-shot deer. Originally I hoped to compare the behavior of gun-shot deer to that of bow-shot deer but this proved impossible for a variety of reasons. More than 40 percent of the recovered gun-shot deer died within sight of the hunter, thereby reducing the sample size of wounded deer considerably. Gun hunters recovered a noticeably higher percentage of the deer they wounded and this meant the number of unrecovered deer was quite small. And finally, very few gun hunters in

Table 1. Observed reactions of recovered and unrecovered deer immediately after being wounded.

Reaction Of Deer	Gun-Shot Deer		Bow-Shot Deer	
	% Of Recov. Deer	% Of Unrecov. Deer	% Of Recov. Deer	% Of Unrecov. Deer
No Visible Reaction	15.6	19.5	8.2	7.8
Deer Dropped Dead Within Sight	42.5	0.0	16.8	0.0
Deer Walked Away	5.7	7.3	8.0	12.0
Deer Ran Away	57.9	82.9	80.9	89.5
Deer Reared Up	7.2	10.4	3.4	5.9
Deer Hunched Its Back	8.7	11.6	8.7	7.1

Note: The totals in each of the "%" columns exceeds 100 because some hunters observed several types of reactions by the wounded deer.

this survey waited any length of time before pursuing a wounded deer so it became impossible to compare the behavior of wounded deer with the length of the waiting period.

Bow hunters responding to this survey provided useable data for 1,114 wounded deer. This included 715 deer the bow hunters recovered and 399 deer they failed to recover. With the information supplied regarding these deer, we can examine several questions relating to the theory of typical wounded deer behavior: (1) How far do wounded deer run (or walk) before dying, bedding down or before the hunter loses the trail of the wounded deer? (2) What percentage of the deer wounded by archers bed down? (3) Do recovered or unrecovered deer bed down more frequently? (4) Do recovered or unrecovered deer travel farther before bedding down? (5) If not disturbed by the hunter, do bedded deer die in their beds? (6) How does the distance travelled and bedding activities of wounded deer affect the probability of recovering wounded deer?

On average, wounded deer travelled relatively short distances from the point where wounded to where the bow hunter either recovered the deer or lost the trail of the wounded deer (see Figure 2). Of the 715 recovered deer, 549 (76.9 percent) travelled 200 yards or less. Hunters lost the trail of wounded deer within 200 yards 41.4 percent of the time (165 of the 399 unrecovered deer).

Many variables undoubtedly influence the distance travelled by wounded deer. These variables might include the severity of the wound inflicted by the bow hunter, whether the hunter "pushed" the deer and how soon after shooting, and the type of activity the deer was engaged in at the time of the shot. Regardless of which factors exert the greatest influence on how far a wounded deer travels, this distance noticeably affects recovery and wounding rates and does so quite quickly. Table 2 clearly illustrates that recovery rates decrease sharply as the deer moves away from the spot where the hunter wounded it. This change in the recovery rate surfaces as soon as the

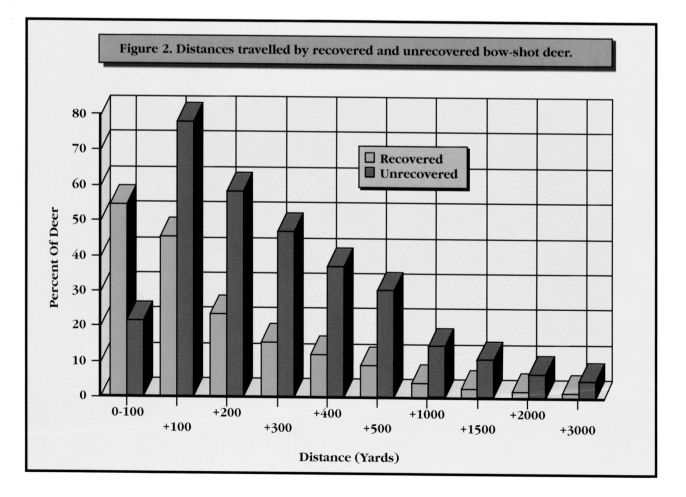

Figure 2. Distances travelled by recovered and unrecovered bow-shot deer.

deer travels as few as 100 yards. Of the 1,114 bow-shot deer, hunters recovered 64.2 percent of them. The recovery rate declined to 51.2 percent for deer that travelled more than 100 yards and beyond 200 yards bow hunters recovered less than half (41.5 percent) of the deer they wounded. It appears that when the hunter fails to recover a deer within 200 yards, he faces a difficult trailing job with a much-reduced likelihood of recovering the deer.

Since recovery rates decrease as the deer moves away from the hunter, it becomes desirable to take whatever measures are necessary to minimize the distance travelled by a wounded deer. According to the theory of waiting, hunters will achieve this objective by waiting for a period of time before trailing a wounded deer because the deer will bed down and die within a short distance if not disturbed. The data from this survey, however, contradict that portion of the waiting theory.

Using that data, the distance travelled by recovered deer was correlated to the length of the waiting period reported by bow hunters. Unrecovered deer were omitted from the analysis of distances travelled versus waiting periods because the fate of these deer remains unknown.

Figure 3 reveals that as bow hunters increased the length of time they waited before beginning pursuit, the distance the deer travelled before dying increased considerably. Bow hunters who pursued within five minutes, for example, recovered the deer an average of 163.1 yards from where it was wounded. Those who waited the longest periods of time (more than two hours) found it necessary to trail the wounded deer an average of more than 500 yards before recovering it.

It would be misleading to suggest that the distance a wounded deer travels is related solely to how long the hunter waits before beginning pursuit. It seems almost certain that shot placement and the resulting severity of the wound inflicted influences how far a wounded deer travels. The data from this survey, in fact, document substantial variations in distances travelled by deer that hunters recovered when compared to shot placement (see Table 3).

The analysis of distances travelled by bow-shot deer included only deer for which the hunter reported he injured one organ or part of the deer. In many other cases, the hunter indicated he damaged several organs. For example, some hunters stated their arrow pierced

Table 2. Recovery and wounding rates of bow-shot deer versus the distance (yards) the deer travelled or the distance the hunter was able to trail the wounded deer.

Yards Trailed	No. Deer	Deer Recov.	Deer Not Recov.	Recov. Rate (%)	Wound. Rate (%)
All	1,114	715	399	64.2	55.8
+100	639	327	312	51.2	95.4
+200	400	166	234	41.5	141.0
+300	298	110	188	36.9	170.9
+400	236	88	148	37.3	168.2
+500	189	68	121	36.0	177.9
+600	168	58	110	34.5	189.7
+700	155	53	102	34.2	192.5
+800	135	48	87	35.6	181.3
+900	119	42	77	35.3	183.3
+1000	90	31	59	34.4	190.3
+1500	60	18	42	30.0	233.3
+2000	41	12	29	29.3	241.7
+2500	38	12	26	31.6	216.7
+3000	29	9	20	31.0	222.2

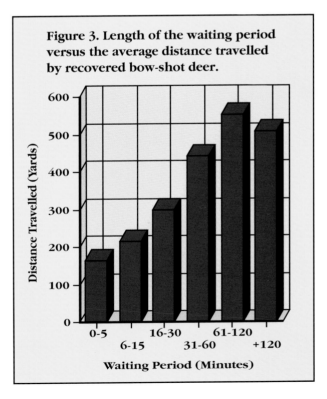

Figure 3. Length of the waiting period versus the average distance travelled by recovered bow-shot deer.

both the paunch and liver. Rather than try to determine if, in this example, the injury to the paunch or the liver contributed more to the death of the deer, I deleted these types of bow-shot deer from this portion of the analysis.

The information presented in Table 3 will surprise few bow hunters. Deer shot in the heart and/or lungs are, on average, recovered quite quickly. Paunch-shot deer, however, travel considerably farther before being recovered. This data, even though expected, stress the importance of shot placement. Basically, if the archer's arrow penetrates either the heart or lungs of the deer, he will recover the deer in a relatively short distance and probably with a minimum of effort. A paunch-shot deer, however, in most cases necessitates following the wounded deer a much greater distance.

Paunch-shot deer often become the focal point of the philosophy of waiting. Many hunters concede that heart- and lung-shot deer can be pursued immediately because they die shortly after being wounded and before travelling very far. In the case of a paunch-shot deer, however, waiting is usually deemed the best, if not the only, way to recover the deer. If the hunter pursues too quickly, it is alleged, the paunch-shot deer travels much farther than if the hunter waits and allows sufficient time for the deer to die.

Table 3. Average distance (yards) travelled by bow-shot, recovered deer wounded in various parts of their anatomy.

Where Wounded	Number Of Deer	Average Distance
Lungs	226	158.5
Heart	39	111.3
Heart/Lung	53	124.6
Paunch	43	695.4
Neck	36	273.9
Hindquarter	34	648.2
Liver	30	249.7
Spine	16	139.1
Shoulder	9	1,406.7
Leg	9	1,192.2
Head	6	58.3

The data from this survey raise some serious doubts regarding the efficacy of waiting before trailing a paunch-shot deer. On average, bow hunters waited much longer before trailing a paunch-shot deer than they did for most other types of wounds. In spite of this longer wait, paunch-shot deer travelled an average of nearly 700 yards before hunters recovered them. This proves little, however, because it takes into account all paunch-shot deer, regardless of the waiting period between the time of the shot and the commencement of trailing. When we compare distances travelled by paunch-shot deer to waiting periods of various durations, the data become more meaningful.

Apparently not all bow hunters subscribe to the philosophy of waiting because nearly 30 percent (27.9) of those who paunch-shot a deer began pursuing almost immediately (within 15 minutes). Those hunters recovered paunch-shot deer in shorter distances than those who waited for longer periods of time before trailing. Hunters who trailed within the first 15 minutes found paunch-shot deer after trailing an average of 313.2 yards; for those who waited one hour or more, the average distance increased to 818.2 yards; those who waited three hours or more found their paunch-shot deer in an average of 350.0 yards. Thus, the data indicate that waiting fails to decrease the distance travelled by paunch-shot deer.

What do we know about the unrecovered, paunch-shot deer? Unfortunately, some very important information about these deer could not be gathered through this survey. We don't know how many of these deer eventually recovered from the wound or how many died. Of those that died, we do not know how far they travelled before dying. We do know that bow hunters were able to trail the unrecovered paunch-shot deer, on average, nearly as far as those they recovered (624.0 yards versus 695.4 yards). Therefore, the unrecovered deer were apparently not the result of a lack of trailing effort on the part of the bow hunters.

Average waiting periods were also essentially the same for recovered and unrecovered paunch-shot deer. Those who recovered paunch-shot deer waited an average of 104.8 minutes while those who failed to recover the deer waited an average of 96.9 minutes. Bow hunters who recovered paunch-shot deer were more likely to pursue quickly, however. Approximately 28 percent of the recovered deer were

trailed within 15 minutes after being wounded while 19 percent of the unrecovered deer were pursued after a similar waiting period.

Analysis of the data regarding paunch-shot deer documents what many bow hunters already suspected. These deer usually travel considerable distances and recovery rates for paunch-shot deer are lower than for deer which receive other types of wounds, especially heart- and lung-shot deer. The data further suggest, however, that hunters who pursue paunch-shot deer shortly after shooting find them closer to where they wounded the deer; longer waiting periods do not reduce the distance travelled by paunch-shot deer. In essence, longer waiting periods fail to compensate for what must be considered poor shot placement and will not increase the bow hunters' chances of recovering paunch-shot deer.

Bill Vaznis

All the evidence from this survey indicates that the length of the waiting period noticeably influences recovery rates of bow-shot deer but in the opposite way the proponents of waiting have claimed for so many years.

The data from this survey contradict that portion of the reason for waiting which claims that if the hunter pursues quickly, he will alarm the deer before it dies and cause it to travel a considerable distance. To the contrary, deer pursued quickly actually travelled shorter distances than those trailed after a longer waiting period. But that only contradicts one part of the waiting theory. Supposedly, a wounded deer beds down after running a short distance and, if the hunter waits an appropriate amount of time, the deer dies in its bed.

Analyzing the bedding patterns of wounded deer, based on the data gathered through this survey, poses more of a problem than the analysis of how far wounded deer travel. The problem arises because when a wounded deer beds down, it usually does so after moving out of sight of the hunter. Thus, if the hunter finds no evidence of bedding but recovers the deer, we cannot say with assurance whether the deer bedded and then died or if it fell dead while on the move.

With that limitation in mind, I began the analysis of wounded deer behavior by examining the behavior of deer remaining in sight of the bow hunter from the time it was wounded until it died. Deer meeting this criteria totaled 115 of the 715 bow-shot deer recovered by hunters. Twenty-one (18.3 percent) of these deer dropped dead in their tracks and, therefore, did not bed down. The remaining 94 either ran or walked off after being wounded. None of them displayed the alleged typical behavior pattern of wounded deer, i.e. move off a short distance, bed down and die. Three (3.2 percent) of the deer that died within sight of the hunter did bed down, but each one arose and then died while on the move — still within sight of the hunter. For all practical purposes, deer that died within sight succumbed within 100 yards of where they were at the time of the shot. Only one deer that died within sight moved off more than 100 yards before dying.

Bow hunters also recovered an additional 274 deer within 100 yards of where they wounded it even though the deer moved out of sight before dying. It now becomes virtually impossible to ascertain what percentage of these deer bedded down before dying, but the number that bedded and then arose is known, based on evidence of a deer bed found by the hunter while trailing the wounded deer.

Of the 274 deer recovered within 100 yards but

out of sight, bow hunters found evidence that 22 (8.0 percent) bedded down. All but one of those deer arose from its bed prior to dying. How many of the 252 deer that left no evidence of bedding did in fact bed and then die in that bed? While the answer to that question remains a mystery, it seems likely that the majority died while on the move. I draw this supposition from the fact that only slightly more than three percent of the deer that died within sight (within 100 yards of where shot) bedded down before dying.

To further complicate the analysis of the frequency of bedding by wounded deer, we must take into account the deer bow hunters failed to recover. In the case of unrecovered deer, we do know how many bedded up to the point where the hunter lost the trail of the wounded deer. What the deer did, or its fate, beyond that point remains unknown. Bow hunters lost the trail of a wounded deer within the first 100 yards on 87 occasions and found evidence that only five (5.7 percent) bedded down. It may be only coincidence, but this figure almost matches the percentage of recovered deer who left evidence of bedding within 100 yards of where wounded.

Rather than speculate on how many of the wounded deer bedded down, let us focus our attention on those that definitely did. Survey respondents provided data on how often they found evidence of bedding by wounded deer, how far these deer travelled before bedding and how far they trailed the wounded deer after it left its bed.

A total of 242 of 1,114 (21.7 percent) wounded deer trailed by bow hunters left evidence of bedding one or more times. As deer travel greater distances from where wounded, it would seem logical that a larger percentage would bed down. This, in fact, is exactly what the data reveal (see Table 4). Despite the increase in bedding frequencies, Table 4 also illustrates that relatively few deer left evidence of bedding. Proponents of waiting claim that wounded deer will bed down within a short distance, but this does not appear to be the pattern. While what exactly constitutes a "short distance" becomes quite subjective, Table 4 shows that even among those deer which travelled more than 500 yards, only slightly more than 50 percent bedded down at some point.

The deer bow hunters failed to recover bedded slightly more frequently than those the hunter recov-

ered (24.0 versus 20.4 percent, respectively), but the deer were also more likely to travel greater distances prior to bedding (see Figure 4). Of those deer that did bed down, 57.9 percent of the unrecovered deer did so within 200 yards. A noticeably higher percentage (75.3) of the recovered deer bedded down within a similar distance.

Table 4. Bedding frequencies of bow-shot deer versus the distance (yards) the deer were trailed.

Yards Trailed	No. Trailed	No. Bedded	% Bedded
All	1,114	242	21.7
+100	642	212	33.0
+200	408	174	42.6
+300	307	149	48.5
+400	244	124	50.8
+500	198	101	51.0
+600	175	89	50.9
+700	163	86	52.8
+800	140	72	51.4
+900	125	66	52.8
+1000	96	56	58.3
+1500	65	38	58.5
+2000	51	35	68.6
+2500	44	29	65.9
+3000	31	24	77.4

Table 5. Bedding frequencies of bow-shot deer versus various waiting periods (no. of minutes).

Waiting Period	No. Of Deer Trailed	% Of Deer Bedding
0-5	248	9.1
6-15	237	20.3
16-30	274	20.4
31-60	202	22.8
61-120	98	34.7
+120	55	43.6

Waiting before pursuing a wounded deer based on the assumption that it will bed down within a short distance and then die in that bed if not disturbed by the hunter will frequently lead to disappointment because the facts contradict that assumption. First, only a small percentage of wounded deer actually bed down. Second, those that do bed down may travel a considerable distance before bedding. And third, even if undisturbed, the deer does not necessarily die in the spot where it bedded.

The data from this survey also provide information about bedding frequencies versus how long the hunter waited before pursuing the wounded deer and what the recovery rates were for deer that bedded versus those that did not bed. As shown in Table 5, bedding frequencies of wounded deer increased somewhat when the waiting period exceeded 60 minutes. We must keep in mind, however, that these deer arose from their beds rather than dying in the beds.

The fact that a deer beds down appears to only slightly affect whether or not the bow hunter eventually recovers the deer. Respondents to this survey reported, contrary to what might be expected, recovering a slightly higher percentage of the deer that did not bed down. While bow hunters recovered 65.1 percent of the deer that did not bed down, they recovered 60.4 percent of the deer that did bed down.

Although very few wounded deer left evidence of bedding within a short distance of where they were wounded and even fewer died in the bed, we cannot ignore the fact that some wounded deer do bed down.

The final part of the philosophy of waiting claims that if a hunter pursues a deer shortly after wounding it, he will jump the deer from its bed and it will run a considerable distance. The data fail to substantiate this contention.

For the purpose of comparing distances travelled by deer after leaving a bed, only the data on recovered deer were used because we know how far each of these deer travelled after leaving the spot where they first bedded down. From the data obtained in this survey, however, we cannot determine how far an unrecovered deer travelled or if it later died as a result of the hunter-inflicted wound.

On average, as bow hunters increased the length of the waiting period, deer travelled greater distances after leaving a bed. For example, deer that bedded and were pursued within 15 minutes travelled an average distance of 321.9 yards from where they initially bedded to where they were recovered. If the hunter increased the waiting period to between 16 and 30 minutes, the distance travelled increased to 589.0 yards. Finally, those hunters who waited more than 60 minutes before pursuing a wounded deer that bedded down, trailed the deer an average of 821.8 yards beyond the point where the deer first bedded.

Contrary to the philosophy of waiting, the results of this survey indicate that bow hunters who pursue wounded deer shortly after shooting find them closer to where they initially bed than do hunters who wait for longer periods of time before beginning their pursuit. Whatever the reason or reasons might be, it appears that longer waiting periods increase the likelihood of having to trail a wounded deer for a considerable distance beyond the point where it initially bedded.

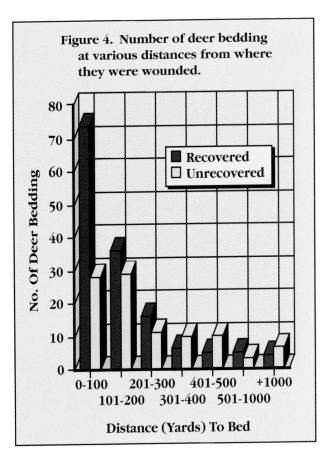

Figure 4. Number of deer bedding at various distances from where they were wounded.

Summary Of
Wounded Deer Behavior

The common belief that an undisturbed, wounded deer typically runs a short distance, beds down and dies is, at best, a gross oversimplification of wounded deer behavior. The results of this survey indicate that this type of behavior represents the exception rather than the rule for bow-shot deer. It seems more accurate to state that wounded deer exhibit no simple, predictable behavior pattern. In all likelihood, the absence of a clearly identifiable pattern of "typical" wounded deer behavior relates to the innumerable variables involved. Some of these variables might include the severity of the wound inflicted by the hunter, the health and vigor of the animal wounded and the activity the deer was engaged in at the time of the shot. And perhaps, the length of the waiting period also influences the behavior of wounded deer, but not in the way many deer hunters think it does. Although the results of this survey fail to provide a concise description of "typical" wounded deer behavior, the data clearly indicate that wounded deer do not typically run a short distance, lie down and die. Yes, after being wounded, most deer run off and some only run a short distance before dying. Those deer most likely do not bed down and die, however, but die while on the move as the result of a well-placed arrow which kills quickly and cleanly. Indeed, more than 75 percent of the bow-shot deer recovered by hunters died within 200 yards of where they were wounded. This single snippet of information probably says much about the efficiency of archery equipment for the hunting of deer. There seems little doubt that a well-placed arrow kills deer very quickly.

But not all wounded deer are recovered and many of those that are travel quite far from where they were wounded. What is the behavior of these deer? Do they bed down after running a short distance? Do they then die while bedded if not disturbed by the hunter for an appropriate period of time? The advocates of waiting claim that doing so results in a quicker (in terms of distance) recovery of wounded deer and that hunters will recover a greater percentage of the deer they wound. Data from this survey indicate that just the opposite occurs. As the waiting period increased, the distances travelled by wounded deer also increased and as the distances travelled by bow-shot deer increased, the recovery rate decreased.

Regardless of the distances travelled by wounded deer or the success of bow hunters in recovering them, this survey revealed little evidence of bedding on the part of wounded deer. While it is true that most of the deer that bedded did so within a relatively short distance, only 20.4 percent of the recovered deer and 24.0 percent of the unrecovered deer left evidence of bedding after being wounded. Thus, the results of this survey contradict the claim that a wounded deer generally runs a short distance and beds down.

Some deer wounded by hunters participating in this survey did bed down, however, so it became necessary to analyze the effect of waiting versus quick pursuit of wounded deer. According to the proponents of waiting, hunters who pursue quickly will alarm the deer from its bed, the deer will then run a considerable distance and make recovering the deer a difficult proposition. On the other hand, if the hunter waits for an appropriate period of time before pursuing a wounded deer, it will supposedly die in its bed. Once again, the data contradicted the theoretical behavior of wounded deer. Hunters who quickly pursued bedded deer recovered a higher percentage of them, and in shorter distances, than hunters who adhered to the philosophy of waiting.

The results of this survey indicate that the philosophy of waiting is based on a false premise. Wounded deer do not typically run a short distance, bed down and die. The bow hunter who waits for a period of time before pursuing a wounded deer bases his trailing strategy on at least two false assumptions: (1) it is unlikely that the wounded deer will bed down and (2) it is even more unlikely that it will bed down and die in that bed.

Even though the data acquired through this survey refute the alleged typical behavior pattern of wounded deer, upon which the philosophy of waiting is based, this does not automatically prove that pursuing wounded deer quickly represents the best strategy for hunters.

Despite the fact that wounded deer seldom run a short distance, bed down and die if left undisturbed, other factors could be involved that still make it advisable to wait for a period of time before taking up the trail of a wounded deer. Regardless of the actual behavior of an individual wounded deer or the behavior of wounded deer in general, we must study the recovery rates of hunters who waited before pursuing and compare them to recovery rates of hunters who

pursued wounded deer either immediately or very soon after shooting.

Waiting Versus Quick Pursuit

As stated previously, I originally planned to compare recovery and wounding rates versus the duration of waiting periods for both gun-shot deer and bow-shot deer. With this as an objective, I began tabulating recovery and wounding rates for gun-shot deer.

Firearms hunters responding to this survey reported wounding a total of 958 deer. They recovered 793 of those deer for an overall recovery rate of 82.8 percent and a wounding rate of 20.8 percent. Tabulation of the data revealed that firearms hunters pursued wounded deer shortly after shooting in most cases. Perhaps this was because firearms hunters frequently saw the wounded deer die within sight. Another potential explanation for the quick pursuit by firearms hunters is that they feel this represents the best strategy in areas of intense hunting pressure to avoid having another hunter claim the deer. Whatever the reason or reasons, 645 (67.3 percent) of the firearms hunters pursued their wounded deer within five minutes after shooting. At the other end of the range of waiting periods, only six (0.6 percent) hunters waited more than 120 minutes before trailing a gun-shot deer. This small sample size for the longer waiting periods made it impractical to make meaningful comparisons between the recovery rates for various waiting periods during the firearms season.

Despite the small number of deer trailed after longer waiting periods during the firearms season, the data hinted at higher recovery rates (and lower wounding rates) for those hunters who pursued shortly after shooting. For example, firearms hunters who pursued within five minutes recovered 89.6 percent of the deer they wounded; waiting up to 30 minutes reduced the recovery rate to 83.7 percent; and those who waited more than 30 minutes recovered 66.7 percent of the deer they wounded. I urge caution, again, before drawing hasty conclusions from this data because relatively few firearms hunters waited more than 30 minutes before trailing a wounded deer.

The problem of small sample sizes for the longer waiting periods vanished during the bow season. The bow hunters in this survey were more prone to wait for longer periods of time before trailing wounded deer. This permitted a meaningful analysis of recovery and wounding rates for various waiting periods.

The hint of increased recovery rates by firearms hunters who pursued wounded deer after a minimal waiting period became a very pronounced pattern when the data for bow-shot deer was tabulated. Table 6 and Figure 5 show the strong correlation between recovery and wounding rates versus the duration of the waiting period. Bow hunters reported steadily declining recovery rates (and increasing wounding rates) as they increased the duration of the waiting period after wounding a deer. At first, I suspected this pattern might be influenced by bow hunters who pursued quickly those deer that died within sight. Even

Table 6. Recovery and wounding rates of bow-shot deer versus the waiting period (no. of minutes) between the shot and the commencement of trailing.

Waiting Period	All Wounded Deer				Excluding Deer Dying Within Sight			
	Number Recovered	Number Unrecovered	Recovery Rate	Wounding Rate	Number Recovered	Number Unrecovered	Recovery Rate	Wounding Rate
0-5	203	48	80.9	23.6	134	48	73.6	35.8
6-15	159	80	66.5	50.3	135	80	62.8	59.3
16-30	161	121	57.1	75.2	150	121	55.4	80.7
31-60	113	92	55.1	81.4	106	92	53.5	86.8
61-120	55	47	53.9	85.5	52	47	52.5	90.4
+120	27	27	50.0	100.0	27	27	50.0	100.0
Total	**718**	**415**	**63.4**	**57.8**	**604**	**415**	**59.3**	**68.7**

after excluding those deer from the analysis, however, the same pattern of lower recovery rates and higher wounding rates for the longer waiting periods remained. At the extreme ends of the various waiting periods, the wounding rate for bow hunters who began trailing within five minutes was 35.6 percent. Bow hunters who waited the longest period of time (more than 120 minutes) reported a wounding rate almost three times as high (100.0 percent).

The survey results presented in Table 6 and Figure 5 strongly contradict the theory that waiting for a period of time before trailing a wounded deer increases the likelihood of recovering the deer. The more than 1,100 bow hunters participating in this survey recovered a noticeably higher percentage of wounded deer if they began trailing shortly after shooting.

The discussion concerning the advisability of waiting could, perhaps, end at this point. When taking into account all bow-shot deer, immediate pursuit represents the best strategy based on the results of this survey. However, we must examine the possibility that not all bow hunters arbitrarily either pursue wounded deer quickly or wait a predetermined amount of time each time they wound a deer. In

other words, an advocate of waiting might pursue a lung-shot deer after a much shorter wait than if his arrow enters the paunch of the deer.

Indeed, the data suggest that many bow hunters base their decision of how long to wait on their assessment of how severely they wounded the deer. Waiting periods varied considerably from hunter to hunter but appeared to be somewhat dependent on where the bow hunter's arrow struck the deer (see Table 7). Bow hunters waited the longest period of time, on average, when they paunch-shot a deer.

These paunch-shot deer provided an opportunity to analyze the effectiveness of various waiting periods. Proponents of waiting after shooting a deer strongly urge the bow hunter to wait after paunch-shooting a deer and generally recommend waiting longer for this type of wound than any other. They claim that if the hunter pursues paunch-shot deer too quickly he will disturb the deer, cause it to run a considerable distance, make trailing a difficult proposition and reduce the likelihood of recovering the deer.

Earlier it was pointed out that paunch-shot deer travel a considerable distance, on average, regardless of the waiting period. When we compare the recovery rates for paunch-shot deer to various waiting peri-

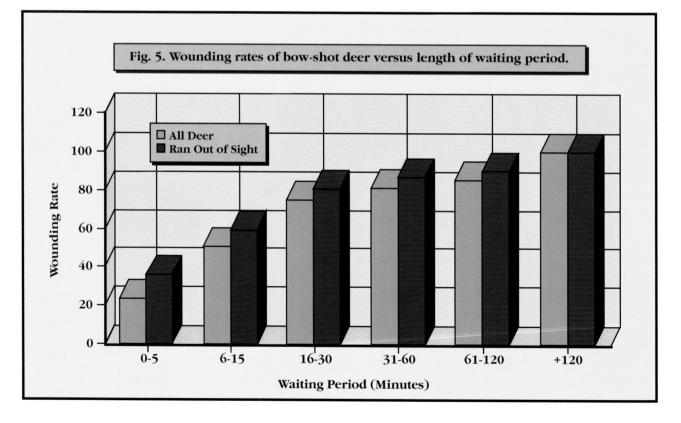

Fig. 5. Wounding rates of bow-shot deer versus length of waiting period.

ods, the results of this survey continue to contradict the theory that paunch-shot deer should not be pursued shortly after the hunter shoots. Even though the average waiting period for paunch-shot deer was longer than for any other type of wound, a significant number of bow hunters pursued rather quickly. It will surprise many bow hunters to learn that waiting for long periods of time before trailing paunch-shot deer does not increase the chances of recovering the deer.

Waiting periods for paunch-shot deer ranged from zero to 840 minutes. Bow hunters who began trailing within 15 minutes after shooting recovered 63.2 percent of them. For those who waited the longest periods of time before trailing, recovery rates failed to improve. Bow hunters who waited four hours or more before trailing paunch-shot deer recovered 62.3 percent of them, but when the waiting period increased to six hours or more, the recovery rate declined to 50.0 percent. Contrary to what the proponents of waiting claim, recovery rates for paunch-shot deer did not increase as the waiting period increased. Actually, recovery rates varied minimally for waiting periods of various durations, but bow hunters who waited the shortest period of time recovered a higher percentage of paunch-shot deer than did those who waited the longest period of time. Thus, while proponents of waiting argue most forcefully in favor of this strategy for paunch-shot deer, immediate or quick pursuit resulted in recovery rates similar to or even slightly better than those recorded by bow hunters who waited a considerable time before trailing paunch-shot deer.

The average waiting period for recovered and unrecovered paunch-shot deer was quite similar (104.8 and 96.9 minutes, respectively), but this was not the typical pattern. For other types of wounds, the general pattern was a noticeably shorter waiting period for recovered deer. Hunters who recovered wounded deer waited shorter periods of time than those who failed to recover the deer in the following situations: heart-shot deer, lung-shot deer, neck-shot deer, spine-shot deer, shoulder-shot deer, and leg-shot deer. The only exception to this pattern were deer wounded in the hindquarters. Hunters who wounded deer in the hindquarters did, however, wait an average of more than one hour before pursuing these deer regardless of whether they eventually recovered or failed to recover the deer.

Summary And Conclusions

The origin of the philosophy of waiting before pursuing a wounded deer can be traced back to at least the mid-1800s. Indeed, this philosophy probably predates the deer hunting literature because we find references to the advisability of waiting in even the oldest writings about the sport. To this day, the majority of recognized authorities on deer hunting advocate waiting for a period of time before taking up the trail of a wounded deer. They base their argument on what they allege to be typical wounded deer behavior: If not disturbed by the hunter, a wounded deer runs a short distance, lies down, "stiffens up" and dies.

From time to time a dissenter surfaces who recommends immediate pursuit of wounded deer, but the opinions of these nonconformists are either ignored or severely criticized. The debate periodically returns, however, because neither the proponents of waiting nor the advocates of immediate pursuit ever, to my knowledge, attempted to offer any proof for their claims.

In the February 1986 issue of *Deer & Deer Hunting* magazine, readers were asked to participate in a "Wounded Deer Survey" designed to delineate factors

Table 7. Average waiting periods (minutes) by bow hunters who wounded deer in various parts of their anatomy.

Where Wounded	Number Of Deer	Average Wait
Head	9	14.8
Heart	41	21.1
Heart/Lung	53	27.8
Lungs	262	31.9
Liver	34	32.2
Leg	28	42.1
Neck	61	43.0
Spine	31	59.4
Shoulder	73	66.8
Hindquarter	60	86.4
Paunch	79	101.2

that influence the recovery of gun- and bow-shot deer. One of the many factors studied focused on the effect of waiting periods of varying durations on the recovery of wounded deer.

The analysis of the data began with an examination of the alleged typical behavior pattern of wounded deer, the premise that forms the basis of the philosophy of waiting. Information submitted by more than 1,100 bow hunters clearly contradicted the widely held belief that a wounded deer, if not disturbed

> *Waiting before pursuing a wounded deer based on the assumption that it will bed down within a short distance and then die in that bed if not disturbed by the hunter will frequently lead to disappointment because the facts contradict that assumption.*

by the hunter, normally runs off a short distance, lies down and dies. The survey results indicate it would be far more accurate to state that individual deer react to wounds in such a variety of ways that it is impractical, if not impossible, to classify any pattern of behavior as being "typical" of wounded deer.

In reference to actual wounded deer behavior, the survey data revealed the following: (1) Deer that run only a short distance after being wounded apparently die while on the move rather than bedding and then dying. (2) As the distance travelled by a wounded deer increases, the percentage of wounded deer

recovered by hunters decreases. The distance travelled by wounded deer increases as the bow hunter increases the amount of time he waits between shooting and commencing the trailing of a wounded deer. (3) Very few wounded deer bed down and even fewer bed down within a short distance of where they were wounded. The distance travelled by wounded deer that did bed down increased as the waiting period increased. (4) Bow hunters recovered a higher percentage of those deer that did not bed down as compared to those that left evidence of bedding.

Although the survey data revealed many falsehoods in the alleged typical behavior of wounded deer, this did not automatically prove that waiting reduces the bow hunter's chances of recovering wounded deer. The possibility remained that other factors might still make it advisable to wait for a period of time after shooting.

And so, we return to the original question: Does the waiting period affect the likelihood of recovering wounded deer? All evidence from this survey indicates that the length of the waiting period noticeably influences recovery rates of bow-shot deer but in the opposite way the proponents of waiting have claimed for so many years. Bow hunters who participated in this survey recovered a noticeably higher percentage of the deer they wounded when they began trailing the deer either immediately or shortly (within 15 minutes) after wounding a deer. The pattern of increased recovery rates after minimal waiting periods remained quite consistent for all types of wounds and in no situation did the data indicate increased recovery rates by bow hunters who waited longer periods of time after shooting. The combination of all this information produced the ultimate conclusion that trailing wounded deer immediately or very shortly after shooting represents the best strategy for bow hunters.

Editor's Note: "The Philosophy of Waiting" was originally published in the December 1986 issue of Deer & Deer Hunting *magazine.*

The Philosophy of Waiting

■ SUBJECT NEEDS FURTHER DISCUSSION

I want to thank you for the fine magazine and ask you to keep publishing the excellent articles about deer behavior and especially any article about tracking wounded deer such as Al Hofacker's "The Philosophy of Waiting" in the December 1986 issue of *Deer & Deer Hunting*.

I believe the subject of tracking wounded needs further discussion. It's sometimes easy to think that your shot wasn't as good as you first thought. Then your recovery, or loss, of the deer makes you realize there is a whole puzzle and you have to remember to put it together one piece at a time.

— *Vin McCarthy*
Westminster, Massachusetts

■ HE WAS SKEPTICAL

My hat's off to Al Hofacker for his article, "The Philosophy of Waiting," in the December 1986 issue. When his "Wounded Deer Survey" was published in February 1986, I was skeptical. I guess I didn't realize the value of the information a survey of this type could provide. Hopefully, the information provided through this survey of deer hunters will help dispel many of the "old wives' tales" that have been expounded by the so-called experts.

The quality of articles being written about bow hunting improved a thousand percent in recent years. Yet, until Rob Wegner's article on tracking (*Deer & Deer Hunting*, August 1985) and now Hofacker's survey results, the information being written about tracking wounded deer has been not only bad but actually detrimental.

Over the years I have helped track several hundred bow-shot deer. Although the average bow hunter in my area can easily position himself to get a shot, I am continually amazed at their lack of tracking ability. Most lose the trail of the wounded deer before the tracking even gets close to being tough. Information abounds on how to get a shot, but we find little information on the most important aspect of the hunt — finding the wounded animal.

I'm glad *Deer & Deer Hunting* provides a forum for, and has the guts to publish, articles about a tough subject like that of wounded deer.

— *Keith Monson*
Cooperstown, North Dakota

■ THE WORD IS "WAIT"

I usually don't correspond with hunting magazines even though I subscribe to several. An article written by Al Hofacker, "The Philosophy of Waiting," caused me great concern, however.

Hofacker stated, based on data obtained from a hunter survey, that it is better to follow up paunch-shot deer immediately and that the recovery rate is much better employing this method rather than waiting. I disagree with this philosophy most strenuously!

I have been hunting deer with bow and rifle since I was 15 years old and am now 41. I've taken 20 deer with a bow. This statement is not made to brag, but to show I have some experience in trailing wounded deer. In my early years of deer hunting, I lost a paunch-shot (bow) buck because I followed immediately and kicked him out of his bed. I couldn't get a second shot and efforts to find any blood trail met with negative results. I swore to myself I would never follow up another paunch-shot deer immediately. Since that day, I have never lost another solidly hit deer, mainly because I always wait before tracking a wounded deer.

I am sure some hunters who followed their deer immediately and recovered them may have struck the liver or ruptured the diaphragm or pyloric artery, and thought they only struck the paunch. I feel a deer shot in the paunch with an arrow should be given six to seven hours before following up and one to two hours if shot with a rifle. In my experience, a paunch-shot deer, if not disturbed, will not travel more than 200 yards before bedding down and after six to seven hours will be very sick and not hard to finish off.

Just this past year, I paunch-shot a nine-pointer at 20 yards. My shooting lane was too wide and the deer was trotting. I released too late as he passed my lane. The buck ran and from my stand I watched him as long as possible. Needless to say, I was sick with the shot. I left the woods, came back seven hours later and found the deer approximately 150 yards from where I shot it.

Upon my approach, he got up but could hardly stand. I put a finishing shot through his lungs and recovered him 30 yards from where he was struck the second time. Had I followed immediately, I am sure my task would have been much harder, if not impossible.

Borderline hits (not fatal) may leave a lot of blood but dry up after several hundred yards and the deer will usually not bed down in the immediate area. Lung, heart and arterial hits will usually drop the deer before he thinks about bedding and, of course, drop him on the spot.

So, in my experience, and the experience of other archers I know, the word is "wait" and wait I will!

— *Joseph J. Azzato*
Russell, Pennsylvania

A hunter who can place a shot into the correct spot in a few seconds is likely to kill so quickly that the deer "has no time to die" — and the hunter has no time to get buck fever.

Charles J. Alsheimer

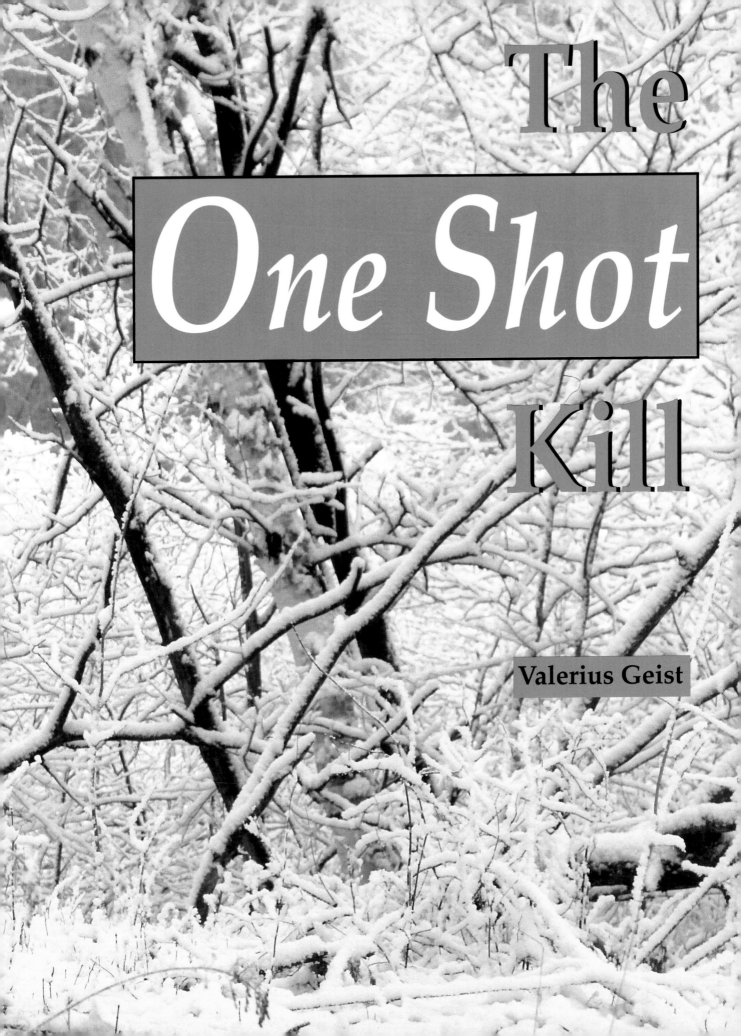

The One Shot Kill

Valerius Geist

The One Shot Kill

Making quick, certain kills should be every deer hunter's primary goal. It ensures success when one finally sees the quarry after a stalk and delivers good, palatable meat to the family table. Equally important, it conserves wildlife. The loss of wounded deer saddens the ethical hunter. We know only too well that he who shoots and loses an animal may continue hunting and possibly repeat his earlier mistakes. He who wounds and loses a deer is likely to continue wounding and losing deer. We should not tolerate that pattern. Hunters must strive to kill quickly, without pain, and to make the recovery of dead animals certain and quick.

Making consistent, one-shot kills on deer requires good marksmanship, correct anatomical knowledge, and a rifle that shoots a bullet that will penetrate and destroy vital organs. Sporting journals tell us much about the latter. Gun writers dwell endlessly on rifles, cartridges, bullets, sights and accessories. They say little about how to improve one's marksmanship, however, and even less about the anatomy of big game animals.

Unfortunately, some of what passes as anatomical knowledge in sporting journals and even reputable books is false and can only promote crippling, suffering and the loss of wounded animals. The trilogy of marksmanship, knowledge and equipment need equal attention. Big calibers, high velocities and super bullets cannot compensate for poor shooting, and even a good marksman will leave a lot of dead, unclaimed wildlife in the field if his equipment or anatomical knowledge is faulty. To advocate heavier and heavier calibers promises not more clean kills or more meat on the family table, but more woe at both ends of the rifle. Promoting big bores will only promote flinching, poor aiming and psychic blockages at one end of the gun and, therefore, a lot more wounded and lost deer at the other. The proper rifle for one-shot kills is one the individual hunter can shoot comfortably with ammunition selected intelligently.

Marksmanship, Anatomy & Equipment

Is writing about good marksmanship less exciting than writing about a new super magnum caliber? Money can buy a better gun, a gun of larger caliber or different ammunition, but it cannot buy better marksmanship. One must learn marksmanship and maintain it through practice. Formerly, military service ensured wide acquisition of marksmanship skills. However, with more than 20 shots per deer legally harvested documented by recent studies, we need to find ways to make marksmanship important to hunters. To learn how to make consistent, one-shot kills requires dedication to learning, discipline and practice; there is no other way.

Let's assume that you have thoroughly familiarized yourself with the equipment you use, that you keep it in good repair and that you take care to maintain and improve your marksmanship. I hope that you still dry-fire and call your shots, that you practice dropping into a solid sitting position once in a while — just like you sometimes do in the field. I hope that you try to shoot from some kind of a rest whenever possible and that you minimize offhand shooting, shots at running animals, shots at long distances, shots in poor light and shots at animals well-screened by brush. I hope that you check the screws on the stock and scope mounts to make sure they are tight, that you know how to put on a shooting sling and occasionally use it, and that you visit a rifle range to re-sight your rifles before each deer season. That's the least a responsible hunter can do, even if he is very busy. If you do this and practice with a .22 once in a while, then correct anatomical knowledge will help you to improve your ability to kill deer quickly and humanely, to reduce crippling losses, and thus become a more successful hunter.

No matter how much we consider "Old Betsy" a thing of beauty or perfection, "Old Betsy" is first and foremost an instrument of termination. That's why it was bought. Therefore, we must treat it as such and learn to use it well and appropriately.

In my opinion, some of the experienced gun writers demonstrate a fair knowledge of where to aim on big game and what bullets do in the body. However, their instructions will not deliver one-shot kills consistently and will lead to some losses of well-hit animals when visibility and tracking conditions are poor.

The crux of the matter is that some well-hit animals run a considerable distance before falling. While hunting I have found dead deer, hit in the lungs and heart, that ran deep into cover and were not found. In each of these cases, the hunter apparently failed to check for signs, because these deer left adequate blood trails on snow-covered ground. One early fall day in British

Columbia, I spent an anxious hour tracking a black-tailed buck hit through the heart at 15 paces. The buck dove into the thick salal thickets of the Pacific coastal forests. It ran only 120 paces, but it made two, right-angle turns and then slid dead into a tangle of ferns underneath a fallen tree. The blood trail was sparse despite a good-sized exit hole left by the 139-grain bullet of my 7x57mm Mauser. Had I shot at dusk or during a rain, I probably would have lost that highly excited rutting buck. The blood trail would have been next to invisible in the beam of a flashlight, or it would have been washed off the wet vegetation.

Heart-shot deer, in extreme cases, can run several hundred yards before expiring; invariably they make a sharp turn just before dying and will be found well off the direction of their earlier trail. I once lost a cow elk shot just behind the shoulder with a 173-grain RWS 7mm bullet with a hollow, copper point and an H-jacket shot out of a 7x57. I clearly saw the large entrance hole created by the mushrooming copper point. I lost the blood trail within about 200 yards and could not find her in the failing light. It had been a very warm early fall day and the night was not much cooler. When I found her, the meat was spoiled. She had made a sharp turn before dying and lay in thick but low cover of rose and snowberry bushes barely 20 paces from where I had lost her trail.

Since I have killed many animals with heart shots and tracked the animals on snow to where they dropped, I have noted this sharp turn just before collapse on a good many occasions. When there is no snow for tracking, when rain or snow is falling, or when darkness begins to descend, heart shots can lead to the loss of wounded animals. When tracking conditions are poor, one must shoot to drop the animal on the spot.

One cannot kill deer quicker with heart shots by using more power. A white-tailed buck, for instance, that I shot with a 160-grain Nosler partition bullet from a 7mm Remington Magnum at about 70 paces ran more than 100 paces before collapsing. Upon autopsy, I found the heart completely detached and floating within the congealed blood in the rib cage. The bullet had hit the top of the heart and sheared it

Len Rue, Jr.

The trilogy of marksmanship, anatomical knowledge and equipment needs equal attention if the deer hunter wants to consistently make one-shot kills.

off, as well as the trachea and the gullet. Despite an exit hole, I found very little blood on the snow. A 37mm cannon could not have done better! Yet the buck must have run at high speed for about 10 seconds after being hit.

Unfortunately, too many sources instruct hunters with anatomically false drawings, which can only increase crippling loss. Some of the worst offenses occur in advertisements of rifle scopes, with completely incorrect placement of cross hairs on animals. Some makers of animal targets for bow and gun hunters also misinform by drawing lines in the wrong places. Thereby they portray kill zones that are, in reality, crippling zones. The aiming areas on such targets are usually much too large; the real quick-kill zones are much smaller. Targets like that can only generate false security among careful hunters who would otherwise acquire better anatomical knowledge and aiming habits. To consistently drop deer on the spot requires that a hunter has a precise mental image of where to aim.

Knowing exactly where to aim is important, for deer may offer an opportune shot for only a few seconds. Routine practice in quick, accurate aiming overcomes buck fever, at least partially. A hunter who can place a shot into the correct spot in a few seconds is likely to kill so quickly that the animal "has no time to die" — and the hunter has no time to get buck fever. With a little practice and dry firing it becomes second nature to aim correctly.

The chief advantage of the modern hunting rifle over the bow and arrow resides in the fact that properly constructed bullets can penetrate and shatter bone. This gives one a choice of killing either by causing instant massive hemorrhage or by delivering so hard a blow to some bone structures that vital functions come to a halt. To attain both with one shot is, unfortunately, difficult and unrealistic. Let us consider the nature of both options.

Heart & Lung Shots

A heart-lung shot kills by massive hemorrhage and often by instantly disrupting breathing or circulation. It may also lead to instant unconsciousness. Often it does not. Unconsciousness may follow within seconds, and usually within a minute. Consequently the animal, though mortally wounded, may run a fair distance from where it stood when first hit.

Outdoor writers commonly advocate the heart-lung shot. Its advantages are a large target area, a fairly quick kill, a carcass well bled out, only a modest amount of meat spoiled, and the high likelihood of hitting other vital organs by near misses such as the spine, the neck or the liver. In open country where you can keep a hit animal in sight, or when conditions provide excellent tracking, the heart-lung shot is a good choice. It is most effective if it shears off the top of the heart and thus instantly cuts circulation and breathing. Under such circumstances an animal will not go far, improving your chance of recovering it.

Unfortunately, the heart shot has a minus side: A shot through the tip of the heart or the lungs disrupts circulation and breathing only partially. In aiming low at the heart on an animal quartering away, a near miss may only break a leg or hit the paunch. Also, some heart-shot animals run off as if not hit and then collapse shortly after disappearing from view. The hunter, doubtful of having hit the animal, may not find signs of cut hair or blood and walk away thinking that he missed. One must rigorously inspect where the animal stood at the time of the shot as well as follow for some distance the trail of the animal — provided that is possible. Some well-placed shots, even when the bullets exit, may not provide blood trails for a number of reasons: The exit hole may be blocked by the hide, fat and organ fragments; or the bullet holes are high on the body, precluding the exit of blood. An experienced hunter looks for any unusual behavior of the animal he shot at, but some well-hit animals show no signs of being mortally wounded. Consequently, if an animal runs off as if unhurt, you should still look for signs of a hit and follow the trail for at least 300 paces. You may find it dead with a perfect heart shot. It has happened to me.

The rib cage offers relatively little resistance to a bullet, which should mushroom fairly fast and cause maximum damage within the rib cage. If the bullet leaves two big holes on either side of the rib cage, the lungs will collapse causing quick death. Conventional soft-point bullets, as loaded for most big game calibers, will fill the ticket here. However, in high-velocity cartridges of small caliber firing light bullets, fragile conventional soft-point bullets that kill quickly with lung shots may fail to penetrate bone. Such loads are therefore not appropriate for shots through bone. Keep this in mind, particularly for large, heavy-boned animals such as elk, moose, big bull caribou, and bears. Conventional soft-point bullets of light weight for a given caliber may only be good for heart-lung shots. If so, it reduces for an ethical hunter the opportunities of bagging such an animal because he simply must pass up all shots except those that offer his fragile bullet unobstructed passage through the rib cage. Such a hunter must be a better and more patient hunter. That patience will be well rewarded, for the kills are likely to be spectacularly quick when a bullet explodes inside the rib cage of even large, tough big game animals, let alone within a fragile pronghorn or deer.

When tracking conditions are poor, when daylight fades on warm evenings, when it rains or snows, or when there are many hunters afoot to claim downed game, it is necessary to drop an animal on the spot or chance losing it.

Aim For The Shoulder

How does one drop an animal on the spot?

The best shot is squarely through the middle of both shoulder blades. Such a shot will almost certainly hit the spine, causing instantaneous unconsciousness

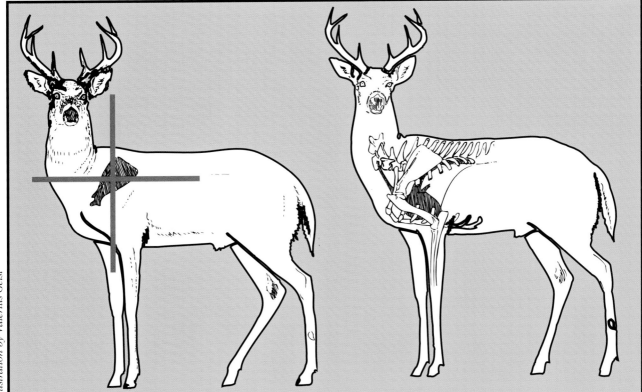

Illustration by Valerius Geist

A shot through the center of the shoulder blade of a standing deer invariably hits the spine as well as the major nerve bundles emanating between the first four thoracic vertebrae of the spine. These big nerve bundles control the muscles of the rib cage and of the front legs. Consequently, the deer drops to the ground unconscious, unable to breathe or move its legs; it expires quickly. This aiming point is very forgiving for shots straying left, right or low. A stray shot to the front hits the spine and may damage the carotid artery or the jugular vein. A stray shot to the rear may hit the spine, the aorta or the lungs. A stray shot

hitting low destroys the valve area of the heart or punctures the lungs. Only a shot straying high, hitting above the shoulder blade, will not kill, though it will drop the deer for a few seconds to a minute — time enough to get a second shot. While an aiming point for the heart is forgiving for shots straying high, it is not forgiving for shots straying to the front, rear or low. A stray shot to the rear results in a paunch shot and most likely an unrecovered deer. A stray shot to the front or low hits the legs or the brisket, both shots that promise a long trailing job and probably also a lost deer.

and paralysis. A hit through the shoulder blades will damage the large nerves that emanate between the first four thoracic vertebrae and which control breathing and the movement of the front legs. Therefore, the animal so hit is unconscious, paralyzed, and unable to breathe. Death could not be quicker.

"Karamojo" Bell, the famous African elephant hunter, was a fanatic on shots through bone. He succeeded due to precise anatomical knowledge and superb marksmanship. Bell studied keenly the anatomy of African big game. Consequently, he cleanly killed hundreds of elephants with brain shots using solid bullets in his 7x57mm Mauser and 6.5x54mm Mannlicher rifles. He also advocated the kidney shot on lesser game. This tricky shot requires exquisite anatomical knowledge and precise marksmanship. Usually the animal drops unconscious because of the blow to the spine and quickly hemorrhages to death through the ruptured kidneys or attached large blood vessels. I do not recommend kidney shots, however,

Learning how to make consistent, one-shot kills requires dedication to learning, discipline and practice; there is no other way.

because one must know precisely where these small targets are located; a narrow miss merely gut-shoots the animal. If successful, it fills the gut cavity with blood, resulting in an awfully messy gutting job. Bell, of course, had African porters to do the gutting.

The shot through the shoulder blades and spine, understandably, requires a bullet that can penetrate bone. A conventional soft-point bullet that opens up rapidly may fail here. In particular, if the bullet hits the shoulder blade at an acute angle, it may skid along the bone, fail to penetrate, and leave the animal wounded. That happened to me once in a rather freak situation. I had followed a wounded mountain goat billy into a steep cliff. When we met, the billy was above me barely 10 paces away. A snap-shot to his shoulder only caused him to turn, lower his horns and lunge at me. I had to jump aside rather quickly. He missed me by a couple of feet and sailed off the cliff to land with a crash some 30 feet below. A neck shot finished the goat. The 7mm 139-grain soft point bullet had hit the shoulder blade at an acute angle and skidded the length of the blade and right out of the goat. It had done little damage. Such an experience is exceptional, however.

A shot through the shoulder blades not only kills quickly, but the shoulder blade is also a fairly large target. Near misses are likely to hit the vertebrae of the neck, the lungs and aorta, or the spine. Too high a shot, however, only hits the neural spines and while the animal falls, it is only stunned and will, within seconds or a minute, rise and run off. Any animal dropping as if hit by lightning may only be hit through the neural spines. In every case when the animal drops instantly get ready to shoot again and watch to see if it raises the head. If it does, shoot at once. Alternatively, approach quickly with your rifle at the ready so as to shoot instantly should the animal try to rise. The animal may recover very quickly from a hit in the neural spines, as I can attest from bitter experience in losing a ram and a mule deer buck after neural spine hits.

A shot through the shoulder blades with a partition bullet damages less meat than a shot with a conventional soft-point bullet through the ribs right behind the shoulder blade. This may surprise you, but due to layers of loosely fitting muscles behind the shoulder, a bullet exploding here may drive blood between muscle layers over the whole quarter. That requires a lot of patient cleaning with a very sharp knife to save the meat. The muscles on the shoulder blade and along the spine are more compact; with Nosler partition bullets, I have found the meat damage to be quite modest. In either case, I have found the loss of meat to be minimal. One must weigh it against the likelihood of losing a well-hit animal, be it as a result of poor tracking conditions, darkness or other factors.

For shots through bone one clearly needs either heavy, thick-jacketed bullets that open up slowly or partition, H-jacketed bullets or bullets with hard lead cores in the rear. Such bullets penetrate deeply. Conventional heavy, soft-point bullets may give marginal performance on lung shots. However, once in a while a reputable manufacturer releases a fragile lot of otherwise tough bullets. I ran into one such lot of 175-grain 7mm bullets. They exploded on contact even on fragile antelope bucks and were worse than useless on elk. German H-jacketed bullets also have served me poorly; the soft front part exploded away on impact while the tough rear portion drilled a thin wound channel through the animal, leading to long blood trails and loss of game. Partition bullets gave excellent results.

One attribute of bones is their ability to deflect bullets within the body. My son made one such freak shot on a mule deer buck at about 100 yards with a 160-grain Nosler bullet fired at about 3,000 feet per second from a 7mm Remington Magnum. The buck stood broadside. The bullet hit the upper end of the humerus, about one inch below the joint with the shoulder blade. The bullet penetrated the big bone, shattered the head of the humerus into three pieces, but deflected sharply downward, leaving the buck's lower neck dead center. The bullet, while causing considerable damage, hit neither the large blood vessels of the neck nor the spinal column. The buck, fortunately, stopped soon and was brought down with a second shot. This is but one example of the heavy bone at "the point of the shoulder" deflecting even a reliable bullet of excellent design. A hit two inches higher would have dropped the buck instantly with broken shoulders.

Avoid Neck Shots

In my opinion, a shot to be avoided is the neck shot; ditto for the head shot. My experiences with head and neck shots are all bad. Once I shot a chunk of bone out of the lower part of the fourth neck vertebra of a very big caribou bull. The bull was resting

when hit. Instantly I saw four legs in the air. In the next moment he was on his feet and about to depart. A shot through both lungs dropped him. The 139-grain soft-point bullet from my 7x57, after knocking out a chunk of neck vertebra, had penetrated the neck and lay under the skin on the far side. None of the 250-grain Nosler bullets hand-loaded for my .338 Winchester Magnum penetrated the necks of big rutting bull elk. Neither did the same load knock down two elk with near misses of the spinal cord, nor did a 160-grain Nosler bullet knock out a big bull moose with a near miss of the spinal vertebrae of the neck. The vertebral column is a very small linear, curved target, well hidden behind deep, sometimes massive, muscles and camouflaged by neck and mane in elk. The chances of losing a badly-wounded animal with a neck shot are good. Never take it!

Excellent killing shots with bullets that penetrate deeply are, at short range, frontal shots into the rib basket. Two rams I so hit expired instantly. Several mule deer and antelope bucks I hit from the other end also dropped dead instantly. Raking the body lengthwise with a well constructed bullet is lethal, but it does taint meat with gut contents and may ruin a haunch. Such must never be a consideration if the animal is already wounded. Killing it quickly is then the only recourse.

One who practiced the shot through both shoulder blades was John W. Spencer, who related his experience in W.P. Taylor's *The Deer of North America* (1956). Spencer dropped, with one shot each, four bull elk, 17 mule deer bucks and three buck antelope with a .30-06 using 180-grain bullets. One bull elk only went 30 feet, the others dropped on the spot; more than half were instant kills.

Then Spencer switched to a .270 Winchester with 130-grain silver-tip bullets and dropped 18 mule deer bucks and two antelope bucks with one shot each. That's 44 consecutive one-shot kills! One can hardly get better recommendations for the shoulder shot. Spencer was an exceptionally careful hunter and rifleman, however, who paid close attention to the vital trilogy: equipment, marksmanship and anatomical knowledge.

Editor's Note: "The One-Shot Kill" was originally published in the November 1990 issue of Deer & Deer Hunting *magazine.*

When The
Pressure Is On

Charles J. Alsheimer

With proper preparation, a hunter can be successful hunting escape routes, whether it's opening day or the end of the season.

Charles J. Alsheimer

The frigid northwest wind bit into my face as I walked through the predawn darkness. Finding my stand in the dark isn't always easy even when I know the terrain like the back of my hand. When I left the house, the temperature hovered around eight degrees above zero. During the night, two inches of fluffy snow had fallen. With each step, I wondered why I bothered to hunt whitetails in such conditions.

I followed familiar landmarks and after the 20-minute walk arrived at the ground stand, set up my seat and cleared the leaves from underfoot so I could move silently if necessary. The woods started to brighten as dawn approached. Only the trickle of the nearby stream and the slight breeze blowing through the trees were audible as I gathered my thoughts. Aside from the severe cold, I'd been through many forest awakenings like this in my 20 years of white-tailed deer hunting.

There is no guarantee a white-tailed buck will always do the same thing under a given set of circumstances. But when pressured by hunters, a buck's escape route or routes can be fairly predictable.

With New York's deer season nearly half over, I knew most hunters would stay out of the woods because of the cold and windy conditions. But I also knew the cold would keep any hunters brave enough to fight the elements on the move. Because of this, I was sure my morning stand would be productive if I could sit it out long enough.

First shooting light came and went. Nothing, not even a chickadee, moved about in the cold. The wind velocity increased and the wind chill dipped well below zero. In the distance I heard the first shot ring out at eight o'clock. Suddenly, I heard a twig snap on the other side of the ravine. I could tell deer were headed in my direction. Across the small stream they bounded. First one, two, then a third deer came into view — a doe and two fawns. All three halted less than 20 yards away. I knew if I moved they would spot me and I was determined not to alert them, sensing a buck might be hanging back.

The doe checked her backtrack, twitched her tail and hurried through the woods behind me as fast as she had come. Her body language told me more deer were probably coming. I didn't have long to wait. Down the bank, across the stream and up the time-worn trail bounded a beautiful buck. In one motion I threw the gun to my shoulder, clicked off the safety and pulled the trigger. At the shotgun's roar the buck reeled sideways, ran another 30 yards and fell in the snow.

Hunting pressure in my part of the country (northeastern farmland) is intense. Because of this, most deer hunters who haven't scored by the second day of gun season usually feel their season is over. History, experience or whatever has taught them that after the second day their chances of scoring on a buck greatly diminish.

Unfortunately, this shouldn't be the case. In my 20 years of hunting in high-pressure areas, I've killed 26 white-tailed bucks. Of these, only 12 were killed on the first or second day of the season. Consequently, I've learned to use hunting pressure to my advantage.

First of all, I hunt whitetails much differently after the second day of gun season than I do during the archery season and the first two days of the firearms season. During bow season and the opening two days of gun season, I hunt over or near active scrapes. Because of New York's liberal bag limits, I've never been finished hunting after the second day of gun season, but I do switch my tactics after the second day.

At that point I switch from scrape hunting to hunting the whitetail's escape routes. In my opinion, this style of hunting is completely different than the type of hunting I prefer, which is scrape-related hunting. With proper preparation, however, one can be successful hunting escape routes, whether it's opening day or the end of the season.

Like humans, whitetails are creatures of habit. Throughout their life they act and react to circumstances in a more or less predictable way. Obviously there is no guarantee a buck will always do the same thing. When pressured by hunters, however, a buck's escape route or routes can be fairly predictable.

Finding the escape routes of whitetails often requires many years of scouting a certain area. As a result, it is very difficult to locate escape routes during the pre-season (August and September) unless you get lucky and hit it right.

Over the years I've concentrated on finding escape routes after the firearms season ends. In the farm country where I hunt, deer do not yard up to any degree so I scout extensively from mid-December until March. During this time I hunt with a camera and if there is deep snow, I often follow deer when I jump them to see where they go. By patterning them in such a fashion, I've been able to determine the best blind locations along their various escape routes.

Though deer will flee in almost any direction, my experience indicates that they tend to move downhill when pushed in hilly country. As a result, deer crossings a short distance above stream bottoms or on a natural bench on a hill's midpoint can be excellent high-use escape routes. In a ravine or gully that is more than a half-mile in length, there will usually be several escape routes. However, one will invariably be the key route. Heavy sign and worn trails crossing a stream or wash will be a good indicator of the route. Intentionally tracking deer in the off-season will also reveal which route is the most heavily used. These routes usually remain the same for generations unless extensive logging or some other alteration of the land takes place.

In terrain that is fairly flat, with smaller woodlots, bucks seem to use connecting cover to their advantage. This could be nothing more than a hedgerow or diversion ditch. It could also be a narrow patch of woods. Over the years, I've found that the key fea-

Charles J. Alsheimer

Finding escape routes often requires many years of scouting and it is very difficult to locate escape routes during the pre-season.

ture to look for is an area which connects two or more cover zones.

I've also found that camera hunting from mid-December to March can be very rewarding when trying to pattern a particular buck. For one thing, you won't need to worry about pushing him into another hunter. Also, once jumped he'll reveal a great deal about how he moves throughout his territory. This can pay off greatly in preparation for the next season.

Time and experience are keys in hunting escape routes. Three highly successful New York hunters, Arlan Button, a dairy farmer from western New York; Bob Avery, an Adirondack guide; and Larry Watkins, an avid Adirondack hunter, have used years of experience in determining white-tailed deer escape routes. All of these hunters use stands and also drive deer.

Button has farmed and hunted the same large area for more than 13 years. This past season he added a large eight-pointer to his collection of trophy deer. He has been very successful in hunting pressured whitetails and shared with me some of the reasons for his success.

"When we first moved here more than 13 years ago, we spent the first couple years figuring out which way the bucks would run. But you know, since then it has been amazing. There is one tree on the property where many bucks have been killed over the years. Any deer in that woods runs right past that tree when pushed by hunters. Take the mountain behind the barn. When we drive it in a certain way, the bucks almost always try escaping through one section where a logging road connects two thick portions of the mountainside. They really are predictable once you learn an area.

"My son Darrell is just starting to deer hunt and last season when I put him on stand he questioned why that spot was better than others. I told him it may not look as good as others, but years of experience had proven it to be the best location. If I hadn't been there to post him, he would have gone to a less favorable place."

Well, that speaks for farm country whitetails, but what about deep woods bucks? One of the better known Adirondack deer hunting guides is Bob Avery of Arietta, New York. For more than 50 years Bob Avery and his family, using their inn as a base, have guided hunters. The tract they hunt encompasses an area 20 miles long and seven miles wide. The number of hunters Bob has guided in any given year has varied, but the best season as far as deer take occurred in 1960 when his clients killed 63 bucks. The group also harvested 11 bears during that same season. From the early 1900s until the late 1960s, their clients harvested a yearly average of 45 bucks.

Escape routes used by deer usually remain the same for generations unless extensive logging or some other alteration of the land takes place.

Avery's use of driving techniques, though not necessarily unique, are worth passing along. He told me, "The key to drive hunting in the Adirondacks is knowing the mountains. You need to know where the deer are going to run when disturbed. I started deer hunting 54 years ago as a kid and my father had me drive all the time back then. It was good experience because I learned where the deer would be at all times. I also learned which runways they'd use to escape the drivers. That was the key to learning how to hunt these mountains — learning the runways.

"You know, things are traditional. Over the years we've had as many as 50 bucks killed from the same runway. Regardless of the year, the deer always seem to run the same way when pushed. Once a man figures out the deer's pattern, it is just a matter of driving an area. Sometimes we'd drive only 500 yards and sometimes two and a half miles. It all depended on how many guys we had and what mountain we wanted to drive. Of course, you really had to know the lay of the land to be successful. We were most successful pushing a mountain lengthwise. Water boundaries and wind direction also played a big part in how we drove things.

"There were some drives, like Iron Lake Mountain, that were successful only when driven one way. And then, if there was a buck on it, he'd only use one of three runways. These were the things we learned about escape routes over the years."

Another Adirondack hunter, Larry Watkins of Dolgeville, has been very successful over the years deer hunting near beaver dams and the ponds associated with these dams. He revealed that the way he hunts these areas depends upon the age of the dam and the flow of water created by it. Older dams will have dead trees in the middle of them and he has found that the deer will cross in one of two places: on the dam itself or where the stream flows into it. On newer ponds, it has been his experience that the deer will not cross at the dam, but usually cross where the stream flows into the beaver pond.

As a teenager, I used to wonder what it would be like to feel confident about killing a buck late in the season. I also envied deer hunters in the western United States who could hunt unpressured whitetails throughout their deer seasons. Although at times I'm still a bit envious of them, I long ago stopped feeling defeated after the second day of gun season.

Like Avery, Button and Watkins, deer hunters across America are discovering how productive deer hunting can be when the escape routes are found. Certainly it takes longer to figure out how deer will move when pressured. But once an area's escape routes are located, your confidence will soar — keeping you in the woods past the second day.

Editor's Note: "When the Pressure is On" was original-ly published in the November 1988 issue of Deer & Deer Hunting *magazine.*

Part Three
The Deer Hunt

Forgive me my deer counting because I simply can't forget the excitement that each of the sightings brings. They have become part of my hunt's official record, something to be called up for periodic review.

Counting Deer

Patrick Durkin

If I had the power, I would have reset the clock and rolled back the late-morning sky to the day's cold, thin dawn. Several hours had passed since I first hunkered into the blind, my eyes trying to pencil in deer among the forest's dark shapes. My luck seemed in no hurry to change. It idled away the time, even after sunlight burned away the shadows.

Before noon I questioned my judgment about this stand, prompting my wish to start the day all over. But experience advised me to be patient and to deal with reality. Time never pauses to give us two swings at a single event. Besides, how many times had seemingly futile days changed to heart-stoppers, all in a matter of seconds, all in the turn of a head? Surely one of deer hunting's lessons is to take pleasure in what we have already seen, and to look at everything beyond that as a bonus.

So I stayed with the stand that day, figuring there is some virtue in sticking to a commitment. Shortly before noon my eyes snapped to the right after detecting a shiny flicker about 75 yards away. The picture was fuzzy at first, but then I could see a doe shaking herself off, having just crossed a nearby creek. Two fawns and a yearling doe followed the old girl's lead, silently wading the creek and then shaking off the water. They stood there in a loose bunch, licking their coats and shuffling nervously, their noses sifting the air for danger. Eventually, they melted into the tag alders, four gray ghosts departing the small world that was solely mine for the moment.

The sightings reinforced my decision to stay on this stand, even though those four deer had never offered a clear shot, and no buck ever crossed the stream to catch up with them. Once I was alone again, I mentally recorded the four whitetails in my mind's journal and told myself: "Well, they can't take

Charles J. Alsheimer

How many times have seemingly futile days changed to heart-stoppers, all in a matter of seconds, all in the turn of a head?

138

those away." I now had at least four deer sightings to report when I returned to camp, and the day was not quite half spent.

I know I probably shouldn't place such a premium on deer sightings, having read a bellyful of "Hunter Sensitivity Training" articles in recent years. But I still count deer, without apology. Which isn't to say I don't appreciate other wildlife. I do. I've marveled many times at nuthatches clinging upside down to jack pines. I have also cheered on ermines as they hunted voles in a snow-free forest, their white fur waving like a handkerchief among the low-hanging branches. And I've been pleasantly shocked to see a sow black bear leading three cubs on a late-November foray, no doubt spurred from their den by a brief warm front.

Such observations are a big part of the hunt, and the woods would be a poorer place without them. But you know what? Those occasions don't race my hunter's heart nearly as much as the sight of deer legs mincing through a cedar bottoms.

There's a reason for that, and I'm sure it's linked to some predatory instinct I don't fully understand. For instance, a few years ago a researcher hooked a heart monitor to a hawk and then recorded its reactions when it spotted various prey. When the hawk saw a pigeon or other quarry it couldn't easily capture, its heartbeat rapidly increased but then quickly tailed off to normal. When the hawk saw a field mouse, however, its heartbeat shot up and stayed there as it set up for an attack.

The hawk's reactions sound surprisingly familiar. Whose heart hasn't jolted into high gear upon hearing the snap of a twig or seeing the flash of a tail? If we identify the source as a squirrel, our hammering heart soon resumes its normal rhythm.

Our heartbeat doesn't abate, however, if a legal deer steps out of the brush. We're now in position to make a kill, to take a life in order that our own may continue. It's a pressure-packed moment, soon to be followed by elation or despair, often depending on how we handle the tension.

Try as we might, it's impossible to get that prolonged adrenalin rush as a spectator. For example,

consider how you react in the March woods during a scouting trip. Deer you see then are not prey, and you'll view them about the same as you did the crows, cardinals and chipmunks the previous autumn. Sure, there's a rush at first sight, but then your perspiration cools and your senses return to normal.

> **Experience advised me to be patient and to deal with reality. Time never pauses to gives us two swings at a single event.**

That might also explain why "hunting" with a camera will never quite measure up to hunting with a bow or firearm. We're in the woods for far different reasons and those motivations dictate which emotions or instincts will surface. We can take great pride in capturing something on film, but it's still vastly different from living out our role as one of nature's predators.

So forgive me my deer counting because I can't forget the excitement that each of the sightings brings. They are part of my hunt's official record, something to be called up for periodic review. I could recount each of the sightings for you, but inevitably their value would get lost in the translation.

And because I can't even give such memories away, I don't have to worry about someone walking off with them. They're mine alone to treasure.

Editor's Note: "Counting Deer" was originally published in the March 1992 issue of Deer & Deer Hunting *magazine.*

Charles J. Alsheimer

The Snoose Trail Buck

Don L. Johnson

As a longtime outdoor writer, I have listened to countless hunting yarns and, believe me, if there was a record book for hunting yarns, some of them would rank close to the top.

During more than 40 seasons as a deer hunter, I experienced my share of good fortune — not only in the form of some memorable bucks but also in the opportunity to share our hunting heritage with kindred spirits.

There is, after all, much more to the hunt than that which can be measured in points and pounds.

In fact, to me the best part of tagging a deer may not be the backstraps or a trophy rack. Often it's the story that goes with it.

The Snoose Trail Buck

Stories, after all, are my stock-in-trade. As a long-time, full-time outdoor writer I have listened to countless hunting yarns and, believe me, if there was a record book for hunting yarns, some of them would rank close to the top.

Here's one I heard more than 20 years ago. I have never forgotten it and I'll wager you won't either.

The year was 1966. January. I'd been doing a story on ice fishing along the Mississippi River in southwestern Wisconsin. Chilled to the marrow at the end of the day, I checked into a motel in Prairie du Chien. After thawing out in the shower, I bundled up again and walked down the street for some nourishment and a drink or two.

I'd just gotten seated in the nearly empty restaurant when the man at the next table came over. "Aren't you the outdoor writer for *The Milwaukee Sentinel?*" he asked. I admitted it warily. "Well, we have some mutual friends," he said, grinning around the stub of a cigar. And so we did.

He was a traveling salesman. A cheerful-looking man of middle age and size, he had ruddy cheeks, twinkling eyes and sandy, curly hair. The grin made him instantly likable.

It took him all of 10 seconds to mention that he had the darndest experience last deer season. Would I like to hear about it? Sure, I said. Why not?

He asked the waitress to bring his meal to my table, relit his cigar and settled back with a dreamy look in his eyes.

"You'll remember the 1965 season started out on a sour note," he began in the rambling way all real hunting yarns are told. "Lots of wet snow fell on Friday and it packed on the roads. Couldn't get anywhere without tire chains and it wasn't until 8:30 Saturday morning that I was able to find a pair in Rhinelander, where my partner and I were staying.

"Getting a late start on opening day didn't matter though. Nothing seemed to be moving. The woods were beautiful, but the only wildlife we saw all day was a whiskey jack flitting around and looking for a handout.

"Hiking back to the car at dusk, I started reminiscing about the Old Snoose Trail country in the Chequamegon National Forest. That's where I shot my first buck more than 30 years ago. I was just a boy then. Had a crude, remodeled Army rifle, but it got the job done. The buck was a dandy. A big, dark,

10-pointer. The old-timers called one like that a swamp buck. I still do.

"Quite a few of the real, old lumberjacks were still around in those days. They were great woodsmen and they taught me a lot. When I was a youngster, I thrilled to the tales those old loggers told about the giant trees they felled and the huge bucks that roamed the primeval forest.

"My favorite story was about the time they found a fawn buck and its dead mother in the woods. They told me how they took that little deer back to camp and raised it. It became the camp mascot and, like its benefactors, it developed a craving for an occasional snit of whiskey and a pinch of Copenhagen.

"The fawn grew to be a giant buck. The loggers called him 'Big Ole.' They'd deck him out with red ribbons for the hunting season and all of the local folks knew better than to take a shot at him. Despite

Richard P. Smith

"I shot my first buck there more than 30 years ago. The buck was a dandy. A big, dark, 10-pointer. The old-timers called one like that a swamp buck. I still do."

that, one November he was found lying in the woods. Badly wounded, he'd made it almost all the way back to camp. They carried him the rest of the way on a horse blanket, put him in the horse barn and nursed him back to health.

"Big Ole lived several more years. During rutting season he'd parade through camp with his does, as if to show the boys who was king of the woods. He was never too proud, though, to beg for a little booze and a pinch of snuff."

> **"He was a big swamp buck. Eight points. Weighed more than 190 pounds when we got him to a scale. I wasn't looking forward to dragging him back to the road."**

The yarn-spinner paused, solemn now. He studied his soggy cigar stub and continued in a quieter, almost wistful voice.

"Well, on the way back to town that day, I began talking about those old haunts. My partner said he wanted to go there, so we got an early start and were on the Old Snoose Trail not long after daybreak Sunday, despite the slow drive on slippery roads.

"The snow-laden branches were beautiful but visibility was bad. We just poked along quietly, keeping our eyes open. After walking about a mile, we stopped for a while. I tried to light the cigar in my mouth, but it was chewed beyond salvaging, like this one. I left it on a stump. Then we moved slowly on, seeing nothing. The woods seemed deserted.

"We were retracing our steps that afternoon when I thought I saw something out of place in the brush about 65 yards away. Gradually, I made out the outline of the back and hindquarters of a deer. Then I saw a black nose; then horns! Finally, I could see part of the rib cage through an opening in the brush. I slipped the safety off quietly and the old '06 cracked. The deer dropped right there.

"He was a big swamp buck. Eight points. Weighed more than 190 pounds when we got him to a scale. I wasn't looking forward to dragging him back to the road. I knew it was about a mile, for I'd dropped him right near where we'd stopped to rest that morning.

"Now here's the funny thing. As we prepared to field dress him, I moved his head. And you know what? There was my cigar butt clenched in his mouth!"

There was a catch in the man's voice. He stopped to gulp from the beer he'd ordered with his dinner. Then, blinking, he continued.

"I'll tell you, the memories flooded back. It had to be more than coincidence. I had surely shot one of Big Ole's direct descendants and he must have passed all of his traits down to that fine buck. Even his penchant for tobacco.

"I suppose that's why I caught him unawares. The snow muffled all sounds as well as obscured vision that day, but that buck's biggest disadvantage was that he couldn't smell anything else while he was savoring my cigar.

"And you know, I'm sorry I pulled the trigger," the storyteller concluded gravely. "Being a nicotine addict myself, I would not have knowingly taken advantage of a buck like that."

That was some story, I admitted. Later, back in my room, I jotted down some notes while the details were still fresh. Just for the heck of it I intended to check out some things. I especially wanted to locate a "Snoose Trail" in the Chequamegon. I never did.

I came across the notes again a couple of years ago and my curiosity was renewed. I made some phone calls and was sorry to learn that the cheerful, cigar-smoking buckslayer had passed on. His widow said his old hunting partner was still around, however, and she gave me his name.

I called the man. Yes indeed, he remembered the day and remembered the shot just as it had been described to me. He also remembered helping drag that big buck for a mile, "mostly uphill."

But no, he didn't remember that cigar butt.

It was a helluva good story anyway.

Editor's Note: "The Snoose Trail Buck" was originally published in the November 1988 issue of Deer & Deer Hunting *magazine.*

Ian McMurchy

Buck Fever

Rob Wegner

> *Buck fever affects veteran and novice deer hunters alike and appears in about as many different guises as there are individuals who succumb to this frenzied derangement of deer hunting behavior.*

"Any sportsman who can kill his deer without the tingling spine, the quick clutch at his heart, the delicious trembling of nerve fibers when the game is finally down, has no place in the deer woods."
— *Larry Koller, 1948*
Shots at Whitetails

The "delicious trembling of nerve fibers" as Larry Koller, that great Catskill deer hunting guide, suggests, represents an essential ingredient of buck fever. But what is buck fever and how does it affect man, the hunter? When we consult the scientific journals, we find no such concept. We don't find it listed under the subject headings in the card catalog of the public library either. Yet, deer hunters all across this land confront it and pour their soul into understanding and coming to terms with this vicious and contagious malady. Although absent as a concept in standard bibliographic references, the literature on the subject of American deer hunting contains countless examples of how buck fever affects hunters and how they describe that fever and search for a cure.

Buck Fever

I get buck fever when I merely take Eldridge Reeves Johnson's classic book on the subject, *Buck Fever* (1911), in hand. Sneaking this $300, rare, blue-chip deer book past my wife is what I call buck fever! Paying that kind of money for a single book gradually undermines the cement of the marriage contract even though my wife is a deer hunter.

The musty, ancient smell of *Buck Fever,* the black and white plates with printed overlays and the watered silk endpapers paralyze my emotions. If read in the deer forest, this volume will render the deer hunter, regardless of his mental constitution, foolishly helpless upon the sighting of any buck. Published in 1911, this privately printed jewel seriously questions the universal notion that buck fever only affects ama-

> *As most buck hunters learn sooner or later, the chief end of a trophy buck focuses on one basic instinct: keeping his head on his own shoulders rather than above your mantelpiece or as a statistic in the record book next to your name.*

teurs and then disappears as the deer hunter gains experience. Johnson remained convinced that buck fever is far more reaching in scope and certainly more tenacious than the popular conception would indicate.

Like many deer hunters, Johnson confessed to being hopelessly susceptible to buck fever, or to what he called that "expensive, intermittent, business-disturbing mania." He rightly compared this intermittent mania to malaria because you can depend on it to return at certain times of the year.

In his explanation of buck fever, Johnson observed that this interesting disease does not limit itself to the single matter of marksmanship but runs deep into the blood of the human condition. "Buck fever," Johnson writes, "is a blood affection; it is contagious and hereditary. A well-developed case will impart the disease to many innocent persons in a comparatively short time, if opportunity can but secure them as an audience. Buck fever, in truth, is nothing less than a tormenting desire to go and rough it a bit — a continuous longing to get back close to Mother Nature, who is always calling to her truants."

Like many deer hunters before him, Johnson believed that a mild dose of buck fever does little harm but actually adds a little spice to the deer hunt. We all miss bucks sometimes and Johnson acknowledged that it takes a good deal of experience and a tremendous amount of self-control to gracefully acknowledge missing a close, easy shot. Most deer hunters like to fall back on those weird tales of buck fever to explain their misses, but these tales often constitute little more than what Johnson calls "disappointed, disgusted Mr. Missed-the-Buck's explanation of why it happened." Whatever buck fever may be, he thought it had a lot more to do with hunting than the mere incidence of missing a very close and easy shot. He experienced buck fever as a longstanding, irritating, restless attack of one age-old thing: a haunting desire to hunt and hang a trophy white-tailed buck on the meat pole.

That haunting desire drove Johnson to the deer forest each fall to pursue a buck. He called his deer camp "Harvey's Inn," named after one of his guides. While deer hunting out of Harvey's Inn, Johnson experienced buck fever in various degrees of intensity. One day shortly before returning to Harvey's Inn, he spotted a buck entering a small clearing at an easy trot. He recalls the incident in *Buck Fever:*

"I suspended breathing and threw every nerve and muscle into the aim; I never aimed quite so hard before. Bang! Now I will see a deer do some running, flashes through my mind. But no, the deer stops short and looks in my direction. No amount of reasoning can forecast what a deer is going to do at such a time, but I am astonished. Didn't even scare him, is my thought. Bang! again. The deer turns and goes slowly on. Bang! Bang! and goodbye. Well, I couldn't expect to make a long shot like that, I say to myself by way of comfort, but it is no comfort. When the shooting is over, I am all out of breath from the strain.

"Missed, just missed! What an awful thing it is to miss. Three thousand miles and two days' waiting for a shot and missed! Missed! I can never become reconciled to that experience."

The disease affects hunters in the deer forest all across America. In checking *The Bucks Camp Log* (1974), a Wisconsin deer camp diary, we find the following record of a severe case of buck fever dated November 25, 1917:

"The bunch drove the vicinity of Poise stump this afternoon. Mr. E.W. Hill, Sr. was feeling well enough to join the bunch. A lead mine could be started with the bullets we left down there. We had five deer surrounded. The bombardment sounded like an English barrage. Deer were running everywhere. They were so thick around Mr. Hill, Sr. that he had to push them away beyond the end of his gun so he could shoot them. He got buck fever so bad that he was shooting in a circle. Mr. True said the air was so thick around Mr. Hill, Sr. that he could not shoot through it."

This kind of buck fever has no scientific name nor does the medical profession recognize it. As one medical doctor exclaimed while deer hunting in the Adirondacks with William Monypeny Newsom, that great popularizer of white-tailed deer information: "Why should any healthy man dissolve into nervous hysteria in one form or another merely at the sight of a deer? As far as I've seen in my own practice, I don't believe it is possible." The doctor made this statement while on his first deer hunt with Newsom. Shortly thereafter, he walked down a trail for an afternoon stand.

Several hours passed when Newsom suddenly heard a shot from the ridge the doctor had headed for. "Evidently the doctor had gone into action," Newsom thought to himself. Newsom arose from his stump to listen. He heard only one shot; that could have meant anything or nothing. Newsom listened for ten minutes. Then down the trail came the bewildered doctor in great haste. Newsom noticed that the doctor's face took on a pale, peculiar yellow tint. He trembled to such a degree that he could hardly hold on to his rifle.

Len Rue, Jr.

For many deer hunters, buck fever is a real barrier to good shooting and sometimes to any shooting. It sometimes throws the hunter's aim so far off that the deer couldn't be safer.

He started to speak to Newsom, but stuttered, hesitated and stopped — before trying again.

"A b-b-b-buck!" he finally blurted out as if he made some world-shaking discovery. "I d-d-don't b-b-believe I e'er t-t-touched 'em," he continued.

Newsom took the frenzied doctor up the ridge again to investigate and discovered that a buck had stepped out from behind a windfall and stood broadside less than 25 yards from the doctor's stand. Fifteen feet to the right of where the buck stood, Newsom found a birch sapling with the top broken off. The fresh cut made the mark of the bullet plainly visible. The doctor had missed the buck by 15 feet.

Newsom became so fascinated with the whole question of buck fever that when he returned to New York City, he sought out an eminent psychiatrist who pronounced these words of wisdom on the subject of buck fever and its victims:

"Of course buck fever is a violent form of nerves, but there's a good reason for it. You will notice it is more apt to hit a man who goes from the city to the deer country. Before he goes he says he 'needs a rest' or he 'ought to get away.' In other words, he's saying he is out of adjustment with his city environment. Perhaps he doesn't realize it but he's antagonistic to and fighting against his city life and the hurry of it all. Quite unconsciously he's pulling against the stream instead of pulling with it, though he doesn't see the current. Naturally, when he hits the deer woods, he's out of adjustment with that environment, too. He goes from one bad adjustment to another bad adjustment. Then, instead of taking it easy mentally, he fusses and frets over little things like a late start in the morning. He is mentally pushing himself along harder than he should. Besides which he usually overworks physically the first few days or so walking too far, getting overtired, and perhaps not sleeping well the first few nights. But always striving mentally toward the deer. The natural result is, without his knowing it, the nervous system is overtaxed and breaks under the strain when the climax comes and the object of the trip is sighted. And that is particularly true of short deer hunts because there is much jammed into a short space of time and there's a constant rush to get it done. There is little chance to become adjusted under such circumstances."

Some deer hunters refer to these circumstances of buck fever as the shakes and a strange sort of craziness. In the south, hunters sometimes call it "buck ague." One deer hunter from Louisiana defined it this way: "When a person endures rain, wind, cold, heat, mosquitoes, thirst and hunger and even forgoes tobacco, coffee and almost anything to be out in the woods deer hunting, he has what is known as buck fever. It is a contagious disease and each year in Louisiana it becomes increasingly more difficult to contain."

Others think that this mysterious, humorous malady afflicts only greenhorns. For many it is a real barrier to good shooting and sometimes to any shooting. It sometimes throws the hunter's aim so far off that the deer couldn't be safer. The initial symptoms remain familiar to most deer hunters: Your heart speeds up, your temples pound and your arms and legs weaken. One deer hunter in Ohio referred to it as an unpredictable and unconscious thing forcing the hunter to choke up and freeze. Ben East, the longtime field editor for *Outdoor Life,* called it "a very queer affliction and I have yet to hear a really good explanation of it. It can result from excitement, fear, a trance-like concentration on getting game, even from fascination, or from a combination of all of them."

In trying to explain buck fever, deer hunters talk about palpitations, jammed cartridges, incoherent mumbling and quick jolts of adrenaline. Russell Thornberry, a trophy hunter from Alberta, explains it as a product of fear. He argues that the "number one fear is that the buck will get away due to the hunter's inadequacies in delivering a fatal shot." I find this explanation particularly relevant to the bow hunter. While buck fever never plagues me during the gun season, it haunts me during the bow season when the odds greatly favor the buck. The only partial cure I have found for buck fever revolves around spending more time in my tree stands throughout the entire year and learning to live with live deer so closely that you can hear them chew acorns and break wind. But as Thornberry warns us, we will probably never find a 100 percent cure for buck fever, nor should we:

"It is only fitting that there should be no 100 percent cure for buck fever in a sport that offers no guarantees anyway. When the biggest buck you ever have seen walks out in front of you and you feel no surge of adrenaline, check your pulse to be sure you still are alive. If you find you still are among the living, go home and hang up your gun or bow. It would be a crime for a hunter with no thrill left in his veins to bag such a magnificent creature. It is not that we desire to eliminate buck fever, because that is part of the thrill of the hunt. We only want to learn to function with control through it. The thrill of the opportunity combined with the sweet taste of success is the combination we seek."

Other deer hunters such as John Madson, that poetic outdoorsman from the prairie land of Illinois, compares buck fever to "a form of shell shock" that so overwhelms the mind and paralyzes the nervous system that some deer hunters "perform amazing maneuvers that have absolutely no logical connection to the job at hand, such as jacking a magazineful of hulls through the rifle without firing a shot and maybe even yelling 'bang!' each time they throw the bolt." Madson mourns for the hunter who's never experienced a glowing flush of buck fever and rightly doubts whether he has ever really been hunting. After all,

> *In trying to explain buck fever, deer hunters talk about palpitations, jammed cartridges, incoherent mumbling and quick jolts of adrenaline.*

who really has the most fun Madson asks. The cold, detached, clinical deer hunter? Or the shook-up buck hunter who bites through his pipe-stem when a white-tailed buck jumps into sight?

Indeed, buck fever is perhaps as common as wet feet. A classic example of an attack of buck fever occurred when Emil Winter, the one-time President of the Pittsburgh Steel Company, went deer hunting at the Woodmont Rod and Gun Club in Hancock, Maryland with Henry Bridges, the secretary and gamemaster of the club. Winter wanted to kill a buck for a stag party he planned to give in his Pittsburgh home. After a good deal of effort while moving deer around on the Woodmont acreage, one of this country's finest hunting clubs, Bridges finally got Winter within 500 yards of a magnificent white-tailed buck coming along an oak ridge.

When Winter, a big game hunter with many years of experience, finally saw the sun glinting off the buck's massive rack, he bolted upright from the stump he had been sitting on. He seemed startled; sweat beads popped out on his forehead. The buck seemed to float through the oaks in a ghostlike manner as it approached the hunters. Bridges saw Winter's hands begin to tremble; the foreign-made, custom-built rifle in his hands wobbled and shook. Winter's glassy eyes stared straight ahead; his mouth hung wide open.

The buck approached the two hunters and soon stood broadside between two white oaks, less than 50 yards away. "Shoot!" Bridges whispered to his agitated colleague. "Shoot him!"

Winter looked at Bridges dumbfounded and gasped for air. "I can't shoot him, Henry. I can't even see him!"

"There he is, Emil! Right in front of you," Henry whispered again. "Shoot!"

"Henry, I can't see any buck! I tell you I can't see him," Winter insisted somewhat in a state of delirium. "Henry, you shoot him!"

"No!" Henry whispered. "He's your deer. You shoot him!"

While trembling and shaking as the fever intensified, Winter sat back on his stump. He mumbled inaudible sounds and looked blindly about himself. "I can't see him, I can't see him," he kept muttering in muffled tones.

Henry very slowly raised his rifle and aimed it at the buck. Incredibly enough, the buck still stood there, patiently offering a perfect broadside shot. "Look down my rifle. It's aimed at the buck. Now, pull the trigger, Emil," Henry whispered.

Winter leaned forward and squinted down Henry's rifle barrel. He trembled with such excitement that he could hardly keep his head above the barrel. "I don't see any buck," he finally blurted out loud. The buck tensed up, ready to spring forward.

"Shoot!" Henry said. "He's heard us — he's ready to bolt!"

But Winter just sat there and trembled as the buck bounded off. So Henry shouldered his rifle and shot twice. The buck staggered but managed to keep going. Henry's two shots seemed to break Winter's fever, for he now jumped to his feet and shot just as the deer stumbled and went down.

After walking over to the fallen buck, Winter somewhat dazed said: "Henry, did I — did I get him?"

149

Trying to keep the humor off his face, Henry replied, "Yes, you hit him and I missed."

Winter stood there shaking his head and breathing hard, as if coming out of a delirious dream. A moment of silence occurred, followed by this one-liner: "Henry, my boy," Emil proudly pronounced, "I want you to come to my stag party and if we find two bullets in this buck, I'll give you credit for one of them!"

Indeed, buck fever affects veteran and novice alike and appears in about as many different guises as there are individuals who succumb to this frenzied derangement of deer hunting behavior. Whether it be loss of judgment, helpless confusion or utter loss of composure, it differs only in its effect on the hunter and the intensity of the feverish attack. The proximity of the deer often plays a considerable part in stirring the hunter's emotions. A buck standing off at a great distance does not seem to excite the fever as much as when that same buck comes close enough for the deer hunter to see the intricate details of its anatomy and the distinct structure of its rack. The booming of the deer rifle and the sight of a mortally wounded buck struggling to regain the spark of life also play a strong psychological role in that complex affair we call "buck fever" that embraces so many variables.

Regardless of the variables or the different ways it's experienced, the end result remains pretty much the same: The buck escapes to higher timber. That might strike some of us as an excellent state of affairs, at least from a selfish point of view. If buck fever did not exist, few white-tailed bucks would be left in the deer woods for the rest of us.

I doubt whether any wildlife ecology student in America has yet received a Ph.D. degree for a doctoral dissertation on the subject of buck fever, but the problem has received attention in the technical literature. While trying to explain this confused state of mind and body we call "buck fever," Harry Ruhl, the one-time Chief of the Michigan Game Division, offers us this technical interpretation:

Bill Phillips c/o Leonard Rue Ent.

A buck standing far off does not seem to trigger buck fever as much as when that same buck comes close enough for the hunter to see the intricate details of its anatomy.

"What happens? Under great emotional stress, a temporary block momentarily occurs between the straining mind and the willing but uncontrolled muscular system. The effects are different in individuals.

> *The only partial cure I have found for buck fever revolves around spending more time in my tree stands throughout the entire year and learning to live with deer so closely that you can hear them chew acorns and break wind.*

Some persons are simply paralyzed. Others are victims of muscular incoordination so pronounced that the simple act of pointing a gun becomes impossible. Others may perform complicated muscular maneuvers, but their actions may have no logical relation to their immediate objective. Hunters have been known to rack their guns until every cartridge in the magazine lay unexploded on the ground. One of the most regrettable reactions may be the peculiar visual aberration whereby a man, cow or other animal appears to the victim as a deer. In such a case, the old story of shooting a man for a deer may be reenacted.

"Buck fever is a peculiar variation of the situation referred to by medical men as nervous shock. Mind and body do not function as a unit. Each responds intensely to the sharp stimulus of the sight of big game. All of those fine adjustments built up through the years suddenly break down. The heart speeds up. Blood pressure rises. Hormones are spilled into the blood with reckless abandon. Blood sugar rises, then drops. The whole voluntary and autonomic nervous system goes awry. The more the victim struggles, the worse his condition becomes. The last flick of a white tail disappearing in the distance is likely to break the spell. The hapless victim revives with electric suddenness. The self-condemnation and maledictions sent in the direction of the vanished deer are scarcely less violent than the inward struggles occurring at the height of the 'fever.' "

However we define it, many different things cause buck fever to stir in my blood regardless of the season. Finding a fresh scrape with a pool of urine in it does the trick or seeing a massive eight-pointer at my corn feeders the day after the gun season closes. Encountering a rutting buck trotting down a major runway with its tail standing straight out and with its nose tight to the ground in hot pursuit of a whitetailed doe in estrus fires the fever. Observing a buck licking an overhanging branch in the middle of July or watching a fashion show of 14 different bucks in an alfalfa field with the sun in the sky in early autumn intensifies and sustains the fever throughout the year. Finding shed antlers in the deer forest in spring, seeing newly-shed velvet hanging from bloodied antlers in late summer and locating the devastating buck rubs of the "Birch Bark Buck" all inflame the heat of the fever.

As a young Nimrod of 12, the convoys of covered trucks heading north toward deer country on the highways and back roads brought forth the first traces of buck fever. But the fever peaks for me when I watch the sun rise in the east while the moon slowly sets in the west next to Doc's Rock during the closing days of the bow season and as I stare at a large, gray, antlered image moving through the young birch stand in front of Doc's Rock, I then think of the deer hunters' eternal paradox: Why do I kill the object I love best?

While thinking about this eternal paradox, these lines from Ortega y Gasset's *Meditations on Hunting* (1942), always come to mind: "Every good hunter is uneasy in the depths of his conscience when faced with the death he is about to inflict on the enchanting animal. He does not have the final and firm conviction that his conduct is correct. But neither, it should be understood, is he certain of the opposite." Because of this eternal paradox, buck fever will always afflict man, the hunter.

Editor's Note: "Buck Fever" was originally published in the August 1987 issue of Deer & Deer Hunting *magazine.*

151

THE IRON HAND

Ken Preston

In one strangely devout instant of thrill, desire, need and want, a shot broke the silence of the snowy woods and the great buck lay dead.

The old man reached through the darkness and shut off the alarm clock. It hadn't sounded yet, but he knew it would in about 10 minutes. He wasn't sure why he even bothered to set the alarm anymore. He awakened an hour before daylight everyday for so many years that he didn't need an alarm. It had somehow become instinctively etched into his subconsciousness.

The deer camp's air was cold and he slid deep into his sleeping bag to savor the trapped warmth from his own body. As soon as he mustered the courage, he rolled quickly from the sleeping bag and felt his feet hit the icebox surface of the linoleum floor. He scratched a wooden match on a strip of sandpaper tacked to the center-support post of the camp. He turned on the propane light and held the flame beneath the fragile mantle. The flame licked the mantle until the accumulating gas popped and blew it out. The mantle filled itself with a blood red color, then turned a soft yellow and finally into white.

> **It was always his opinion that when any living thing dies quickly, it dies with its self-respect. When it dies slowly, it loses more than life.**

His myopic eyes squinted with adjustment and he moved with a certain lameness toward the wood stove. The cast-iron door on the old stove opened with a familiar squeak. He harrowed the coals with a poker and small red coals winked slowly out at him. It were as if they, too, had just awakened. He crumpled a half-dozen pages of newspaper and tossed them onto the coals. They had already ignited by the time he could chuck a few slender pieces of cedar kindling onto them. Quickly, the kindling ignited and the old man added a couple chunks of well-seasoned maple. He shut the door and adjusted the damper.

He stooped close to the wood stove until the heat increased enough to flush his face and warm the thighs of his long johns. He moved to the gas cookstove and lit a burner beneath a teakettle of water. When the kettle whistled, he poured a mug full and dunked in a tea bag. He poured himself a bowl of cereal and began to eat, pausing now and then to jig the tea bag until the water was sufficiently stained.

As he ate his breakfast, he looked around his tiny, one-room camp. Deer racks were nailed to the walls everywhere. His eyes picked out a couple and he relived the kills as if they had just happened. His sense of recall had diminished on many things, veiled with age. Memories of his hunts, though, lived vividly in his memory. The 10-pointer from Baker Brook in the deep snow; and the nontypical 17-pointer that was the last of four deer to leap over a blow-down. He remembered each of those moments with perfect clarity.

After finishing breakfast, he placed the dirty dishes in the sink. He felt the old nagging pain in his hip. His shoulder muscles were sore, too, from lugging his deer rifle all day yesterday. He looked into the small shaving mirror over the sink, dragged his knuckles slowly over the white stubble on his chin and thought about how damned old he looked — how damned old he felt.

He dressed in his wool hunting clothes and laced up his boots. He took his old .30-06 from the crude gun rack on the wall. He was using an '06 before it was popular to use one — back when everyone else carried lever-action .30-30s. He turned off the gas light and stepped out onto the porch. The snow that began to fall last night had left about four inches of dry powder. The east looked like a light behind a thin, white curtain. A few scattered flakes sifted down but, for the most part, the mid-November storm was over.

He opened the door of his pickup truck and brushed away the dusting of snow that swept in onto the seat. He hung his rifle in the rack and started the truck. He adjusted the heater up to the windshield and slapped the accelerator with his foot to reduce the idle speed. He stepped out of the truck and took his snow brush from behind the seat and began to clean the freshly fallen snow from the windows and hood.

He had almost finished when he felt the Iron Hand; the first time since back in early September while he was splitting wood. It came as it always did, suddenly. It pressed hard against the center of his chest. He called the sensation the "Iron Hand" because it felt heavy and far stronger than himself. It wasn't a painful thing, just a powerful, ominous pressure that held the oxygen out of his lungs briefly. It was a cruel and foreboding tease.

The Iron Hand seemed to dare him to think about death; a death that he was 73 years closer to than ever before. It made him wonder which time the Iron Hand would refuse to let up; which time would it press heavy against his chest long enough to stop his heart? This time? No. It went away as quickly as it had come. Still, he knew it would return. It was a part of his own mortality, a part of being old.

His heart beat feverishly with anxiety, trying to make up for the momentary lack of breath. The rapid beating reminded him of the jubilant wagging of a dog's tail — rapid, genuine happiness. He leaned against the hood of his truck and rested until his knees solidified enough to carry him to the driver's seat.

As he drove down the snowy logging road, he crossed several deer tracks. One was a large one, but he kept going. He was too old for tracking now. The buck might lead him too far from the road. Even if he were to kill it, how would he get it out? That would be a sure invitation for the Iron Hand to return.

Ahead in the road, a doe and her fawn paused briefly, then bolted across an old clear-cut of waist-high spruce trees. Their bounds were graceful and dainty. He watched their tails float like white butterflies through the evergreens. The doe stopped momentarily at the edge of safety to look back. Her small fawn pranced nervously around her. Then, with one more leap, they both vanished into the stand of mature timber.

A mile farther down the road he turned the truck off onto a logging road. He stopped and jerked the transfer case shifter into four-wheel-drive. Brush had begun to swallow the old trail and it scraped and squeaked against the sides of the truck. At the end of the trail, he turned his vehicle around in the rem-

Charles J. Alsheimer

To the old man there was nothing as wonderful as a November day in the woods hunting deer.

nants of a cul-de-sac, shut off the engine and stepped out, sliding his rifle from the rack in the rear window. Deep in the pocket of his wool pants he found several cartridges and loaded them into the rifle. He silently eased his truck door shut and started into the woods.

At first the brush was dense and the snow sifted down on him, leaving his wool clothes powdered with white. The brush turned into a mixture of hardwoods and softwoods for 200 yards, then sloped up into open beeches. He moved stealthily. He prided himself on his "soft" steps, and had been a successful hunter because of them. Beneath the snow-laden brim of his hat, his eyes glanced furtively in all directions. Even after all these years there was still a hunger — a yearning that all predators must feel if they are to be successful. Slowly and silently he eased through the forest. He learned long ago that a good hunter, a truly good hunter, must be in the forest without the forest knowing he is there.

> *The old man felt embarrassed by the spotlight of praise; hunting and its successes were a personal thing to him.*

At the top of the beech ridge, he looked for the tree. He'd know it when he saw it because of its huge, bulbous growth. After locating the tree, he stalked his way over to it and looked up at the odd growth. It was about 10 feet up the trunk and the size of a washtub. It looked even bigger this year, he thought. He carefully pushed the snow and leaves away from the base of the tree with his boot, until he was able to stand on the quiet, black humus beneath. The pungent, mildewy odor of rich soil drifted to his nostrils. He leaned his back against the tree and cradled his rifle in his arms. From here, he could watch down the side of the ridge and wait for a deer to make its way into his sights. It had happened here before. He took several deer over the years standing in this very spot. He looked up at the big growth

above his head. Yes, this very spot.

After an hour, he felt the urge to sit down, but from past experience he knew better. If he sat, the cold would hammer against his hip like an anvil. The resulting ache would sometimes last for several days. He shifted his weight to the other foot and remained standing. He hunched his shoulders against the chill.

A patch of brown moved behind a large beech. The corner of his eye caught the movement and he raised his rifle before the deer could emerge and detect his presence. The same sense of thrill that he always felt reached deep into his gut and tugged. When the deer showed, he knew instantly that it was a doe. Ascertaining that she was not accompanied by a buck, he eased the rifle back into its cradling position. Never mind that the Fish and Game Department's laws prohibited the shooting of does. He had never shot anything but bucks and for many years had shot nothing but big bucks.

The sun finally melted its way through the wispy, leftover clouds. It warmed the wool of his jacket and made him drowsy. He tried to force away the heavy feeling in his eyes. He took a roll of butterscotch Lifesavers from his pocket and put one in his mouth. A gray camp jay lit on a branch in front of him. It studied him with great curiosity for several minutes, then flew away.

To the old man, there was nothing as wonderful as a November day in the woods hunting deer. The beauty, the challenge, the thrill . . . even the loneliness; he loved it all. The loneliness was his own doing, but he far preferred it to the alternative. At one time other hunters came to his deer camp each year but, for him, the company ruined the atmosphere. It always seemed that they drank too much, ate too much and hunted too little. If any one of them was lucky enough to blunder into a deer, they showed much too little respect for the animal. All his old hunting companions were gone, those old friends who hunted in the same manner as he did — religiously, reverently. Now a new breed of hunter roamed the woods, and they were not fully understood by the old man. Times change, he thought. People change, too, but it was the thought of deer hunting changing that distressed him most.

Nearly two hours passed before another movement diverted his eye from the same spot where the doe appeared earlier. The deer was moving swiftly, following the doe's track, with it's head low to the ground. He would have known it was a buck just from its movements even if he had not been able to see the massive rack the deer sported on its head.

In one strangely devout instant of thrill, desire, need and want, a shot broke the silence of the snowy woods and the great buck lay dead. His legs kicked to quickly fading signals of adrenaline and steam escaped from the animal's warm, wet body. As the old man approached the downed animal, he felt the odd duality of proud accomplishment and respectful remorse that always rushed through his mind and heart. The old man lifted the deer's head from the snow and admired the handsome rack. It spread nearly two feet wide with 10 points more than an inch long, one point less than an inch and one point broken off in a fight earlier in the rutting season.

He gutted the deer, saving the heart and liver. He then took a short coil of rope from his belt and tied it around the base of the deer's antlers. After a brief admiration of the animal, he began dragging it down the slope toward the truck. The snow made the task easier, but it was still an arduous task. The deer's body was huge and the old man labored under the strain. His rangy frame was still very strong despite its years, but he stopped often and rested; always apprehensive that the Iron Hand would hear his loud breathing and come rushing in.

While resting on a stump, he thought that perhaps a heart attack wasn't such a bad way to die. A heart attack would be quick, like a bullet. Certainly he would prefer it to, say, cancer. The old hunter didn't like the thought of a tumorous growth lying dormant, deep inside him and then, one day, for no known reason, slowly awakening. He envisioned it stretching its tentacles out in all directions seeking a vital organ to consume, as a snake might swallow a mouse. No, he didn't want to die a slow, agonizing death from cancer. That would be too much like winter-kill. God knows this old-timer saw enough of that in the winter deeryards. He would never forget the dull, sunken eyes of once proud animals, reduced to hide and skeletons. It was a horrible torture, lasting for weeks, and ending in the same death that might have come in an instant. It was always his opinion that when any liv-ing thing dies quickly, it dies with self-respect. When it dies slowly, it loses more than life.

When he reached his truck, it was late afternoon. The sun had been replaced by a lead-gray sky which hung low and heavy, threatening more snow. The old man snaked the deer up onto a bank on the edge of the road, backed his tailgate up to the deer and slid it in. He drove slowly toward town to register the deer at the deer check station. He adjusted the rearview mirror so he could take an occasional glance at the magnifi-cent trophy. He felt an elevated sense of manhood and of worth. After all, how well a man hunted was a large measure of his value by the old man's standards. Those standards were handed down to him from his father and his father before him. They came from a time when simple things and concepts worked and simplicity was all that was needed. His life remained that way and he felt very thankful for it. Beyond that, the old deerslayer understood perfectly the concept of biological balance and Nature's intriguing, prearranged romance of predator and prey.

The Iron Hand was pressing against his chest again. Gently at first, but turning suddenly angry and pressing so hard it felt as if his chest might collapse. The old man managed to stop the truck and gripped the steer-ing wheel with anguish. The Iron Hand taunted him by alternately increasing the pressure and then offering to leave. Eventually, it did leave and the old man hunched limply over the steering wheel, panting. After a period of rest, he rolled down his window and felt the cold wind seal his perspiring brow. It had begun to snow again and icy granules slanted into the cab, stinging the side of his face. He put the truck in gear.

By the time he reached town, it was dark. The check station was at the tiny general store, where a handful of hunters milled about in the cold, waiting to see the deer that would be brought in. Excited chatter bubbled from the crowd as the old man's buck pushed the scale's needle to 266 pounds. The old man felt embarrassed by the spotlight of praise; hunting and its successes were a personal thing to him. It was a mea-suring stick by which he rated himself, not something he did to gain the awe of others. The hoopla made him self-conscious and anxious to register his buck and return to the sanctuary of his camp.

A middle-aged woman was leaving the small store

as the old man's deer was being reloaded onto the tailgate of his truck. She balked at the sight and told him that he was a despicable scum, totally lacking in humanity. The veteran hunter said nothing, but stared her squarely in the eyes as she cast her judgments. He knew who she was, or at least had heard of her. She lived in the city, but owned a large farm on the outskirts of town, which she used as a get-away place. He didn't know why anyone would live in a place they had to get away from, but that was her business. As was the fact that all of her land was posted to hunting, fishing and/or trespassing.

> *He had found truth in what he had always known — predation was the best way to die. It was an honorable death.*

When she finished her holy reprimand, the old man's stare escorted her to her Mercedes wagon. He said nothing. Ignorant ears hear less than deaf ones, he thought. There were, in fact, so many things he would have liked to have said. Things such as:

"Take a long look at your own world, Lady. It isn't so perfect. Don't come here from a place where you kill people, rape children and ignore your neighbors' cries for help. Don't come here from a place where the water and air are only masses of garbage in motion. Don't come here and criticize our annual harvest of birds and animals which we have managed despite your destruction of the environment. Each year your city newspapers print anti-hunting articles. Soon those same newspapers become used as blankets for the homeless, or sop up the blood from a battle over illegal drugs. Think about where your priorities are and where they should be. Try to understand your own world before coming here and trying to change mine. Lady, I won't go to the city and tell you how to treat people and the environment we live in if you won't come here and tell us how to manage wildlife. You live in your world, Lady, and we will try to live in ours despite you."

Those were some of the things he would have liked to have said, but he knew the futility. He also knew that making such narrow-minded statements would make him no better than her. The old man got into his truck and returned to his camp.

Working by the truck's headlights, he winched the stiff carcass high up on the meat pole. The deer twisted gently on the rope and the old man put his hand to its side and steadied it. He took one more long, scrutinizing look at the animal and a slight smile warmed his stony visage. He shut off the truck's headlights and went into the camp for the evening.

When the camp was lighted and the fire was built, the old man poured a generous portion of blackberry brandy into a tin cup. He sat in an ancient rocking chair close to the woodstove and sipped the brandy. When the bottom of the cup showed, the old man's face blushed with a warm, alcohol fever. His head felt light and he was tempted to doze. He shook off the urge, rubbed his eyes and stood. When he did so, the exertion of dragging the big buck began to show itself. The sore muscles had begun to stiffen in his back, arms and legs. He moved lamely to the cupboard, took down a can of stew, dumped it into a small saucepan and set it atop the wood stove.

He made his way to the small bunk and sat down. Forcing his tired back to bend, he unlaced his boots and pried them from his feet. He then dropped the heavy wool trousers and stepped out of them. Now clad in only his long underwear, he felt remarkably unburdened. The stew had begun to bubble on the woodstove. He took it to the table and ate it from the saucepan with a tablespoon.

With a full stomach, he felt both sedated and exhausted. He put a large chunk of maple into the woodstove and dampered it down. He shut out the light and felt his way to the bunk, where he slid deep into his sleeping bag and listened to the snapping wood fire and, outside, the growing howl of a north wind. He lie there thinking about how he counted his years in deer seasons. Another year was gone.

He had come to know the Iron Hand well and sensed its approach even before feeling its pressure on his chest. Tiredly, he waited for it to complete its stalk. The Iron Hand struck his chest and squeezed the oxygen from his lungs. It punched the biceps of his left arm, sending a sharp pain the entire length of it. The Iron Hand denied him his breath longer than it ever had before. It seemed to demand the old man panic but he lay still and quiet, like an emaciated deer waiting to die in a winter deeryard. The Iron Hand had come too many times for the old man to fear it anymore. It had made itself too familiar and had given him too much time for acceptance. At last, the Iron Hand left his chest, but the old man knew it hadn't gone very far, or for very long. It remained in the camp with him but, then again, it had the right to be there. Just as he had the right to enter the woods and prey on deer.

The old buck hunter felt restful and his sore muscles were soothed. An intoxicating drowsiness lifted him and he felt himself drifting away. All of his life he had been a deer hunter. Many times he pondered what it would be like to find himself on the other end of the predator/prey spectrum. Now he knew, for he was the prey and the Iron Hand was the predator. It wasn't so bad, he thought; it was natural and he liked that. He had found truth in what he had always known — predation was the best way to die. It was an honorable death; idyllically poetic.

An hour before dawn, the buck twisted slowly on the meat pole. Its vacant eyes stared up at the dark, November sky. Its hide was covered with icy pellets. The only sound was the whispering swish of snow-covered spruce and the faint ringing of the old man's alarm clock inside the camp.

Editor's Note: "The Iron Hand" was originally published in the November 1989 issue of Deer & Deer Hunting *magazine.*

The Iron Hand

■ OLD MAN AND THE LADY

I am writing regarding the article, "The Iron Hand," in the November 1989 issue of *Deer & Deer Hunting* magazine.

I read a lot and never have I read a story which was so well-written. I just cannot get over the part where the old man was weighing his deer and the lady was giving him hell for shooting a deer. Best of all was what he might have said. I have read this at least five times and no truer words were ever spoken. That is exactly the way it is here in our state and town. Again, what a fine job!

— *John Webb*
Bernhard's Bay, New York

■ A MESSAGE FOR ALL HUNTERS

I have been a subscriber to *Deer & Deer Hunting* magazine for several years and it is by far the very best deer hunting magazine on the market.

I read all of the hunting articles and the information sections, but I do not usually read the fictional stories, until the November 1989 issue. In that issue there was an article by Ken Preston called "The Iron Hand." I have read this over and over. Not only is it a good story, but there is a message in it for all hunters, both young and old: the importance of being in shape for the hunting season and not taking your health for granted.

A lot of hunters, myself included, are couch potatoes for 10 or 11 months of the year and then opening day arrives. You dust off your bow or gun and head out, walking a long ways, climbing hills, getting into tree stands and if you're lucky enough to bag a deer, you then have the job of dragging your trophy who knows how far to your vehicle. Anyone who has ever tried to drag a deer any distance soon finds out how humbling a task that can be, especially if you are more than 40 years old.

A hunter should prepare himself long before the deer season opens. Doing some daily exercise, walking, jogging, squats for the legs, building up your endurance. It would even be wise to get a physical from your family doctor prior to the hunting season.

Some people will think that all of these precautions are a waste of time, but many hunters each season end up like the old man in "The Iron Hand," with the sound of the buck hanging from the twisting rope and the sound of the alarm clock.

— *Dan Watkins*
Des Moines, Iowa

The .30-30:
An Overrated Caliber For Deer?

Richard P. Smith

Consistent, clean kills and 100 percent recovery of wounded deer should be the goal of every deer hunter. In the author's opinion, the use of a .30-30 reduces the chances of achieving that goal.

• • •

Richard P. Smith

I have never used a .30-30 for deer hunting and, given a choice, never will.

That may sound like an extreme statement, considering this caliber's popularity among deer hunters, but there are good reasons for such a strong opinion. Frankly, I think the .30-30, and other calibers with similar ballistics, is overrated as a deer rifle and try to discourage as many hunters as possible from deer hunting with it. Simply stated there are a number of better calibers to choose from.

> *I'm convinced that hunters who choose to hunt deer with a .30-30 do not realize they are risking the loss of wounded whitetails.*
>
> • • •

I realize that innumerable deer have been brought down with .30-30s, and rifles in that caliber will continue to account for many whitetails each year. In my opinion, however, bullets from those rifles don't produce clean kills as consistently as other .30-caliber slugs. This sometimes accounts for the unnecessary loss of a wounded deer.

Deer hunters must overcome enough handicaps to fill a tag without creating another one by using a centerfire rifle that is not best suited for the task. If you've hunted with a .30-30 very long, or know another hunter who has, you may know what I mean. Although I have not hunted with a .30-30, one of my regular hunting partners (my brother) does, and I've also shared deer hunting experiences with other hunters using the same caliber.

Brother Bruce came darn close to losing a six-point buck that he mortally wounded with a .30-30 slug during the 1984 deer season. We were posted about 250 yards apart opening morning. At 8:45 a.m. I heard a shot from his direction and it sounded like the bullet connected. I took it for granted the season was off to a good start, with Bruce quickly filling his tag, until he approached my stand an hour later.

"I hit a buck, but I can't find him," Bruce said with obvious concern in his voice. "There's hair on the ground where he was standing when I shot, but I can't find any blood. He was only about 25 yards away, standing broadside, when I shot so I'm sure I hit him well. I was aiming for the middle of his shoulder."

We returned to his stand to reexamine the hairs knocked off the buck by the 150-grain bullet. We found a lot of short white hairs and also several that were gray and tipped in brown, indicating a possible hit in the lower shoulder. Bruce could watch the buck for only about 50 yards when it ran off after he shot. We spread out and carefully searched the ground the buck ran over, as well as the terrain beyond in all directions, looking for the smallest speck of blood to indicate the buck's course of travel. We came up empty.

Without further evidence of a fatal hit after a thorough search of all possible avenues the buck might have taken as far as 175 yards from where it had been hit, I was ready to conclude that the bullet just grazed the whitetail. In fact, I started to return to my stand, convinced that was the case. And then I spotted a deer carcass.

It was Bruce's buck. The animal traveled at least 200 yards from where it was hit. Although the .30-30 slug passed completely through the animal, there was no blood on the ground until a short distance from where it went down. Apparently, the body cavity filled with blood before any blood leaked out.

Bruce's bullet did strike the deer in the lower shoulder, angling back instead of going through the body. Nonetheless, the lungs and liver had been damaged. The buck went farther than I think it should have with such a hit. I'm sure the same hit with a 150-grain bullet from my .30-06 would not only have put the deer down sooner, it would have resulted in a decent blood trail to follow, if following the animal proved necessary.

I shudder to think how close we came to not finding that buck. Even worse, though, are recollections of two incidents in prior years when the scenarios were dreadfully similar, only we did not find the bucks Bruce shot at. The bucks were bigger in both cases, each sporting racks with at least eight points.

In one case, the buck jumped at the shot and we found hair that confirmed a hit. The buck was close and in the open at the time of the shot so there was every reason to suspect the hit was a good one. However, our efforts to locate blood or the deer failed. Perhaps we didn't look long enough or far enough. At the time, I expected a deer hit solidly with any .30-caliber rifle bullet would not travel much more than 100 yards and there would be ample blood sign to follow in cases where the deer ran out of sight. The experience in 1984 with the six-pointer changed my opinion.

Another close shot — 20 to 30 yards — was involved with the second buck Bruce shot at with his .30-30 that we failed to recover. That time we couldn't even find hair to verify a hit, but under the circumstances it was hard to conceive of the bullet missing the deer. We made another fruitless search, lasting hours, without a clue as to what happened to that buck.

We finally concluded, due to lack of evidence to the contrary, that the shot must have missed the whitetail. In retrospect, I think we should have looked longer and farther away from where the deer was at the time of the shot. There was a river in the direction the deer ran. We made no effort to look for blood or the deer on the other side, but we should have. That's what I would do if the same thing happened again.

In both cases, our conclusions may have been correct and the bucks survived. I hope so. A nagging doubt in the back of my mind, however, prompted me to write this article. I'm ashamed to think that either one of those bucks possibly lay dead beyond the scope of our search pattern. These are some of the reasons why I wouldn't choose to carry a .30-30 in the deer woods, and there are more.

In 1985, Bruce shot a spike buck with his .30-30 on the third day of the season. The deer was 30 to 40 yards away when he shot, breaking one shoulder and knocking the whitetail off of its feet. However, the small buck managed to get up and run off. Fortunately, Bruce kept the deer in sight and got off two more rounds.

The second bullet missed, but number three was on target, putting the buck down for good. With a bullet through the lungs and a broken shoulder, the whitetail ran about 75 yards from where it was initially hit before a second bullet stopped it. How far would the animal have travelled if Bruce hadn't hit it a second time?

No matter how far the buck would have travelled,

Bruce would have recovered it because there was snow on the ground. Although the snow wasn't necessary to track the deer in this case, it revealed something else of interest. From the point where the buck was hit, it ran about 50 yards before leaving a drop of blood, and that was with complete bullet penetration. Without snow and a view of the deer's departure, that buck could have been another tough one to trail and recover.

Also during the 1985 deer season, I ran across a hunter from another group who wounded a buck with a .30-30. My tag was already filled and I was walking toward my vehicle when I passed another hunter. He shot a minute or two later, after I entered a patch of cover, so I retraced my steps to see how he made out

Richard P. Smith

The .30-30 has been a traditional favorite among deer hunters and its value as a deer rifle is seldom questioned. The author believes it is time for that to change.

and to investigate the possibility that I might have moved a buck past him.

As it turned out, the guy's shot connected on a buck with a "big rack," but it was a poor hit. There was blood and hair where the buck had been at the time of the shot, and we found the mushroomed bullet laying on the leaves. Intestinal matter was mixed with the blood. Plenty of blood was present initially, revealing the buck's course of travel, but it soon petered out.

I left the hunter after he jumped the buck for the second time, and suggested he wait a few hours before continuing to trail it. There was snow in the swamp where the whitetail took refuge, but none in the open. If the deer was pushed out of the swamp, it would be difficult, if not impossible, to follow it with no blood trail.

Several days later I saw another member of the hunter's party and asked if the big buck had been recovered. The answer was no.

A poor hit is a poor hit, regardless of rifle caliber. However, I can't help but speculate about the outcome had that buck been hit with a bullet from a rifle with better ballistics than a .30-30, such as a .30-06 or .270. I can only guess, but I believe that the odds of recovering the buck would have been greater if shot with a rifle in one of those calibers due to greater shocking power and accompanying tissue damage.

I know the knockdown power of a .30-06 on whitetails very well and can't help comparing the results I've experienced with that caliber to those of the .30-30. My records reveal that I've shot 19 whitetails over the years with a .30-06, always aiming for the shoulder or chest. Twelve of those animals were dropped on the spot. Another four went down within sight, one of which was hit twice.

Only three of those 19 deer went out of sight after being hit. Two of the three, both does, were out of sight almost instantly due to the terrain, but they only ran 20 to 25 yards before dropping. The carcasses were easily visible as I approached the spots where they stood when I shot.

One out of 19 deer travelled a significant distance after being hit — about 100 yards. It was a spikehorn that was running when I shot. There was a good blood trail in that case, though, enabling easy trailing and quick recovery of the animal.

I counted 12 whitetails my brother shot and recovered with his .30-30. Half of those dropped on the

spot and stayed down. However, four of those six were felled with either broken necks or backs. Instant paralysis results from any caliber bullet that strikes those areas. Five of the 12 deer Bruce shot dropped within sight and one (the six-pointer in 1984) ran out of sight.

The raw figures don't show a significant difference between the recovery of deer hit with a .30-06 or a .30-30. With each caliber only one whitetail was docu-

> *Some hunters will continue to use .30-30 rifles when pursuing whitetails. They are urged to learn the limitations of this caliber and take extra care when searching for a wounded deer.*
>
> ● ● ●

mented as having travelled any distance, but there was a significant difference in the ease with which those two deer were recovered. Also of significance are the question marks surrounding two bucks Bruce shot at that were not recovered.

Without considering the two "unknowns," Bruce almost lost one out of 12 (8.3 percent) whitetails he hit. If one or both of the unrecovered deer actually were killed, the rate of loss was either one out of 13 (7.7 percent) or one out of seven (14.3 percent). Using these figures, is it realistic to project the loss of whitetails to hunters using .30-30s across North America at between 7.7 and 14.3 percent?

Maybe. Maybe not.

From my point of view, the answer to that question is irrelevant. What is important is the answer to this question: Is hunting deer with a .30-30 worth the risk or possibility of losing a single animal? My answer is no. I want to attach a tag to each and every deer I hit solidly, and I'm sure every other deer hunter feels the same way.

With that in mind, I'm convinced hunters who choose to hunt deer with a .30-30 do not realize they are risking the loss of wounded whitetails. Perhaps they have been fortunate enough to avoid the problems Bruce experienced with that caliber. I know Bruce doesn't, or at least didn't, think he was risking the loss of a deer he might hit by going afield with a .30-30. And I want to make it perfectly clear I'm not trying to be critical of Bruce in any way, or anyone else who hunts with a .30-30. His experiences with a .30-30 serve as convenient examples because I'm familiar with many of them.

The primary purpose of this article is to alert hunters who hunt with a .30-30 of the potential problems they might encounter in recovering some deer. In addition, I want to bring attention to the fact that there are calibers better than the .30-30 for deer hunting, and the .30-06 isn't the only one. Others include the .270, .308 and .300 Savage.

A look at a ballistics table will help explain why. According to figures for Federal ammunition, 150-grain .30-30 bullets leave the rifle's muzzle at 2,390 feet per second and have 1,900 foot-pounds of energy. A similar bullet out of a .30-06 travels more than 600 feet per second faster and has almost 1,000 more foot-pounds of energy at the muzzle. Bullets from a .30-06 also maintain velocity and energy better than those from a .30-30 out to 100 yards and beyond.

Ballistics for both the .270 and .308 (again using a 150-grain bullet) are almost as good as the ought-six. There's an increase of 240 feet per second and 400 foot-pounds with a .300 Savage versus a .30-30.

Better ballistics than the .30-06 are available from rifles in 7mm Remington magnum and .300 Win-chester magnum. Only a 180-grain bullet was listed for the .300 magnum in the Federal chart. That bullet has a muzzle velocity comparable to a 150-grain .30-06 slug, but 3,500 foot-pounds of energy versus 2,820. Velocity and energy of a 150-grain 7mm magnum bullet are, respectively, 3,110 and 3,220.

The .30-30 has been a traditional favorite among deer hunters and its value as a deer rifle is seldom questioned. I think it is time for that to change, however. There was a time when the .30-30 was one of the best calibers available for deer hunting in terms of ballistics, rifle design and weight. That has long since changed. Short, light rifles with fast actions have been available in better deer hunting calibers for many years.

Consistent, clean kills and 100 percent recovery of wounded deer should be the goal of every deer hunter. In my opinion, the use of a .30-30 reduces the chances of achieving that goal. Nonetheless, I realize some hunters will continue to carry rifles of that caliber when pursuing whitetails. They have the right to make that choice. I would urge those hunters, however, to use extra care when searching for an animal they either know they hit or feel strongly that they did, even in the absence of a blood trail. They may be glad they did.

Editor's Note: "The .30-30: An Overrated Caliber for Deer?" was originally published in the December 1986 issue of Deer & Deer Hunting *magazine.*

The .30-30

■ STICKING WITH HIS .32 SPECIAL

I am writing in regards to the article by Richard P. Smith on the .30-30. He brings up some very good and interesting observations. I am constantly amazed at how one hunter's experiences can be so drastically different than another's.

For comparison, I have hunted for many years with a .32 Special, a caliber almost identical to the .30-30. I have also hunted with other people who use a .30-30. In my experience, I have had quite a few one-shot kills with my .32 Special. For example, four years ago I shot a buck at a distance of 40 yards. The bullet hit the animal in the center of the chest, directly through the lungs. He ran about 20 yards before falling and there was more than enough blood if tracking had been necessary. The 170-grain bullet was laying against the far side of the hide and was a perfect mushroom about the size of a nickel. I noted in the article that Smith said his brother hunts with 150-grain bullets. The people I hunt with who use .30-30s all swear by the 170-grain bullet.

Another point I would like to bring up is the pure "shootability" of the .30-30. Recoil is not excessive, so most hunters can shoot it very accurately. If a hunter can't shoot accurately, he might as well use the old deer-wounder, the shotgun.

Our observations on the caliber may differ, but then every hunt is different. I guess that's what makes it so enjoyable. I'll stick with my .32 Special and hopefully continue to have good luck with it. I guess a cartridge that's been killing deer for almost a century can't be all that bad.

— *Brad Larson*
Williams Bay, Wisconsin

■ COMFORTABLE WITH HER .30-30

I am writing in response to Richard P. Smith's article, "The .30-30: An Overrated Caliber for Deer?" I must say that I was upset by this article.

I hunt with a .30-30 mostly because at the time I was looking for a rifle it was the shortest, lightest rifle I found that fit comfortably against my shoulder. You see, I am a female deer hunter who is small in size and having a deer rifle that I could easily carry and one that didn't kick like a mule was important to me. Also, I hunt in brushy, thick, out-of-the-way places and having to carry a long-barrelled, heavy rifle would be like having to crawl through a briar thicket with a lengthy two-by-four.

We all deer hunt in diferent ways, use different hunting methods and prefer different weapons. I usually hunt in thick cover which means I take short-range shots. If I occasionally hunt near the edge of a field, I'm not about to try a 175- or 200-yard shot across the field. My rifle has its limitations and I'm well aware that the .30-30 is not a rifle for long distances.

Most of my friends and relatives hunt with rifles ranging in caliber from .270 to .30-06 and 7mm. A lot of these big guns are put away at the end of the season and never touched until opening day of the next season. The heavy recoil on a tender shoulder probably is a major factor. On the other hand, by the time deer season rolls around, I've shot my .30-30 several times, enough to assure me that I can hit where I aim. The recoil is not a problem and I'm familiar and comfortable with my gun before I line up my sights on a deer. I think being a good marksman as a result of being able to adequately handle and fire a rifle is more important than having a big gun that one seldom shoots.

I totally agree with Smith when he says that the goal of every deer hunter should be clean, consistent kills. I try to achieve this by taking open, clear shots and waiting or passing up opportunities that might be risky. I have not yet lost a deer; all I've shot left blood trails a six-year-old could follow. I have known quite a few deer to go unrecovered after being shot with a .270 or a .30-06. Perhaps I've been lucky so far and I may have to change my opinion at a later date. But as long as my .30-30 keeps making clean, quick kills, I'm not about to find a permanent resting place for it in the back of the gun cabinet.

— *Viola A. White*
Windsor, North Carolina

■ EINSTEIN AND THE .30-30

I am a student at Clemson University and an avid deer hunter. After reading the letters from your readers in the April 1987 issue of *Deer & Deer Hunting* magazine, I became gravely concerned about the lack of knowledge of the average deer hunter.

Several of the letters concerned the use of the .30-30 rifle for hunting whitetails. Two of Einstein's equations prove that there are better guns to use for deer hunting. The kinetic energy of a bullet is equal to $1/2 MV^2$. It should be obvious that as you double the velocity you increase the kinetic energy four-fold, while if you double the mass of the bullet you only double the kinetic energy.

The second concern is the knockdown power of a bullet. The momentum of a bullet is equal to its mass multiplied by its velocity. This shows that a bullet travelling twice as fast with half the weight of another bullet travelling half the velocity is equal. Therefore, you lose no knockdown power with a smaller bullet, but you greatly increase the kinetic energy. This should prove to most hunters that there are better cartridges on the market today than the .30-30.

— Les Cooper
Fountain Inn, South Carolina

■ EDUCATE RATHER THAN CRITICIZE

I feel that the article by Richard P. Smith in your December 1986 issue was much too critical of the .30-30, a rifle which has probably been responsible for the demise of more whitetails than any other weapon.

The underlying premise of this article was that the .30-30 should be abandoned as a weapon for whitetails since more efficient weapons are available. If the .30-30 should be abandoned because of the availability of more powerful calibers, what would the author propose we do with bows and muzzleloaders? Certainly these are less efficient than a .30-06, but this self-imposed limitation is part of the pleasure of using these weapons. The .30-30 is very efficient when used within its effective range. Furthermore, smaller calibers tend to ruin less meat and thus the .30-30 is very "efficient."

Three hunter errors contributed more to losing deer in the author's examples than did the choice of the .30-30. First, a 170-grain bullet in the .30-30 packs more punch than does the 150-grain bullet which was used. Secondly, shot placement is more important than the caliber used. A gut-shot deer will not drop in its tracks no matter what caliber is used. Additionally, if a deer has been severely spooked or shot at, it will very likely run after being shot regardless of shot placement. This could explain some of the problems the author reported. The third type of hunter error shown in several of Smith's examples relate to tracking after the shot. A hunter should be willing to expend a great deal of effort to find a wounded animal. A hunter should not track a gut-shot deer immediately after the shot. It is common knowledge that one should not begin tracking gut-shot animals for at least several hours. These are the errors that caused the loss and near loss of the deer in Smith's examples, not the choice of the .30-30.

Velocity and energy are no substitute for marksmanship and hunter knowledge. More could be done to reduce crippling losses by educating hunters than by criticizing the weapons they use.

— Jay S. Anderson
Stevens Point, Wisconsin

■ TOO CRITICAL OF THE .30-30?

It came as no surprise that Richard P. Smith's article about the .30-30 generated a tremendous amount of mail from the readers of Deer & Deer Hunting magazine. Space limitations in the magazine prevented publishing each of the letters received but the preceding letters are a representative sample.

The majority of the letters received were critical of the article. The letter writers generally shared the opinion that Smith's article was too critical of the .30-30 as a deer rifle. Many felt that perhaps the article should have focused on the hunters using the rifle rather than the rifle itself. In short, those commenting on the article believed that unrecovered deer are the result of the hunter's performance and not the performance of the rifle per se.

The debate about specific types of rifles and their suitability for deer hunting will continue as long as deer hunters have a variety of rifles to choose from. Also, no one will ever "prove" that a particular rifle is "best" for deer hunting. With all this in mind, Smith presented his opinions regarding the .30-30 and urged deer hunters using this caliber to exercise caution in regards to shot selection because of the limitations of the .30-30 as compared to larger calibers such as the .30-06. He also warned that deer hunters using .30-30s may sometimes have to put forth extra effort when tracking a deer they wound.

After the publication of Smith's article, some interesting information surfaced pertaining to rifles of various calibers and wounding rates reported by deer hunters. In a "Wounded Deer Survey" published in Deer & Deer Hunting magazine, readers responding to the survey showed a strong preference for .30-30 and .30-06 rifles. Hunters who used the .30-06 reported a wounding rate of 12.3 percent. Hunters who used .30-30s, however, reported a wounding rate nearly three times as high — 34.8 percent. These data seem to substantiate Smith's words of caution to hunters using the .30-30 while deer hunting. It is easy to attribute this substantial difference in wounding rates to the hunter rather than the weapon, but whatever the reason or reasons, it does appear that deer hunters who use .30-30s fail to recover a substantially higher percentage of the deer they wound than do hunters using .30-06s.

As Smith stated in his article, "Consistent, clean kills and 100 percent recovery of game that is hit should be the goal of every deer hunter. Some hunters will continue to carry .30-30 rifles when in pursuit of whitetails. They have the right to make that choice. However, I would like to urge those people to use extra care when searching for an animal they either know they hit or feel strongly that they did, even in the absence of a blood trail. They may be glad they did."

— Al Hofacker, Editor
Athelstane, Wisconsin

Part Four
The Deer Hunter

The Deer Hunting

Experience

Robert M. Jackson and Ray Anderson

We believe there is a recipe for increasing the satisfaction that each of us can find in the hunting experience. The key is in working on aspects of the hunt that you can do something about. That means, first and foremost, your own expectations.

Ask yourself this question: "If for some reason I could not go deer hunting next year or if the season closed, how much would I miss it?" How important to us are the many activities we describe as "deer hunting?" To one of the authors, Robert Jackson, it is so important that he moves his birthday celebration from the date of his birth, August 29, to the day before the opening of the bow season. Forget that I am a year older; let's celebrate that I've lived to the eve of enjoying another deer hunting season!

Many successful deer hunters apparently share similar feelings. When asked, as part of a research project on hunting motivations and satisfactions conducted by the authors, 61 percent of the Wisconsin deer gun hunters interviewed said they would miss deer hunting "more than most or all other interests." Thirty-nine percent stated they would "not miss it much" or would "find other interests." Does it surprise you to learn, however, that 81 of the 100 bow hunters interviewed for our study said they would miss it "more than all other hunting activities?"

Why do we hunt and fish? What motivations and satisfactions lead us to value these experiences so highly? In the past eight years, we conducted a series of studies with Wisconsin hunters to extend our understanding of hunting for the benefit of sportsmen as well as for the wildlife managers and conservation officers charged with people management responsibilities. In conducting those studies, research assistants, trained by the investigators, contacted more than 1,000 deer gun hunters, 600 waterfowlers and 250 deer bow hunters as they left the field at the end of the hunting day. Approximately one-third of these hunters were interviewed again in their homes after the season by professional interviewers (all hunters) who probed in depth and in detail the hunting satisfactions, motivations and values of these men and women. We can, with confidence, describe "what makes us tick" as hunters and outdoorsmen.

Common sense tells us that the nature of hunting

Charles J. Alsheimer

Tradition is one of the key elements in hunting satisfaction and can be controlled by the individual. For many deer hunters, gathering at deer camp and enjoying the companionship of family and friends is a vital part of their deer hunting tradition.

and hunting satisfactions constantly evolve. Hunters today are different than their parents or grandparents because hunting itself has changed dramatically throughout history. The motives of primitive hunters and food gatherers were undoubtedly utilitarian. They wanted meat for the table. It wasn't that different for the early settlers or even those living through the Great Depression in the 1930s. Hunting success, or lack of it, had a real impact on their lives and the resource.

Paul Hunt wrote of early life in western Wisconsin: "Domestic consumption commodities were obtained during the early years in manners customary on the Wisconsin frontier. The forest was a major source of supply in the struggle for survival. It was only the hunters' skill that carried the family through the first year or two and it was called upon to supplement the larder for years to come. Plentiful at first, the supply was radically decreased during the severe winter of 1858. During that winter the snow accumulated to such depths as to prevent the deer from finding food or moving about easily. As a result, many deer froze or starved to death, if they were not clubbed to death by pioneers. Whatever the case, the deer population was virtually wiped out. As late as 1890, the sight of a deer was a neighborhood newsmaker."

Hunting Satisfactions And Expectations

Today, however, hunting motivations and behaviors relate largely to recreational activities, yet wildlife managers still tend to define and measure recreational satisfaction by the number of animals bagged. This, too, can be traced back to the earliest days of wildlife management in North America when a big harvest was assumed to be proof of hunter satisfaction. Incidentally, this rationale for hunting continues to exist, and many equate harvest with successful hunting in a society that measures success by material acquisition. How many hunters and anglers do you know who measure their day, and even their personal worth, by the amount of game they bag? And do you enjoy hunting with them?

In the 1960s, with hunting becoming more popular and hunting opportunities more limited, managers began to look for other measures of satisfaction. Wildlife agencies began to count recreation-days in the field as an evaluation criteria. Bow hunting, of course, stood high: lots of days afield per deer bagged. Then, in the 1970s, professionals like John Hendee recommended that managers look for "multiple satisfactions," a broadening of management objectives to include companionship, experience with nature, solitude, etc.

> **Wildlife management procedures can make hunting so artificial as to make it lose much or all of its value.**

But the urge to equate satisfaction with bag still exists! When one of the authors recently asked a fish manager to justify his job, he pointed to Jackson's creel and said, "I put fish in your basket."

While pursuing that assessment, managers often distorted what many theorists declared to be the intrinsic values and satisfactions of hunting. Aldo Leopold stated, "The recreational value of a head of game is inverse to the intensiveness of the system of game management which produced it." Leopold was saying that management procedures can make hunting so artificial as to make it lose much or all of its value. I wonder what he would say about some of the modern deer gun hunts with the woodlands sometimes containing more than 100 hunters per square mile. When, literally, hunters outnumber the deer by four to one.

Other forms of hunting have been victims of artificial practices. Geese are attracted to, and become concentrated in, baited areas where wetlands have been managed by drawdown, food growing and re-flooding to make the area more attractive. Hunters concentrate along "firing lines" of refuges adorned in tennis shoes to facilitate the footraces for downed birds. In our studies, we interviewed many hunters such as this. One individual told us he always took his youngest son along because "he was the fastest." He told us he never actually aimed the gun at the goose; he just pulled the trigger and sent his son running to retrieve a bird.

Forest trails and roads are seeded to white clover to bait ruffed grouse into a position where they are more accessible to shooters; woody vegetation is cut back along the edges of roads to provide better shooting. The grouse do not need the clover in the fall, a time of the year when a variety of natural foods abounds, but this practice has become synonymous with ruffed grouse management. The number of grouse harvested per mile of road driven has become the measure of success and hunting with a motorized vehicle has become the accepted method. For many, it is the only method.

Derived from Leopold's theorum stated earlier, we proposed a definition of a true recreational hunt as the opportunity to practice hunting skills under conditions in which the animal is permitted its normal behavior pattern (appropriate to the season) in its natural habitat. Consequently, hunting skills must include an intimate knowledge of the quarry's daily and seasonal activities and of the area being hunted. The bow hunter will quickly recognize that, based on this definition, the modern bow hunter — one man and one deer — epitomizes what should be the real challenge and satisfaction of our sport.

But, do the hunters interviewed in our studies support what we theorized about hunter satisfaction and motivation in the modern hunting context? Again, hunting satisfaction is a dynamic quality and there are clear patterns of individual differences. For example, satisfaction varies depending on the hunting method used and the quarry being sought. At the end of each hunting day, hunters in our research studies were asked, "How was your hunt today?" It amazed us

Table 1. Percentage of Wisconsin waterfowl hunter and deer hunter responses to the question: "How was your hunt today?"

Response Category	Deer Bow Hunters	Deer Gun Hunters	Waterfowl Hunters
Excellent	11.4	17.6	9.3
Good	33.1	24.8	21.2
Fair	26.7	23.2	20.1
Poor	28.8	34.4	49.4

when almost half of the 529 waterfowl hunters we interviewed declared that they experienced a poor day (selected from a four-point scale including *excellent, good, fair* and *poor*). The data in Table 1 indicate that only nine percent of the waterfowl hunters felt that they had an excellent day.

Deer hunters were more positive in looking at their day's hunt, but more than one-third of the hunters suggested the day was *poor* and another 23 percent said it was *fair*. The largest percent checking *excellent* and *good* was found among the bow hunters (44.5 percent), followed by the deer gun hunters (42.4 percent) and waterfowl hunters (30.5 percent). These satisfaction data are of particular interest because of the relatively low level of success or opportunities to shoot per hunting day among bow hunters. Only one bow hunter in five actually shot at a deer on the day of the hunt compared to shooting for one of every two deer gun hunters. Bow hunters reported seeing an average of three to four deer per hunting trip. But deer gun hunters, in good deer range, reported seeing 20 to 40 deer per day. One bow hunter explained he was happy seeing fewer deer because it was "infinitely more difficult and challenging to get these sightings hunting by myself rather than in a woods filled with blaze orange."

Can bow hunters really be happier? We wondered and so we dug deeper. When we asked bow hunters to explain their rating of the hunt, 61 percent referred to whether or not they *saw deer* or *other game*. Only eight percent of these bow hunters justified hunting satisfaction in terms of either bagging a deer or competing with other hunters. In fact, bow hunters wanted to talk about nature appreciation (31 percent), escape and solitude (29 percent), and using various outdoor and recreational skills (23 percent). Bow hunters wanted to talk about their encounters with nature (game or nongame sighted, beauty of the woods, etc.) even when we didn't ask questions about it.

The bow hunter apparently develops and builds a different set of expectations about hunting than those of the gun hunter and these expectations affect his feelings of satisfaction. In part, it may be a rationalization by the hunters because bow hunters were more likely to recall companionship, seeing deer and nature when they were unsuccessful, but it also becomes part of the anticipation for other seasons or trips. We think these different expectations explain the higher level of satisfaction bow hunters reported on the day of the hunt. One young hunter, who hunts both ways, stated, "If I don't get a deer in the nine-day gun season, I'm frustrated as hell; I expect to get a deer. But it doesn't bother me to go all season without success when I bow hunt. I have two different standards." Those different standards, or expectations, become the basis for our personal evaluations of hunting satisfaction. Thus, the key to both understanding and developing satisfaction in hunting or any activity is based on knowledge or manipulation of expectations.

Why are winners often dissatisfied with their performance? How can those of us who are not the best in the world at anything ever be satisfied with our own skills and achievements? The answer is that we measure ourselves against our expectations. If I handicap myself in the field by hunting with a bow or muzzleloader, I create a different expectation. A trout fisherman can find more satisfaction in catching four hard-to-get trout in summer than in taking a bag limit in May. In essence, we mentally handicap ourselves like we handicap horses in a race. These adjustments in expectations make it possible for every hunting or fishing trip to be successful or satisfying regardless of the size of our bag.

How else can we explain why 25 percent of the Michigan deer hunters who shot bucks in a recent season did not see a high quality hunt in their evaluation while, in contrast, more than 62 percent of the Maryland deer hunters studied reported good or excellent hunting even though the success rate was three percent and almost half of the hunters did not see any deer? Hunting satisfaction is not necessarily related to kill rates, bag limits or personal success factors. Maryland hunters, with low expectations of success, described their satisfaction in terms of companionship, solitude, food and nature appreciation.

Bill Vaznis

The bow hunter apparently develops and builds a different set of expectations about hunting than those of the gun hunter and these expectations affect his feelings of satisfaction.

Five Stages Of Hunting

It would be foolish to argue that killing is irrelevant. It is part of the hunt. But its importance and its relationship to hunting satisfaction varies from hunter to hunter. For one, it changes over time (years of experience and age). We noted how the statements of hunters about satisfaction, motivation and hunting behavior fell into predictable patterns of development. A few years ago, we conceptualized five stages of hunter development. We suggested that almost all hunters proceed through these stages and that growth from one stage to another may depend upon the passage of time and the need for fulfilling experiences as a prerequisite to the movement.

The first step in this developmental sequence we termed the *shooter stage*. The beginning hunter apparently needs to pull the trigger and test the capability of his weapon. He may shoot at blackbirds, signs, insulators, tin cans or a hawk. Satisfying that need, the hunter moves to a *limiting-out stage* where bagging animals becomes primary and the hunter measures success by the number of birds or animals shot. From this developmental level, he seems to move to the third stage, or *trophy stage*. With waterfowl hunting, this could mean selectivity in only shooting "green

Table 2. Association of years of hunting experience with ratings of hunting satisfaction.

Factor	One & Two Years	Three To Five Years	Six To Ten Years	Eleven To Fifteen Years	Sixteen To Twenty Years	Twenty-One To Thirty Years	Thirty-One Or More Years
Exercise & Outdoor Activity							
Companionship of a Friend							
Companionship of a Family Member							
Utilizing Hunting Skills							
Solitude							
Appreciation of Nature							
Escape From Routine							
Observe Beauty of Nature							
Killing a Trophy Animal							
Doing Better Than My Friends							
Killing Bag Limit							

Lowest   Highest

LEGEND

heads" or those ducks or geese that have definite status. For deer, of course, the rack or weight of a buck were the criteria. The fourth stage, or *method stage* follows. We feel it is characterized by an intensity or almost religious fervor about hunting. The hunter usually owns all the specialized equipment: decoys and retriever, tree stand, programmed cam bow, etc. Hunting becomes one of the most important dimensions of that person's life. It's what he does best and he lives for the opportunity to practice that expertise. Finally, the research findings indicate a *mellowing out* or *sportsman stage* which apparently many hunters do not reach until later in life, or after many years of hunting experience. At this point, the hunter finds satisfac-

> *Many equate harvest with successful hunting in a society that rates success by material acquisition. How many hunters do you know who measure their day, and even their personal worth, by the number of animals they bag?*

tion in the total hunting experience. This hunter no longer hunts to kill but kills to hunt. There is breadth of satisfaction available to him, drawn from contacts with nature, familiar and treasured surroundings, and other important hunting associations. Bagging animals seems more symbolic than essential to the hunting process. Many hunters, influenced by years of experience or perhaps a good model, do not need to kill to find satisfaction in hunting.

To evaluate these hypotheses about the development of motivations and satisfactions through stages, we asked hunters to respond to a list of 20 statements that describe different types of hunter satisfaction (escape, beauty of nature, killing of trophy, getting bag limit, etc.). They rated each of these on a five-point

scale of importance to their satisfaction ranging from *not at all* to *very much.* We compared the ratings of our hunters by years of hunting experience. As shown in Table 2, a pattern of development in satisfaction seems to emerge from these responses. For those hunters with less than five years experience, *killing the bag limit* and *doing better than my friends* received the highest ranking. *Killing the trophy animal* drew the most support from hunters with six to 10 years of experience. For those with 11 or more years, the pattern moved first to *observing nature* and *escaping routine*, next to *appreciating nature, solitude,* and *companionship with family members and friends,* and finally to *exercise* and *outdoor activities* (for those with 30 or more years of hunting experience). Our data seem to support the phase sequence of development about which we theorized. The source of satisfaction changes with experience and with age. We see sequences of development whether we analyze our data by age or by years of hunting experience. We suspect the two are interwoven.

Our findings on satisfaction seem to confirm that these phases of development are also characteristic of bow hunters. We frankly wondered whether these phases of development still held true when the quarry was a trophy animal such as a white-tailed deer. Some hunters suggested that hunting for a trophy represented the ultimate in hunter development and motivation. There would be no further development. Individual contacts and group interviews conducted with members of 20 different bow hunting clubs suggested otherwise. We saw evidence that hunting method (*method stage*) was more important than hunting results (*limiting-out* and *trophy stages*) when hunters talked about selecting and pursuing one particular buck for an entire season. One expert hunter said that he hunted only a wise old doe that he observed for a number of seasons. (She was uniquely marked.) He acknowledged, before other hunters in a group setting, that he passed up more than one buck that season, failed to get the doe, and yet it was one of his most satisfying hunting seasons. We know many bow hunters who returned to the recurve and the longbow after mastering the compound. They told us they were looking for more challenge. For them, satisfaction came more from how they took the deer than from the bagging of a trophy.

Other important data came from a question which

asked the bow hunter to rate how bow hunting attitudes and practices changed since they started bow hunting. As indicated in Table 3, certain hunting behaviors diminished or decreased through years of experience. Responding to a five-point Likkert scale, bow hunters were then asked to rate 17 different factors. Those items showing a decrease included: hunters are *less likely to hunt in groups of eight or more*, are *less likely to participate in both small or large group drives*, and they are *less susceptible to peer pressure to bag game*. In contrast, hunters told us that the following behaviors and attitudes increased: *appreciation of nature, use of tree stands, confidence in filling their tag, shooting and off-season practice, days hunted per season*, and *hunting alone*.

The direction of hunting development over time suggested by the data indicated that bow hunting continues to pull and develop the hunter toward our definition of sport hunting. Spending scores of hours on a stand through a long fall season forces the hunter to become more observant and appreciative of nature; the demands of hunting an animal on a one-to-one basis pressures the hunter to carefully observe habitat and habits. Because of these factors, we believe that bow hunting shapes and directs hunter development and behavior more than almost any other type of hunting.

Compare the bow hunting experience with what one authority described as the essence of environmental education (a curriculum for teaching knowledge and values in our schools). He defined environmental education as a "series of encounters with nature." It is these same encounters with nature that have such an impact on bow hunting and bow hunters.

Table 3. Changes in bow hunters' hunting attitudes and practices over time.

Categories	Percent Decreased	Percent Same	Percent Increased
Interest In Trophy Deer	9.2	36.7	54.1
Susceptibility To Peer Pressure To Bag Game	48.4	41.2	10.3
Shooting, Off-season Practice	13.4	25.8	60.8
Hunting Alone	17.5	37.1	45.4
Hunting With A Partner	20.7	40.2	39.2
Hunting In A Large Group (Eight Or More)	65.6	26.0	8.4
Hunting With Family Members	33.0	38.3	28.7
Distance At Which I Would Normally Shoot	25.3	40.0	34.8
Number Of Hunting Days Per Season	13.5	27.1	59.4
Use Of Tree Stands For Deer Hunting	12.2	21.4	66.3
Stalking Deer	39.6	34.4	26.1
Participation In Small Group Drives	50.5	30.5	18.9
Participation In Large Group Drives (Eight Or More)	72.3	20.2	7.4
Hunting From Ground Blinds	62.3	20.4	17.2
Appreciate Nature As Well As Hunt	0.0	10.4	89.6
Confidence In Filling Deer Tag	6.2	33.0	60.8
Interest In Killing A Deer	21.4	55.1	23.5

We believe there is a recipe for increasing the satisfaction that each of us can find in the hunting experience. The key is in working on aspects of the hunt that you can do something about. Some things you cannot do much or anything about: weather, wildlife populations, activities of other hunters. So concentrate on those factors that you can effectively control.

That means, first and foremost, your own expectations. Do not let the media create your expectations. This is a particular problem with young, inexperienced and self-taught sportsmen who our research suggests are more likely to depend on the media to develop their expectations. Editors and publishers of some magazines decided long ago that their subscribers like to read stories that tell of deer behind every bush, fish all but jumping out of the water into the boat, and trophies abounding everywhere. Obviously, these stories build unrealistic expectations about what hunting really is. And if the writers make the mistake of informing the public about where these bounties are to be found, the sportsman is very likely to discover that these now-famous woodlands are posted because of the increased hunting pressure that emerged from the publicity.

Newspapers do not provide positive expectations when they publicize "big buck" contests and glorify "trophies" with their pictures and stories. Have you ever read a story written by Gordon McQuarrie? His work is now being republished with recognition about how he established a new model of outdoor reporting and writing which emphasized the broad satisfactions to be gained from hunting and fishing. Some other newspapers and outdoor writers approach their assignments with these same values.

Wildlife managers, too, create expectations simply by setting bag limits. Individual users have learned to equate hunting satisfaction with "limiting out." How often have we pushed beyond our physical limits to be able to say, "I filled up." All too many deer hunting parties believe that the measure of their worth is filling up for the party. We talked to one of those parties where one man shot 12 of the 15 bucks bagged by the group. The hunters first bragged about "filling up again this year;" a few minutes later they started muttering about the dissatisfactions they felt with the greedy behavior of the man they called "Killer."

The positive message about expectations is, of course, to shape one's thinking in a way that defines expectations of the hunt in terms of those broader forms of satisfaction that are available whether or not there is a large deer population or whether or not that trophy buck chooses to run by your stand that

> *The authors propose a definition of a true recreational hunt as the opportunity to practice hunting skills under conditions in which the animal is permitted its normal behavior pattern in its natural habitat. Consequently, hunting skills must include an intimate knowledge of the quarry's daily and seasonal activities and of the area being hunted.*

season. Of course, we are referring to exciting encounters with nature, sightings of game and nongame species, and companionship with family and friends. We are convinced that when hunters take time to clarify their values, these things easily emerge in their own value structure as the prime qualities of what really makes hunting so successful and satisfying. Hunters tell us frankly that our interview questions helped them clarify their own values and priorities. We hope, also, that this article triggers some of that assessment among those who read it.

Tradition is another key element in satisfaction and

can be controlled by the individual. When psychologists ask questions about satisfaction that seem difficult to explain, they are often drawn back to an awareness that the satisfaction is to be found where activities have become traditional. Tradition and rituals can elevate any recurring event from mere play to a satisfying lifetime activity. We can also intentionally create our own traditions. (If you have not done that in your own family for Christmas or other holiday celebrations, you are missing something.)

Anticipating and reliving traditional hunting activities dramatically increases satisfaction. It is no wonder, if this is true, that low hunter satisfaction is reported when wildlife managers create "new hunts" under manager-designed conditions. I have tried very carefully to build hunting traditions within my own family. My father did not hunt so I "inherited" none of these. Our rituals and traditions now include a celebration of the beginning of each hunting season through the birthday celebration described earlier in this chapter. We also have traditional hunts at traditional sites the same time each year. We have special breakfasts on the way to the hunt and we have special game dinners.

But the most elaborate traditions and rituals revolve around the deer season. My family may not get home for Christmas, but everyone comes home for the deer season, including a daughter who does not hunt but who recognizes all of the values of the togetherness and celebration that go with this special hunting season. And every year I look forward to this special gathering with even greater anticipation.

Ian McMurchy

Many veteran deer hunters find satisfaction in the total hunting experience. These hunters, influenced by years of experience, do not need to kill to find satisfaction in hunting.

Remember, though, we have not said that we can or should remove the kill from our definition of hunting satisfaction. Bagging animals remains an important element for all of us. But how about helping

> **Editors and publishers of some outdoor magazines decided long ago that their subscribers like to read stories that tell of deer behind every bush and trophies abounding everywhere. Obviously, these stories build unrealistic expectations about what hunting really is.**

North American hunters accept the value that the clean kill is the real standard of successful hunting and not the number or size of the bag. We are not particularly impressed with reports of a hunting party "filling up," or of killing a trophy. We always remember that one-third of all Wisconsin deer hunters did not shoot the deer they tagged. What really did impress us was the fellow who reported he killed each of his last seven deer with one shot. He never said whether they were bucks or does; he didn't need to. That hunter had skill and he had responsibility, more of it than 99 percent of all the hunters we have met.

Finally, the kind of maturity of hunting motivations and satisfactions that we describe depends on a certain degree of maturity and independence in the individual hunter. We believe that the hunting club, group or party usually exerts pressures that hold the hunter back at a lower stage of development. The individual must assert himself, even rebel a bit, to reach beyond the club standards and into the *method* or *sportsman stages*. Put another way, most hunting parties are still at the *limiting-out* or *trophy stage*s in their development. The hunters we interviewed who achieved true sportsman status strike us as individualists; men and women who sorted out their own values and experiences and know who they are and why they hunt. They don't let others determine this for them.

The words of Homer Moe, Wisconsin's former hunter education coordinator, really sum up everything we are trying to say. "You don't go somewhere to have fun, you really take it with you." How great it is if that is true. That means every hunter can control his own satisfaction and success. He does that by dealing with his own self, his expectations and his values.

Editor's Note: "The Deer Hunting Experience" was originally published in the April 1985 issue of Deer & Deer Hunting *magazine.*

EVERYONE IS A HUNTER

Brad Herndon

Some kill wildlife with a gun or bow, some with water pollution and some with habitat destruction. Others kill wildlife with their cars, house windows and in thousands of other ways.

This venison stew is outstanding, Barry! And have you tried that grouse? It melts in your mouth."

I smiled as I listened to the conversations among the guests at my birthday dinner last February 16. I was enjoying watching these people feast on a meal considered a novelty in this day and age — a meal where all the foods served were prepared from items provided by nature, not bought at the grocery store. It was especially rewarding to observe the guests who never before sampled many of the "wild" foods served and to see their faces as they expressed disbelief at how good the foods tasted.

Of course, their reactions didn't surprise me, because delicious wild foods have been commonplace on our dinner table all of my life. My family always hunted, so we never considered meals like this one to be unusual — that is, not until my sixteenth birthday, which was 30 years ago.

For that particular birthday meal, my mother decided to cook only foods that had been killed or gathered from the land. She prepared 12 dishes, all harvested by our family, placed them on the table in front of me and five hunting buddies, and then watched six hungry teenagers wolf them down.

The local, small-town newspaper caught wind of this meal and ran an article on "Herndon's Pioneer Dinner" the next week. The interest it generated among people was astounding. Consequently, since people were so intrigued by the unusual meal, we added new dishes to the menu the next year. From

Yes, I am a hunter and a harvester, but also a caring human being. Essentially, I'm just a middle-aged fellow struggling through life like everyone else.

there our selections simply mushroomed. Some years we served more than 100 different varieties of wild foods that we harvested from the woods and fields of southern Indiana. Several newspapers and a few magazines printed feature articles describing my birthday gatherings. A TV station has even filmed it for its evening news program.

At this meal there are very few foods that I don't truly enjoy. If I had to rank my top 10 favorites, hickory-nut cake would be placed at the top of the list. I believe that if someone tried making off with that cake, a fight would quickly ensue. I've jokingly said that people would kill for that cake.

Which leads me into the heart of this essay: hunting and killing.

As I said, hunting is a way of life in my family.

The meals my wife Carol, daughter JoLinda and I enjoy each day still consist, to a large degree, of foods provided by nature. Venison is our mainstay, while grouse, bluegill, squirrel and rabbit add a diversity of meats to our menu. We also hunt and pick mushrooms, persimmons, wild plums, hickory and other nuts, asparagus and many types of berries.

Harvesting some of these foods requires lining up the sights on a gun, pulling the trigger, and killing an animal. Saying I enjoy doing this — and I do — will be a shocking statement both to hunters and non-hunters alike, because you rarely see this said so openly in print. It should be understood, however, that killing is not the only part of hunting I enjoy. I enjoy figuring out patterns that bring success, especially the challenge of trying to outwit a big white-tailed buck. Being a wildlife photographer, I also derive immense pleasure from the trees, wildflowers, birds and insects that surround me when I'm outdoors. It's a wonderful, fascinating world out there, and I have the greatest respect for God's creation.

But still, when hunting, I derive the most pleasure from harvesting an animal. Most of the time I smile when I'm successful, feeling good about myself for making a good stalk and a humane kill. Sometimes I laugh in happiness, celebrating the culmination of what may be weeks of hard hunting. When I tagged my first white-tailed deer, I whooped and hollered loud enough for someone in the next county to hear me. But there are other feelings, too.

Several times I reverently knelt beside a dead white-tailed buck with tears running down my cheeks, marveling at the majesty of the animal. A deer must die, as we all must die, but my utmost concern is for the animal I harvest to die as quickly and painlessly as possible. And with dignity.

An old Indian proverb says, "To give dignity to a man is above all things." Tragically, we all know that many of the illnesses we humans contract can strip us of all of our dignity before we pass from this earth. Conversely, a deer walking into the sights of a gun held by a competent hunter will suffer no such loss of stateliness.

Yes, I am a hunter and a harvester, but also a caring human being. Essentially, I'm just a middle-aged fellow struggling through life like everyone else. I try to be a decent person and as honest as possible.

And that's what I'm doing now: being honest. Too

many outdoor writers pussyfoot around the edges of hunting, saying the hunt is the most enjoyable part of the sport. Sometimes I wonder why they even carry a bow or a gun. Sure, we all enjoy the hunt immensely, and I have many fond memories of days spent afield when no animal was taken. But if we're honest with ourselves, the hunt isn't comparable to the thrill of success.

Assuming that animals bagged are put to good use, there is nothing wrong with enjoying the killing of them. Ethical hunting only removes the excess animals that sound wildlife management provides. Regulated hunting ensures that populations of hunted animals remain stable from year to year, provided the habitat remains intact. That is a scientific fact.

Nevertheless, some people disapprove of my way of life. They dislike me for what I do.

Their feelings, unfortunately, have been caused by a general lack of understanding about the sport of hunting. I believe that hunters are partially at fault for this because many never take the time to calmly and concisely explain hunting and the wildlife/habitat cycle to non-hunters. One other factor, the Bambi myth, also has been responsible for many of the disagreements between hunters and non-hunters. The Bambi scene usually goes like this:

An unshaven, rough-looking hunter in camouflage clothing lurks behind a tree. In his hands he grips a gun that looks big enough to kill an elephant. Shortly, a motherless white-tailed fawn bounces down the trail and pauses in front of his tree, quizzically looking at the hunter. The hunter picks out one of the 350 spots on the fawn's body, aims and blows it to smithereens. After rushing over to needlessly slit its throat and bleed it out, he pats himself on the back. As if that weren't enough, he then ties the fawn on his car and proudly parades around town, with blood dripping down the side of the car's fender.

That is an unfair and inaccurate appraisal of what actually takes place in the deer woods each fall. Although harvesting young deer is now legal, and necessary, in many states because of deer overpopulation problems, three things should be understood: Fawns are almost as big as their mothers during hunting season; rarely do they have any spots at that time of year; and they are entirely self-sufficient by then.

I readily admit, however, that a few deer hunters do some pretty gruesome things. Disgustingly, some hunters kill too many deer, use other people's tags, poach and cheat in every conceivable manner they can think of. Yes, deer hunting contains its share of crude and dishonest miscreants. Similarly, we also find people of this kind in government, social clubs and churches.

Fortunately, we do find a better class of people overall in good organizations than in bad ones. Wherever we go and whatever we do, we'll run into the good, the bad and the in-between. I once heard a journalist speak who had traveled throughout the world. He said he had learned one very important

Brad Herndon

"Herndon's Pioneer Dinner" has become a family tradition on the author's birthday. The meal consists entirely of wild foods that have been killed or gathered from the woods and fields of southern Indiana.

fact during his travels: "Wherever you go in this world, people are people." With the knowledge that there is a cross section of people in all facets of life, including deer hunting, and that many of them are good, conscientious people, let's move on to why I feel everyone, regardless of our hobbies or interests, is a hunter.

Webster provides several definitions of "hunt." One definition says that to hunt is "to pursue (animals) for food or in sport." Another meaning is "to search carefully for; to attempt to find something." Whether I'm looking for blackberries, hickory nuts or deer, the steps I go through when hunting each one are basically the same. First, I determine where the subject will most likely be found. This is interesting, gives the mind a lot of work, and often involves considerable walking. It also can be challenging. Sometimes, finding a good blackberry patch in a drought year is every bit as hard as killing a deer. This searching, or hunting, for something that you aren't really sure is there is intriguing. To find the very best location is challenging; to harvest the item is fun.

But it's in the harvesting where we encounter mixed terminology, depending on whether one is a hunter or non-hunter. I pick a blackberry; I kill a deer.

Now let's make a comparison between my interests and the interests of a woman my age who lives in a large city to see how we both are hunters. This woman needs a new dress, so she plans to spend a Saturday looking (hunting) through all the dress shops in town for a bargain. During the course of the day she finds several styles she likes but is especially attracted to three particular dresses. Comparing prices, she buys (kills) the one with the best value. After arriving home, she tells her family what a great bargain she got (what a good hunter she is). Then she tries on the dress for their approval (so they can see what a fine specimen it is). During the next three weeks she wears it to a fine restaurant, a wedding reception and to church (to show it to others, much like I do my mounted deer). Everyone is favorably impressed — she is a good hunter.

Most of you, whether male or female, will probably agree it was much more exciting for the woman to buy (kill) a dress than to shop all day and come home empty-handed. To carry the hunting/shopping comparison further, consider that just as there are unethical hunters in the deer woods, so also are there unethical hunters in the dress shops. The lady in my example paid for the dress she bought, while others shoplift dresses or place a lower price tag on them. In all aspects of life, we run into the good, the bad and the in-between.

Obviously, there is nothing wrong with a person going shopping, and there is nothing wrong with me going through the same basic processes to kill a deer. The fact of the matter is that if we studied every aspect of life — job hunting, car shopping, looking for a spouse — we would find that hunting is hunting, regardless of the quarry.

Hopefully, you can see how all of us are hunters; it's only the "game" we pursue that differs. Still, a person who disapproves of hunting animals might agree that he is a "hunter" and still think, "At least I'm not a killer." But, we are all killers, each in his own way. Using true-to-life situations, I will illustrate why this is true.

The first example involves a small woods near my hometown. I've spent a lot of time in that woodlot over the years picking berries, hunting mushrooms and squirrel hunting. Friends have killed quail, raccoons, opossums, deer and several other varieties of wildlife there. For as long as I can remember, it has produced an abundance of delicious wild foods. Last year a decision was made to build a shopping center in that location. In a short time, the bulldozers and other heavy equipment cleared off every tree and leveled the ground in preparation for the coming stores. It won't be long now until the only visible objects there will be stores and an asphalt parking lot.

Never again will that area be a haven for wildlife. The deer, raccoons, foxes and squirrels are only a distant memory now. The songs of numerous birds, such as the robin, bluebird and cardinal, will never again provide cheerful music to the ears of passersby.

I'll let you be the judge. Are there any killers of wildlife involved here? If there are, who are they? The developers? The heavy equipment operators? The people who will patronize the stores? Or possibly all of them?

Let me use another example, hypothetical but commonplace, to explain the destruction of wildlife. This time it's a 200-acre tract of ground near a large metropolitan area. The tract contains gently rolling, wooded hills interspersed with grain fields — a beautiful area for home sites to accommodate the influx of workers migrating to the city. A large realty company buys the property, subdivides it, and within three years a new home stands on every lot. A few trees remain for birds to nest in; the culverts provide a home for a few raccoons. Even a few quail, rabbits and other sundry wildlife can be observed, but for all practical purposes the majority of the wildlife disappeared because their habitat was destroyed. Again I ask: "Are there any killers of wildlife involved here? Who are they? The realtor, the home builders, or the families who bought homes in the subdivision? Or, are they all killers?"

> **Whether I'm looking for blackberries, hickory nuts or deer, the steps I go through when hunting each one are basically the same.**

When I discussed these two scenarios with several people, most of them found it extremely difficult to understand why most of the wildlife died when the woods were destroyed. Most people asked, "Won't the animals just move into another forested area?" I told them, sadly, that the animals might move, yet they would still die eventually.

A given woods will only support a limited amount of wildlife. Even though a woods with green trees may look lush to a person travelling by, its food supply is finite. Reserves of nuts for resident squirrels will be eaten by the added squirrels. Insects may become in short supply for the birds, and there may no longer be a sufficient number of small animals for the predatory animals to feed on. Let me clarify how this system works with an example using people instead of animals.

Imagine that one house in your neighborhood is torn down every year. Each year, when this happens,

the people in the house torn down are forced to move in with you for food and shelter. The catch is, you aren't allowed to increase the size of your house or to buy any more food than normal. Basically, your house and yard will look the same to casual observers, although they might notice a slight increase in human activity. But I ask you, for how many years could this continue before you and the others in your home starved to death? Not many, as you can readily see. This is exactly what happens to wildlife when a woods is destroyed; eventually they die because the forest they move into can supply only a limited amount of food per year. The forest can't increase production on demand.

Other forms of wildlife, such as aquatic life, also suffer from our presence on earth. In June 1988 a sewage treatment plant in Indianapolis quit functioning properly. For eight hours this went undetected while tens of thousands of gallons of raw sewage poured into, first, Williams Creek and then into the White River. As a result, an estimated 14,000 fish died. It really makes no difference on whose waste these fish suffocated, a hunter's, a non-hunter's or an anti-hunter's. Because of their very existence, all of these people were, unintentionally, killers that day.

Insects seem insignificant, and we destroy billions of them each year with electric bug zappers and lawn, garden and farm chemicals. Unknowingly, we also kill thousands of birds by destroying their food supply. Some insects, however, such as butterflies, are considered beautiful. Years ago, while on a vacation trip out west, I kept track of the number of monarch butterflies I hit and killed with my car. When I multiplied that number, 12, by the number of vehicles traveling on our highways that year, I was amazed that there were any monarch butterflies left at all. Now, 20 years later, they are on the concerned species list.

And while we're on the subject of wildlife killed by cars, it's worth mentioning that hundreds of thousands of deer are killed on our highways each year, the majority of them by non-hunters because they comprise a majority of the population. If we added to the list the rabbits, squirrels, snakes and birds killed by motor vehicles, it would run into the tens of millions.

The list of the ways that all of us are killers of

wildlife is almost endless. The windows in our homes break the necks of millions of birds per year and even watching TV, a seemingly harmless activity, kills birds. On September 20, 1957, migrating birds flew into a TV tower in Eau Claire, Wisconsin, resulting in the deaths of 20,000 warblers, thrushes, tanagers and other birds. As I said, the list is almost endless.

> *There are those who disapprove of my life. They dislike me for what I do. Their feelings, unfortunately, have been caused by a general lack of understanding about the sport of hunting.*

Throughout this essay I have tried to show, in my own simple way, how all of us are hunters. Whether it's me hunting a deer, a woman hunting for a dress, a man shopping for a new car, or my mother looking for a new recipe, we all are hunters. And, in my own simple way, I have illustrated how we each are killers of wildlife. Some kill wildlife with a gun, some with water pollution and some with habitat destruction. Others kill wildlife with their cars, house windows and in thousands of other ways.

I hope that each reader can see me for what I am: a hunter who loves wildlife and nature. I have a love for each of God's creatures. Man was given dominion over all the creatures on this earth, and by being an ethical hunter, I am simply exercising a God-given right. On the other hand, those who are non-hunters of wildlife also have the right to enjoy life in their own ethical way. I have the greatest respect for each of them, for I understand that hunting wildlife is not for everyone.

For us deer hunters, that means we need to toughen up and eliminate the poachers, thieves and slob hunters from our sport. If that means turning in a friend, so be it. Others in society need to upgrade their standards, too. Millions of tons of trash are thrown along our roadsides every year by travelers. Our streams are polluted with oil, chemicals and waste; our air is unhealthy to breathe in many regions. These things must be corrected.

Tragically, if we continue on our suicidal path, all the while increasing our country's population every year, we will eventually be a nation consisting only of people and, hopefully, enough land to feed the people. Nothing else will remain.

In summing up, a short movie I saw comes to mind. It depicted the deplorable situation on earth, especially the pollution. Happily, the people finally realized how critical the conditions were and began working together to solve the complex problems. There was hope! Then the screen blackened. Shortly, a slow illumination moved across the screen, accompanied by an eerie wind. Buildings became visible, along with abandoned cars, roads and other landmarks. Immediately one noticed the absence of human activity. There was no greenery to be seen; the barrenness was overwhelming. Gradually the view focused in on a billboard so tattered that its message was not readable. Just then, the wind gusted briskly, just enough to lift the paper on the billboard and reveal its solemn message: "Help Save Earth." The revelation was clear: They had been too late.

Yes, the issue is of more magnitude than hunting or not hunting. Perhaps if each of us sees and respects the other's views, and if all of us join together to instill good ethics in all phases of life, we can preserve this beautiful planet for our children and our children's children. Perhaps we won't be too late.

Editor's Note: "Everyone Is A Hunter" was originally published in the October 1989 issue of Deer & Deer Hunting *magazine.*

Everyone Is A Hunter

ON THE SAME WAVELENGTH

I recently came across the incredible article written by Brad Herndon ("Everyone Is A Hunter") and published in the October 1989 issue of *Deer & Deer Hunting*. The magazine's staff should be congratulated for producing an excellent magazine with informative material such as that written by Herndon. It hit home so hard that I had to respond.

I live in Virginia but was recently in the beautiful state of Wisconsin on business where I happened upon the article in the latest issue of *Deer & Deer Hunting*. My hat is off to Herndon for his well-written article. It is difficult to find people with his obvious love and appreciation of the sport of hunting and of nature. These attributes are seldom found together with the obvious sincerity he holds. To show how close we are on the same "wavelength," let me give you a brief background of myself.

I am 25 years old, married, a devoted hunter and about a year ago I received a position with a company making an impressive salary for a guy fresh out of college. One week ago, I placed my two-week notice with the company for two reasons. First, the job requires working a lot of hours which would significantly cut into, if not eliminate, my hunting. This I could suffer through if it meant providing for my family. But secondly, and more importantly, it requires travel to various locations across the United States where I witnessed myriad industries polluting our skies and waters with smoke and other industrial waste. This got to the point where I could no longer bear to watch it or continue to participate in it. I have been bombarded with ridicule from family and friends for quitting such a lucrative job for such a seemingly ridiculous motive, especially with a family to support and no other employment to fall back on.

I enjoy deer and turkey hunting (gun and bow alike) in the Virginia woods. I have hunted since I was 12, in the very same places where my great grandfather walked three generations ago.

My feelings of great sadness also parallel Herndon's when I come across a dead animal which painfully and wastefully died without being recovered by its human predator. I would be the first to admit to having taken a poor shot or rushed a shot in my excitement to bag a trophy buck, but I'll search all night to find it before giving up.

Well, I arrive home in a week, unemployed and frustrated, but hunting season is open and I'll have time to regroup and plan a job-search from atop my tree stand. Here I can find the strength and courage to face the tribulations of the "outside" world hunters seek to overcome.

— *William E. Corl III*
Portsmouth, Virginia

SUPER PHILOSOPHY

Just a note to commend Brad Herndon on his article, "Everyone Is A Hunter," which appeared in the October 1989 issue of *Deer & Deer Hunting* magazine. It is one of the best I've ever read.

The article was full of super philosophy, but it's too bad it appeared in a publication that few, if any, anti- or non-hunters are going to read. I think it would do a lot of good if we all showed the article to anti-hunters and non-hunters alike. It would clear up a lot of ignorance and negative feelings while, at the same time, opening their eyes to the fact that hunting is here to stay whether they like it or not.

— *Alan D. Martin*
Caledonia, Wisconsin

MANDATORY READING

The article, "Everyone Is A Hunter," by Brad Herndon is, without a doubt, the best article I have read in quite some time. The author does a wonderful job of telling it like it is concerning the human impact on wildlife. I find the ignorance or arrogance of some people, especially the non-hunting public, about this issue to be totally unacceptable. The attitude seems to be that hunters are responsible for the loss of many wildlife species when, in fact, the most serious threat to wildlife is habitat destruction through human encroachment and pollution. It has been my experience that sportsmen (hunters) express more concern about these issues than non-hunters. Perhaps by being involved in the sport of hunting we gain a knowledge and respect for our environment that cannot be gained in other ways.

Deer & Deer Hunting magazine should be proud of Herndon and his article. It says a lot. In my opinion, it should be made mandatory reading at the elementary school level. I look forward to reading more of this author's work, along with the many other informative, educational and entertaining articles I find in this superb magazine.

— *Craig A. Cantley*
Charleston, West Virginia

1993 Harvest Seasons   Premier Issue

DEER & DEER HARVESTING

PRACTICAL AND COMPREHENSIVE INFORMATION FOR DEER HARVESTERS

NEW
DEER
HARVEST
GEAR

BOW
HARVESTING
IN THE 1990s

TRANSPORTING
YOUR HARVEST

TEACHING THE YOUNG DEER HARVESTER

Len Rue, Jr.

Harvesting Deer And Liberating Animals

Lee Nisbet

Why do well-intentioned hunters seem to think they can't tell the truth about what they do? Does a certain part of the hunting population really think there is something wrong with pursuing and killing animals in a sporting manner? Or do some hunters think that by speaking candidly about what they do, why they do it and what they experience, that their honesty will doom the sport?

Imagine that you were unable to go deer hunting on opening day. At noon you phone your buddy who owns the farm where you will hunt tomorrow. You want to find out if he shot a deer. His wife answers:

"Hello Doris. Is Frank still out hunting?"

"He's not hunting; he's out harvesting."

"What?" you exclaim. "On opening day Frank's out harvesting?"

"He's trying to harvest a deer," Doris replies.

You laugh, "OK, OK, so he is trying to kill that big buck!"

"No, no!" Doris protests. "He is not trying to kill him; he's trying to harvest him!"

Scratching your head, you hang up and walk out to the mailbox. Excitedly you pull out your favorite hunting magazine. You look at the cover and notice a shocking change. It's no longer *Deer & Deer Hunting* magazine. Instead, the logo now reads *Deer & Deer Harvesting*. Further, it has a new editor, Charles Chameleon. Up front, in an editorial statement, Mr. Chameleon explains that the former editor, knowledgeable historian of deer hunting as well as expert hunter and writer, produced a magazine that was too candid. Henceforth, no deer will be hunted and killed within the pages of the magazine. Instead, all deer will be "harvested."

Secondly, at the delicate "moment of harvest," deer will not thrash about, spurt blood or run off leaving blood trails. All deer will now drop dead instantly. They will not twitch or foul the environment with bodily fluids. In short, deer at the "moment of harvest" will deport themselves respectably.

As an example of the materials that will now appear in the magazine, the new editor recommends this issue's lead article by Fred Furtive entitled "How To Get Your Harvest Home Without Horrifying Anti-

> *Why do animal rights groups oppose sport hunting even though the consequences for wildlife populations would be disastrous without it? The answers should help cure "harvesters" from travelling the same propaganda route as our animal rights foes.*

Hunters — Actual or Potential." You find that Mr. Furtive recommends (1) transporting your "harvest" only at night on back roads and (2) covering "nature's bounty" with a Christmas tree. Unseemly "displays of harvests," he warns, could doom the entire "harvest of the autumn crop."

Does all this sound ridiculous? It sure does to me. Sadly, this imaginary scenario criticizes an actual vocabulary and set of recommendations and ideas used and advocated by some hunters, writers and wildlife managers here and abroad. I satirize these ideas, recommendations and vocabulary because they are a contrived attempt to cover up the nature of the activity of hunting.

Technically, the term "deer-harvesters" is a euphemism, the substitution of an inoffensive term

for one considered offensively explicit. In short, euphemisms are the propaganda of those who have something to hide. The Nazis and Soviets, for example, referred to their murder campaigns as the "Final Solution" and "liquidation." They sanitized murder by making it sound like a chemical process. Do we hunters have something similar to hide that requires the use of dishonest language and false analogies? As both a hunter and a philosophy professor, I think not. It requires only a little thinking to see that pursuing and attempting to kill a deer according to the legal and ethical standards of the sport have nothing in common with an agriculturalist raising a food crop. Even if one raised deer for the market, he would slaughter them, not "harvest" them.

Wildlife managers maintain deer populations through hunting, but the vocabulary of farming has no relevance to this activity. From the deer manager's point of view, professional cullers could reduce herds more efficiently than sport hunters. Whether the dead deer were simply left to rot or if the meat was sold on the market, the process of stalking deer and killing them bears no resemblance to growing a vegetable crop and harvesting it.

Why do well-intentioned hunters seem to think they can't tell the truth about what they do? Does a certain part of the hunting population really think there is something wrong with pursuing and killing animals in a sporting matter? Or do some hunters think that by speaking candidly about what they do, why they do it and what they experience, that their honesty will doom the sport? Hidden in this latter fear is the assumption that there is something wrong with hunting and, if we tell the truth, other people will see that it's wrong also. I don't think that turning hunters into phony farmers out "harvesting" serves our cause.

If some "deer harvesters" genuinely feel uncomfortable with some aspects of their sport, then they must half believe the propaganda of another group of truth twisters, the "animal liberators." The animal liberation/animal rights movement has indeed gained media attention and, as we shall see, is scoring "victories" against hunting. Do their media and political successes, however, prove rightness in their moral claims? Let's examine the movement and subject its moral assumptions to careful philosophical scrutiny.

Newsweek magazine, in its December 26, 1988 issue, featured the animal liberation movement in its cover story. The article estimated that there are 7,000 animal protection groups in the United States with combined memberships of 10 million people and budgets in excess of $50 million. Other articles regularly appear in the opinion columns of newspapers bearing headlines such as "Animals Are The Victims of Vast Slavery Systems." The wire services carry numerous stories on animal liberation and animal rights groups' activities and causes. In one "direct action," for example, an animal liberation group "liberated" 27 cats from an agricultural research facility and pledged that the cats would "be placed in caring, permanent homes." Unfortunately, 11 of the cats were infected with a disease particularly dangerous to human fetuses.

Other stories feature the work of The Humane Society, which is presently mounting a particularly successful campaign to drive up the cost of research animals to make their use in experiments prohibitive. *The Wall Street Journal,* in a recent editorial against such activities, pointed out that animal rights activists persuaded six states to ban the use of inexpensive pound animals for medical research, forcing scientists to use more costly animals. For example, the successful repeal of the Metcalf-Hatch Act in New York State by animal rights groups has driven up the price of research animals from $20 to $200. The editorial quotes Dr. Michael DeBakey, the world-renowned pioneer in open heart surgery, in testimony before Congress that animal rights groups are succeeding in pricing important medical research projects out of existence.

Legislation before Congress in 1989 would have prevented the National Institute of Health from using pound animals when conducting research, even though five million of those pound animals (strays) will be killed anyway. This bill was opposed by the American Medical Association and the Association of Animal Medical Colleges. Such legislation, as noted, affects research on all sorts of deadly human diseases as well as diseases in animals. Animal research, for example, has been essential for the development of insulin, polio vaccine, rabies treatments, open heart surgery, cancer research, AIDS research, and vaccines for animal diseases. As Dr. John A. Krasney (1984), Professor of Physiology at the University of New York at Buffalo points out, ". . . virtually every biomedical advance can be traced to original critical

studies using animals. Indeed, the extension of the average life span from 45 years at the turn of the century to 70-plus years today is dependent in a major way on animal studies. The value of animal research has been proved beyond any doubt."

Dr. Krasney's view is supported by virtually all of the mainstream researchers in human and animal disease. In September 1988, in response to attacks by antivivisectionists on research using animals, a panel of the prestigious National Academy of Sciences concluded that animals are "critical" to medical research and that no new laws are necessary for governing such research. The panel also concluded that abuse in animal research is uncommon.

Brad Herndon

What hunter seeks to cause unnecessary pain and suffering in animals? We strive to kill the animal quickly by picking our shots carefully and by using a weapon that has the capacity to kill quickly when a vital area is hit.

Another newspaper article quoted Dr. Thomas Hamm of the Stanford University Medical Center: "We are under constant threat of break-in. A number of valuable colleagues are leaving because they cannot adjust to the harassment." The animal liberationist's tactics, however, go beyond harassment and intimidation. On April 3, 1987, a group called the Animal Liberation Front (ALF) set fire to a building being constructed on the University of California-Davis campus to house research on diseases in farm animals. The fire resulted in $3.5 million worth of damage. The ALF says farms are part of the "capitalist agribusiness" which they claim "tortures" animals. In November 1988, animal liberationist Fran Stephanie Trutt was arrested for planting a radio-controlled bomb designed to murder an executive of a company that uses animals for research. Through vandalism, harassment, arson, terrorism, legislation, political lobbying and especially through the adroit use of propaganda, various liberation and rights groups are being successful in limiting the use of animals in research.

A classic example of this deceptive and effective media campaign appeared in *Glamour* magazine. In a feature article in *Glamour,* a magazine read by millions of women, a story appeared on animal research. Its headline read "Do House Pets Belong In Research Labs?" Immediately above the headline appeared the pictures of a lovable puppy and kitten. Reading the article closely reveals that (although the author does not say so) the "house pets" in question are strays or pets given up to the animal shelters and that they will be killed (not "put to sleep") if not sold to research labs. The author recommends that readers write to The Humane Society for a "fact sheet." She provides not only a quote from the president of The Human Society, but their address. She never informs the readers that this group is an animal rights group. The author of this "objective" piece, Margaret Engel, is identified as a reporter for the *Washington Post* and a past winner of a Nieman Journalism Fellowship to Harvard. The fellowship apparently did little for her journalistic ethics.

As hunters are realizing, these same groups want to abolish our sport. These groups are already engaging in outright harassment of hunters in the woods, court and legislative efforts to ban hunting in various federal and state reserves and lands where hunting is now permitted, and have launched numerous attacks on the sport in the print and visual media. These attacks are having an impact. As reported in the *American Hunter* magazine, for example, the U.S. Fish and Wildlife Service, in conjunction with the *Reader and Senior Weekly Reader,* found that 79 percent of the fifth and sixth graders polled disapprove of sport hunting and 42 percent disapprove of hunting for food.

What is the animal liberation movement? Why exactly do animal liberation and rights groups oppose using animals in research regardless of the disastrous consequences for both humans and animals if such research were discontinued? Why do they oppose sport hunting even though the consequences for wildlife populations would be disastrous without it? The answers, I think, will help cure "harvesters" from travelling the same propaganda route as our animal rights foes.

The animal liberation movement of today is self-professedly one of the few remnants of the New Left political movement that survived the end of the Vietnam War. Like many other "liberation" movements, many of the philosophical proponents of the movement claim the right to use whatever means are effective to advance their cause including personal intimidation, vandalism, arson and even murder. The movement's national magazine, *The Animals' Agenda* had, for example, a fascinating debate on the use of arson and terrorism (they call it "direct action") in their September 1987 issue. Some "liberationists" openly approve of terrorism and those who condemn it do so only for tactical, not ethical, reasons: It might bring bad publicity to the movement.

The movement's real effectiveness, however, lies in its skill in using ethical or moral issues to promote its political agenda. These issues are promoted in such a way so as to "raise the consciousness" of the public so that Americans will turn against hunting, trapping, the use of animals in medical research, the use of animals for food and the entire sociopolitical economic system that supports these supposed atrocities. Every hunter should know exactly what these supposed "ethical" arguments are, and especially what their weaknesses are. Once we understand that the animal liberation-rights position has no moral or ethical credibility whatsoever, maybe hunters will feel more confident about discussing and promoting their sport more aggressively and honestly instead of with euphemistic language!

Peter Singer, the Australian philosopher, is regarded by the animal liberation movement as its philosophical founder. Singer, in articles in 1973 and in his book, *Animal Liberation* (1976), specifically connects this newest liberation movement to those of blacks, gays and women. The first concern of animal liberators is "consciousness raising." Singer explains that "a liberation movement demands an expansion of our moral horizons so practices previously regarded as natural and inevitable are now seen as intolerable."

Animals, Singer claims, are discriminated against in exactly the same way blacks, gays and women have been. Their interests have not been treated equally relative to the interests of other groups. He points out that moral equality is not strictly dependent on factual equality. Differences in intelligence between human beings, for example, do not confer greater moral weight to the claims of the more intelligent. Singer (1973) thus raises this question: "If possessing greater intelligence does not entitle one human to exploit another, why should it entitle humans to exploit nonhumans?"

Now we see one reason why Singer and his followers are successful. Those not trained in reasoning may not recognize that Singer's question is leading. It disguises an unproven assertion (nonhumans are exploited by humans) as a question which leads one to answer in the way Singer wants. In short, a legitimate version of Singer's propaganda trick would be this question: Is using animals for human purposes such as medical research, hunting, food, etc. unethical? Singer does not answer with an unqualified "yes" as do those who believe in animal rights. Singer (1987) specifically criticizes the view that animals have absolute rights which cannot be overridden by any consideration whatsoever as insupportable, arbitrary and ultimately ridiculous. If a moose, for example, has the absolute right to be unmolested, then every wolf that successfully kills a moose is "guilty" of violating his rights.

Singer, instead, maintains that animals don't have rights but "interests" which demand "equal consideration" with those of humans. Singer claims that both humans and nonhumans have an "interest" in avoidance of "unnecessary pain." That is, the moral status of animals rests not on the capacity to reason, which they lack, but upon their capacity to experience pain. Any act, therefore, that causes unnecessary pain in any animal, human or nonhuman, is unethical. In sum, we must give the same consideration to suffering in animals as we give to suffering in humans.

According to Singer (1987), this means that an experimenter is guilty of unwarranted "bias for his own species whenever he carries out an experiment in a nonhuman for a purpose that he would not think justified him using a human being . . ." In short, Singer argues that mice, chimps and other mammals are just as sensitive to pain as a human infant and if we wouldn't use a human infant for a particular experiment, we shouldn't use an animal. Likewise, if we can get sufficient nourishment from eating plants which (we think) are incapable of suffering, then we shouldn't use animals for food. Sport hunting, an activity which revolves around the satisfaction gained from pursuing, killing and usually consuming an animal, is also supposedly unethical from the viewpoint provided by Singer's standard.

Bill Vaznis

It is factually wrong to claim that animal pain and human pain are equivalent and deserve equivalent moral consideration. The dimensions of human suffering are of a far greater magnitude and of a different kind than animal suffering

If Singer is correct, then animal experimentation would have to be radically restricted, vegetarianism substituted for meat eating and hunting should be outlawed. This agenda is exactly what animal liberation-rights groups are working so hard at to achieve.

But wait, you say, if Singer claims the "interests" of animals are equally as important as human interests in all cases, that seems just as ridiculous as claiming that animals have "rights" that can never be violated. If you were lost in the Arctic, for example, could you not eat your sled dogs to survive? Singer would agree that ethically you could. He is not claiming that the interests of animals are always of equal importance to those of humans as animal rights advocates do, but rather that the animals' interests demand equal consideration.

> *Once we understand that the animal liberation-rights position has no moral or ethical credibility whatsoever, maybe hunters will feel more confident about discussing and promoting their sport more aggressively and honestly instead of with euphemistic language!*

Singer (1987) uses this example to illustrate his point:

"What, for example, are we doing about legitimate conflicts of interests, like rats biting small children? I'm not sure of the answer, but the essential point is that we do see this as a conflict of interests, that we recognize that rats have interests too. Then we may begin to think of other ways of resolving the conflict, perhaps by leaving out rat baits that sterilize the rats instead of killing them."

Singer means, therefore, by "equal consideration" of interests not that rats count as much as children, but by taking the rats' "interests" into account we might deal with them in a less painful way. Likewise, the anti-hunter now argues that instead of killing deer to keep their numbers in balance with food supplies, reduce auto-deer collisions, etc. a contraceptive drug for deer be developed. Newspaper articles indicate that some wildlife managers are giving this proposal serious consideration, especially concerning deer living in suburban areas.

Many people might think Singer's rat example is ridiculous, but growing numbers might favor Singer's argument when it comes to the white-tailed deer, just as many have found his reasoning quite persuasive when it comes to killing baby seals for fur and using bunnies, doggies, kitties and chimps for important laboratory experiments.

Is Singer right? Should we eliminate meat eating, radically restrict experiments on animals that serve vital human purposes and eliminate hunting? The answer is no and here is why.

Singer's conclusions rest on a number of claims: (1) That animals have interests. (2) That animals suffer exactly the same kind of pain that humans suffer. (3) That the "unnecessary pain and suffering" standard can be shown to be incompatible with experimentation, meat eating and hunting. If any of these claims are false or insupportable, Singer's animal liberation argument falls apart. All of these claims are either false or insupportable.

As philosopher R.G. Frey (1979) points out in an article entitled "Rights, Interests, Desires and Beliefs," to say that animals have interests in the same way humans do is false. To claim, for example, that it is in an individual animal's interest to avoid being shot does not mean that the animal desires not to be shot. As Frey points out, even if it is in a tractor's "interest" to have regular oil changes, we can't say it desires or wants an oil change. It is not only because a tractor lacks feeling that it can't desire, but it can't desire because it lacks speech. Allow me to elaborate. Only through speech, using symbols according to rules of grammar, can we figure out what it is that we want and whether what we want is good or bad for us. Tractors, for the reason of lacking speech, can't desire and neither, for the same reason, can animals. They can't talk. They have no sense of the future consequences of present action. They certainly have needs, but to have desires you must not only have needs but speech.

Deer do communicate through gestures (sounds, tails held erect, etc.) and respond to visual stimuli (rubs and scrapes), but without words they are locked into the present. Without words, deer can't anticipate or know a future. They are dependent on present scent and present auditory and visual stimuli. Their habits developed over time, combined with their senses, determine present response to present stimuli. A big buck doesn't "figure out" how to avoid you. His developed habits functioning in the present through his sensory apparatuses help him to avoid you. A consistently successful big buck hunter is one who has learned a particular buck's habits and knows exactly the limits of the animal's sensory apparatuses. So it may very well be in a buck's interests to sleep through opening day, but they can't know that. To return to Professor Frey's point, animals without speech have "interests" only in the way that tractors do. If we don't give a tractor's interests moral consideration equivalent to humans, we can't give equal moral consideration to the "interests" of animals either, at least for that reason.

The points made above concerning interests and their relation to language destroy another of Singer's key assumptions: The ability to experience pain is the basis for giving animals' "interests" moral consideration equivalent to that of humans' interests. In short, animals not only don't have interests in the way humans do, but the pain of animals is not equivalent to the pain of humans.

Philosopher Donald Van De Veer (1979), in an article entitled "Interspecific Justice," argues that the pain and suffering of more complex psychological beings deserves more moral consideration than that of less complex beings. Why? Consider this example: Would the pain of a steer being castrated and a man being castrated against his will be the same? The answer is obviously no. For humans, there can be much more to suffering then merely painful sensations. A human can, through imagination, project the awful consequences of present suffering into the future and also suffer through the memory of past trauma. In short, Singer is factually wrong to claim that animal pain and human pain are equivalent and deserve equivalent moral consideration. The dimensions of human suffering are of a far greater magnitude and of a different kind than animal suffering. A terrorist's bomb on an airliner will change the entire lives of the grieving loved ones. No such tragedy befalls or could befall an animal mother.

Singer's "equal consideration" argument is based on a false analogy and hence fails.

Allow me to show that Singer's moral standard — we should always seek to minimize pain and suffering — is perfectly compatible with all the activities Singer condemns.

A colleague once invited me to be a guest lecturer at an animal liberationist's class dealing with ethics and animals. When I indicated I was a hunter, he immediately pointed out that hunting was incompatible with Singer's dictum that we should not cause unnecessary pain to animals. As a teacher of logic, I pointed out that Singer's standard was a classic example of the fallacy of begging the question. In plain English, the standard is so broad it's compatible with any of the activities that animal liberationists criticize. What hunter, for example, seeks to cause unnecessary pain in animals? We want to kill the animal and kill it quickly. An ethical hunter picks his shots carefully and uses a weapon that has the capacity to kill quickly when a vital area is hit. Likewise, in medical research, ethical procedures seek to minimize any suffering in the animal and, indeed, many experiments become invalid if the animal is stressed by pain.

After making these points, the animal liberationist seemed perplexed. I then pointed out that in some species, such as white-tailed deer, hunting was necessary for maintenance of the health of the species. That is, not killing a certain percentage of the herd would be incompatible with Singer's unnecessary suffering principle. In short, there is no "unnecessary" suffering in general but only unnecessary suffering in specific cases. That is, even if you held to this standard you would still have to determine in each case whether an animal's suffering was unnecessary or not. But again the standard begs the question of what is "unnecessary suffering," that is, unnecessary to whom? If I want to hunt and kill a deer, I must inflict some pain in the animal. As long as I seek to minimize that suffering, my actions do take the animal into account. I wish to use the animal in a certain way, but I also want to minimize the suffering of the animal. Unnecessary suffering, from my point of view, would be wounding a deer due to use of an inadequate weapon or taking a shot that is knowingly outside of the limits of my abilities.

The liberationist then pointed out that what he meant is that I didn't "need" to hunt at all; that is what he meant by "unnecessary." I pointed out that I didn't "need" to make love either in the sense that I would die if I didn't. I, however, want to make love because it makes my life better. Likewise I hunt because it enriches my life and I am quite willing to sacrifice a wild animal in a way that enriches my life. In short, for me to enrich my life through the hunting of animals it is necessary for me to occasionally kill them. Since wounding them and having them get away ruins my experience, it is necessary to take every precaution to avoid this. Likewise, if a researcher wants to find out certain things, it may be necessary to kill an animal. If this is the best way, or the only way, to find out these things, and if these things have a beneficial impact on human welfare, then how is the animal's suffering "unnecessary?"

In sum, Singer plays games with words. He defines his moral standard so broadly that who could be against it? To deny that it's wrong to inflict unnecessary pain on an animal is impossible and, therefore, it tells us little. It would be like the dictum "treat everyone fairly." Yes, indeed. But it begs the question of what is fair treatment in any specific situation. Singer's "unnecessary pain" principle is so broad that it is compatible with the very activities he criticizes; hence, by itself it is useless as a guide to reflective moral action.

The animal liberation movement is morally empty. Its foundation consists of propaganda, factual errors and deliberate distortions. Its advocacy of and reliance on terrorism, vandalism, lying and other unethical and illegal tactics proves its moral bankruptcy. Its proposals are totally irresponsible not only in terms of their impact on humans but especially for animals. Imagine, for example, if we all became vegetarians as they recommend. What would happen to all the farm animals that liberationists are so concerned about? They would cease to exist since there would be no more need for them. Would we simply release existing farm animals into the wild to become feral? In this scenario, animals that survived would have a tremendous impact on existing wild animals — quite probably negative. Wouldn't this cause "unnecessary pain and suffering" to wild animals?

In short, the whole agenda of the animal liberation-rights movement is ludicrous and potentially destructive for both man and animal. Any hunter who guiltily converts himself into a phony "harvester," because he thinks it will play better to the non-hunting audience, simply gives credence to anti-hunter propaganda.

Instead of "harvesting," we hunters need to form alliances with the medical profession, veterinarians and other scientists who recognize the absolute need for animals in research, if both human and animal well-being is to be served and advanced. We need to support wildlife departments in continuing to scientifically manage wildlife populations for the purposes of recreational hunting.

Above all, we hunters need to talk candidly and proudly about our sport. We need to clearly communicate that the motivation for hunting today is recreation with the potential to teach ethical lessons. Hunting is an activity that quickens one life, infuses it with rich meanings and exciting anticipations; hence, it demands celebration, not polite lies and defensive apologies. When we proudly and honestly advocate what we do, we not only make our enemies squirm, but, more importantly, we encourage our daughters and sons and the kid next door to want to be like us, to be hunters.

Selected References

Krasney, John A. 1984. "Some Thoughts on the Value of Life." *Buffalo Physician.* September, 1984.

Singer, Peter. 1973. "Animal Liberation." *New York Review of Books.* April 5, 1973.

Singer, Peter. 1987. "Interview with Peter Singer." *The Animals' Agenda.* September, 1987.

Frey, R.G. 1979. "Rights, Interests, Desires and Beliefs." *American Philosophical Quarterly,* June, 1979.

Van De Veer, Donald. 1979. "Interspecific Justice." *Inquiry.* Summer, 1979.

Editor's Note: "Harvesting Deer & Liberating Animals" originally appeared in the March 1990 issue of Deer & Deer Hunting *magazine.*

Harvesting Deer And Liberating Animals

■ FIRM UP OUR STANCE

Congratulations to Lee Nisbet on his article, "Harvesting Deer and Liberating Animals" (March 1990). At last an intellectual perspective on the subject. I've believed for some time now that we hunters should firm up our stance. We need to maintain our pride, our integrity, and our responsibilities as hunters. We can only do that by elevating our image and our intellect. Lee Nisbet's article gives all of us an excellent first step toward that end. Further congratulations should go to *Deer & Deer Hunting* magazine for publishing an article like Nisbet's. Well done!

— *Ken Preston*
Plymouth, New Hampshire

■ NOTHING TO HIDE

My hat is off to Lee Nisbet. I share his feelings completely. Ethical, law-abiding hunters have nothing to be ashamed of, nothing to hide. During the birth of this great country, hunting was a trade of survival. The hunter was respected, looked up to, and survival was somewhat based on his success.

Now, things are different. We no longer need to hunt to survive and this raises the question of why a person is allowed to hunt and kill animals such as a deer. Nisbet answers this question beautifully: ". . . hunting today is recreation with the potential to teach ethical lessons. Hunting is an activity that quickens one's life, infuses it with rich meanings and exciting anticipations . . ."

—*Hank Stephens*
Walhall, South Carolina

■ EMPLOYING A LITTLE TACT

I began reading "Harvesting Deer and Liberating Animals" with the initial uncertainty that accompanies an article which deals with personal opinions and attitudes, but I was soon intrigued by the author's philosophical and theoretical evaluations concerning the ethics of sport hunting. I admire Lee Nisbet's shrewd talent in responding to the animal liberationists' inept allegations pertaining to the effects that sport hunting has on the ultimate welfare of wild animals.

However, I do not agree with Nisbet when he adamantly protests the subtle conversion of the term "harvest," as opposed to the use of the word "kill." In today's society, the expressed use of the word "kill" is very closely associated with the conviction of murder. So, how will the hunting fraternity benefit by exalting a flippant decorum when describing the taking of game? Aren't deer considered a natural resource? I certainly think they are. Then why should one feel inappropriate or invalid for simply employing a little tact and discretion when a conversation suddenly turns into an inquiry of one's past hunting successes?

I try to be as discrete as possible while in the company of non-hunters when a conversation involves the killing of an animal for sport. I do not feel as if I'm intentionally hiding behind a wall of pretense. In fact, I rather enjoy an honest and open discussion concerning the ethical and moral issues surrounding hunting, and the existence of hunting for sport as well as for necessity.

On more than one occasion I'm convinced that I played a small role in the adjustment of a person's attitudes toward the right — and privilege — to legally harvest animals for sport, but I'm positive that I would not have had a snowball's chance in Hades if I would have come across as an arrogant, boastful, "deer killer."

— *Steven D. Peters*
Merrill, Wisconsin

■ LET'S GO CONTROLLING

In his splendid academic defense of hunting, Lee Nesbit mentioned the use of the term "harvesting." Having hunted in Germany for the last two years under the "Abschussplan," literally "shooting plan" but known as the "Game Harvest Plan," I had the occasion to meet an educated German forester in Southern Germany. Hunting in Germany is done with a religious fervor by a select minority. The forester always used a sterile term before we went hunting, as if to lend professionalism to his passion. "Let's go controlling." I always found this comical, especially considering the dark German past mentioned by Dr. Nisbet.

— *Sebastian Blahnik*
Wausau, Wisconsin

Giving It Back

Jim Maierle

Len Rue, Jr.

The memories come back in black and white: The shadowy deer, the heavy curtain of snowflakes between us, and the dull thud of gunfire as the sound tried to escape the snow-filled balsam forest. The deer stepped forward onto a collapsing leg and sank into the snow, his head buried except for the 12-point rack of the mature buck.

I was standing over him when Dad appeared. We stood in quiet reverence a moment until he put his hand on my shoulder, removing the spell as I broke into a proud grin. Dad turned away, cleared his throat a few times and lighted his pipe.

With a click of the metallic deer tag, I completed the theft. I stole Dad's deer.

For days I reshot my first deer for anyone who would listen. I was self-centered about the hunt, as though Dad hadn't been there.

But something was wrong.

Why was a cartridge missing from Dad's belt that evening? I spotted that clue when I fed the dogs. He always hung his wool pants in the back shed where we kept the dog food. There had been a shot shortly before mine. Maybe it was closer than I thought. Even my own gunfire had seemed muffled.

Why did Dad clean his rifle barrel that night, rather than just wipe it down as usual when he hadn't shot?

And, now that I think about it, my sight picture had seemed a little high when the gun went off.

On my 15th birthday the next September, I followed a yellow, leaf-carpeted skid trail to the green balsam forest where I had claimed my trophy. I ran my fingers along the partially healed scar on a tree that recorded my bullet's path. "Letter high!" I said out loud and into the silence. I had missed by more than a foot!

Thirty years after my theft, I sat on a snowless and sun-drenched birch ridge that looked down on the edge of a broad hemlock stand. I had stopped there for the weather and the view, and to take a break from a still-hunt that began three hours earlier.

The shot startled me. I turned toward the sound and soon saw a flash of movement through the hemlocks, then another. I slid my elbows slightly over my raised knees and leaned into my carbine just as the third flash revealed antlers in the sun. They were headed straight at me. At 50 yards, the running deer swung slightly to the right and my shot angled in behind his shoulder. My second shot hit his neck, anchoring him.

Thirty seasons flashed by as I stood over a beautiful buck whose rack bore an uncanny similarity to the one carried by Dad's deer. I immediately began to backtrack to see if the earlier shot had drawn blood. I soon ran headlong into an old, familiar situation.

The short gray-bearded old man, breathing heavily under an ancient buffalo-plaid wool coat and britches, moved slowly along the track to where I stood. High swampers nearly reached to his knees.

"Did I get him?" he asked hopefully. "I been after that rascal for three seasons!"

He leaned his octagon-barreled lever-action against a tree and removed his faded orange hat to cool himself. The gray film that seemed to cover his eyes couldn't hide the gleam of excitement. "You've got yourself a beautiful buck," I said without hesitation. "He was down when I finished him off for you." I

shook his hand enthusiastically and flashed a big grin as his excitement caught hold of me.

"Did I really get him?" he asked, tears coming down his face. "I don't see the sights too good anymore. I figured I missed him sure as heck! Ma and me can sure use the meat, too!"

"Follow me," I said, hoping he wouldn't ask too many questions. "I'll give you a hand." I turned quickly to hide my own watering eyes as memories and the old-timer's enthusiasm caught me by surprise. I cleared my throat and reached for my pipe, half smiling at the caricature I had become of Dad.

Moments later the man was kneeling next to the deer, stroking its neck in that strange mixture of affection and victory only hunters understand. "Might be my last one; ya never know," he said almost to himself.

I punched out his paper deer tag while the old-timer began field-dressing his deer. "Remember the old metal tags?" I asked reflectively.

"Sure do," he said. "About a hundred years ago it seems. I can't even seem to read the dern things now. Snip this, punch out that. Back then, one click and she was done."

"Amen," I muttered in agreement.

Two hours and a long drag later the deer was in his tired old pickup. I propped the head on a nest of coiled rope so the big rack would be visible. "Show it off," I said with a grin.

We shook hands and they were gone.

I sat against a tree and lit my pipe. The hunt was over for the day and the long lesson complete. Somehow I had given Dad's deer back, and I felt the same reward he must have known. He had to decide in an instant, just as I did, whether to claim the deer. Somewhere between my smile and the click of my tag he had chosen to remain silent. Now I understand. His motive to act as he did with his son standing there must have been even stronger than what moved me.

I still wondered if I had done the right thing, just as Dad must have wondered years before. But the old man's smile was still with me on the long walk back to camp.

It still is.

Editor's Note: "Giving It Back" was originally published in the September 1991 issue of Deer & Deer Hunting *magazine.*

Index

About the Editor and the Designer

Al Hofacker

Al Hofacker, the editor of *Deer & Deer Hunting: A Hunter's Guide To Deer Behavior And Hunting Techniques*, was one of the co-founders and owners of Stump Sitters Inc., former publisher of *Deer & Deer Hunting* magazine. Al was the editor of the magazine from its inception in 1977 until the magazine was acquired by Krause Publications, the current publisher, in 1992. The magazine was an outgrowth of a keen interest in the white-tailed deer and the sport of deer hunting; Al has been an avid bow and gun hunter for nearly 30 years. More recently, he has added bear and turkey hunting to his list of favorite outdoor activities.

A lifelong resident of Wisconsin, Al pursued a career in the field of electronics upon graduation from high school. After receiving an A.S.S. degree from Devry Technical Institute in Chicago, he was employed as an electronics technician by Kimberly-Clark Corp. from 1969 until 1979. By that time the magazine had grown sufficiently to warrant making it his full-time occupation. During his 15-year tenure as editor, Al helped the magazine grow from six to eight issues per year with a circulation of more than 150,000. He also played an active role in the start-up of *Turkey & Turkey Hunting* magazine in 1991.

Al has also been deeply involved in the politics of wildlife management in the state of Wisconsin. He served as a delegate to the Wisconsin Conservation Congress from 1983-1991 and in 1991 he was appointed to the Wisconsin Natural Resources Board's 12-member Ad Hoc Deer Management Study Committee. He is presently a member of The Wildlife Society, the American Forests Association and several hunting and conservation organizations.

Presently, Al lives in Athelstane, on a 400-acre tract located in Wisconsin's northern forest where he continues to pursue his favorite pastimes of deer, bear and turkey hunting.

Valerie B. Smith

Valerie B. Smith, the designer of *Deer & Deer Hunting: A Hunter's Guide To Deer Behavior And Hunting Techniques,* has been active in the graphic arts field for more than 10 years. Born and raised in Wisconsin, Valerie majored in advertising/illustration at Rocky Mountain College (Montana) and the University of Delaware.

In early 1991, she became the graphic arts director for Graphic Management Corp., a print consulting firm based in Green Bay, Wisconsin. She is self-taught in the use of the Apple Macintosh system and a variety of software which she uses for most of her design work — projects ranging from catalogs to pizza labels to promotional brochures.

Shortly after joining GMC, one of her clients became Stump Sitters Inc., the former publisher of *Deer & Deer Hunting* magazine. Valerie assisted in the typesetting and design of both *Deer & Deer Hunting* and *Turkey & Turkey Hunting* magazines. She also was the designer of *Whitetail Details* and did all the design work for the 1991 and 1992 *Deer Hunters Equipment Annual.*

In addition to her full-time duties as graphic arts director at GMC, Valerie still finds time to do freelance design and calligraphy, enjoys travelling, and occasionally performs with a local theatrical group.